# MASTERING

# GERMAN 1

# HIPPOCRENE MASTER SERIES

*These imaginative courses, designed for both individual and classroom use, assume no previous knowledge of the language. The unique combination of practical exercises and step-by-step grammar emphasizes a functional approach to new scripts and their vocabulary. Everyday situations and local customs are explored through dialogue, newspaper extracts, drawings and photos.*

**MASTERING ARABIC**
*ISBN 0-87052-922-6, $14.95*

**MASTERING FRENCH**
*ISBN 0-87052-055-5, $11.95*

**MASTERING GERMAN**
*ISBN 0-87052-056-3, $11.95*

**MASTERING ITALIAN**
*ISBN 0-87052-057-1, $11.95*

**MASTERING JAPANESE**
*ISBN 0-87052-923-4, $14.95*

**MASTERING SPANISH**
*ISBN 0-87052-059-8, $11.95*

---

*Cassettes for learning (2 for each language) are also available. Each cassette set costs just $12.95.*

---

Books and cassettes may be ordered directly from the publisher.
Send the total amount plus $3.50 for shipping and handling to:
Hippocrene Books, Inc.
171 Madison Avenue
New York, NY 10016.

HIPPOCRENE MASTER SERIES

# MASTERING

# GERMAN 1

## ANTONY J. PECK

### EDITORIAL CONSULTANT
### BETTY PARR

HIPPOCRENE BOOKS
*New York*

First published in the United States of America in 1991 by
HIPPOCRENE BOOKS, INC., New York,
by arrangement with Macmillan Education, Ltd., London.

For information, address:
HIPPOCRENE BOOKS, INC.
171 Madison Avenue
New York, NY 10016

First published in 1989 and reprinted with corrections in 1990 by
Macmillan Education, Ltd., London.

ISBN 0-87052-056-3

# CONTENTS

how to order a meal; how to ask for the bill; how to express the time
*Grammar* – Question forms; interrogatives; expressions of time

# SERIES EDITOR'S PREFACE

The first language books in the Master Series, which are intended primarily for adult beginners without a teacher, should fill a notable gap in an otherwise well-cultivated field. The publishers make no promises of instant mastery, and recognise that no one slim volume can contain more than the basic essentials of any living language. We believe, however, that these books provide a carefully planned introduction to the language as well as a secure foundation for further study.

Existing publications seem either to concentrate on teaching 'how to survive abroad' or else to adopt a mainly academic approach. In these new books, our aim is to assist not only those studying a language for practical – generally touristic or commercial – purposes, but also those wishing to acquire a more formal knowledge of the grammar and structures of the language, with the intention of extending their skills of reading and writing by subsequent study. The dual aims of these books are made clear from the start, so that students may determine their own learning procedures and work through the material in ways best suited to their needs and capacity. The main emphasis is placed on understanding and speaking the language, but due attention has been paid to the importance of reading, especially for interpreting instructions and seeking information, and of writing, for such practical tasks as filling in forms, making reservations and writing simple letters.

The author's introduction clearly explains the content and presentation of the teaching material. The table of contents is specific and informative and the student may see at a glance the ground to be covered. It is advisable to study the introduction very closely, in order to make the best use of this carefully structured course. The presentation of each chapter is consistent, and the dialogues which form the basis of the teaching are followed by a list of new German words in order of their appearance; this vocabulary list provides the English meaning and appropriate grammatical clues, as well as stress marks to help solve one of the major problems of German pronunciation.

Mastery of the spoken language presents one of the greatest difficulties to the student working alone; without considerable linguistic experience, it is impossible to develop an ear for the sounds and intonation of a language by reading the printed page. In *Mastering German 1* there is a detailed guide to pronunciation, in addition to the indications of stress given in the vocabulary lists; but these alone could not convey the true nature of the spoken language. It is true that German has so much in common with English that it is relatively easy at first to make encouraging progress in acquiring a reasonably satisfactory pronunciation. However, the similarity between the two languages will become a decoy unless care is taken to listen to the finer differences and to discriminate between similar but not identical sounds. To this end, there is a most useful 'optional extra' in the form of a cassette, on which the pronunciation key and all the dialogues in the book are recorded by native speakers.

The authors of the language books in the Master Series, who are all gifted teachers of individuality and experience, have tried to ensure that those who use these books thoughtfully may experience the pleasure of successful language study without the direct intervention of a teacher. All concerned with the project hope that the books will establish for the learner a continuing involvement with the infinite variety and endless fascination of languages.

BETTY PARR
*Editorial Consultant*

# INTRODUCTION:
# HOW TO USE THIS BOOK

**LEARNING AIMS**

1. The first aim of *Mastering German 1* is to enable students to acquire the ability to take part in every-day communication with native speakers of German. This means being able to take part in the following two sorts of language exchange:

   (a) You need to be able to 'survive' in the language, and that means being able to take part in a number of transactions which are necessary for your health and comfort. This includes such things as going shopping, ordering meals, reserving rooms in hotels and finding your way around by public transport.

   (b) The other sort of language which you need is the language for making social contact with speakers of German. This social language is particularly important for those students who are likely to meet German speakers either at home or abroad, and will need to spend some time with them in a social setting. Businessmen, in particular, may find this sort of language of great use for helping to create a suitable social atmosphere in which business can be done.

2. The other aim of *Mastering German 1* is to give students a solid foundation of German grammar as a base for further learning at a higher level. Students preparing for public examinations will benefit from the clear explanations of points of grammar and from the exercises on them, which can be corrected by the student working alone, using the answers at the back of the book.

**THE MATERIALS**

*Mastering German 1* consists of a book and a sound recording. Students who are beginning the study of German will find the recording of particular use in helping them to acquire good pronunciation, intonation and stress. A guide to pronunciation is included in the book, and has been recorded. It will be found on the cassette after the dialogues. Students who already have some mastery of the pronunciation of German may still find that the dialogues, using native speakers, will help them to speak not only with clarity, but with a good range of expression.

## HOW TO FIND YOUR WAY ABOUT THE BOOK

When you look at the table of contents, you will see that each chapter is presented under two headings:

1. *Topic* This expresses the main communicative aim of the chapter. It describes what you will be able to do with the language you have learned.
2. *Grammar* Here the main elements of formal grammar are listed.

Students who wish to 'cash in' their study as soon as possible should concentrate first on mastering the topics. The most important parts of the book for them are the dialogues, the notes on the dialogues and the vocabulary, the structures to learn and Section A of the exercises. These are the communicative parts of the book, and will help you learn how to make an arrangement or meet somebody, how to request a service, how to make a suggestion or proposal, etc.

Other students, who wish alternatively, or additionally, to acquire a grasp of German grammar, should pay particular attention to Section B of the structural explanations which takes a point of grammar arising in the dialogue, and gives it thorough and systematic treatment, and also Section B of the exercises, which concentrates on these grammatical points.

## LANGUAGE FOR SPEAKING AND LANGUAGE FOR UNDERSTANDING

The main emphasis in this book is on the skills of speaking and under-standing. Some parts of the language presented will consist of things students will want to *say*, and others will consist of things students want to *understand*. Each student will have a good idea of those things he or she is most likely to want to say, and should consequently concentrate on practising these parts of the language aloud. It is necessary to remember, however, that the better you become at speaking the language, the freer natives will feel in replying to you. In choosing the topics to include in this book, the proposals of the

Threshold Level for Language Learning, published by the Council of Europe, has provided a most useful point of reference.

## STRUCTURE OF THE CHAPTERS

Each chapter begins with a number of dialogues, which give examples of speakers using the language for the purpose indicated in the table of contents. These dialogues are recorded on tape by native speakers of German. The dialogues are translated into English and printed in Part II. They have been set out on a line-for-line basis, so that students can instantly understand them. The dialogues are followed by explanatory notes and a vocabulary list.

After the dialogues and the notes on them, comes a section of the chapter called Structural Explanations. In part (a) of this section, you will find a number of phrases and structural patterns, which will help you to use and build on the language of the dialogues, in order to use German freely and cope with the topic of that particular chapter.

In part (b) you will find some points of grammar which are explained fully and clearly, and which will help you to build up a systematic knowledge of German, based on the points of grammar which arise in the dialogue.

Part 4 of the chapter consists of Exercises. These are divided into two sections. The exercises in Section A correspond to the communicative aims of the chapter, while Section B contains exercises of a more grammatical nature, which will help you to master the grammatical rules which arise from the dialogue.

Students should note that the German alphabet coincides with the English alphabet, except in one case. The symbol ß is the equivalent of 'ss'. The rule concerning the use of ß and ss is a complicated one, and may safely be left until a more advanced stage in learning German. Students simply need to note at this stage that the two symbols are pronounced identically. Students who wish to learn the rule for using ß should consult *German Grammar and Usage* by A. E. Hammer, page 409 (see bibliography).

## HOW TO GET THE BEST OUT OF MASTERING GERMAN

### 1. All students

Every student should be able to derive benefit from studying the dialogues which are written in good, colloquial German and recorded on tape by native speakers. The following procedure is recommended.

(a) Study the aims of the chapter. In particular, look at the *topic* of a chapter to see how it sets out to teach you to use German. This will inform you of what you should be able to do by the time you have got to the end of the chapter, and this in turn will help you to evaluate your own progress.

(b) Read through the German text of the dialogue and listen to it simultaneously on tape. Try to work out the meaning of each sentence as it occurs. Very often the common linguistic ancestry of English and German will help you to find out the meaning. These similarities between English and German will sometimes be more apparent when looking at the spelling of words, and sometimes when listening to the way they are spoken. When you have predicted the meaning as far as you can, refer to the translation at the back of the book, so as to be quite sure that you understand the dialogue thoroughly before proceeding.

(c) If you are working with a book alone, work out the pronunciation of the sentences in the dialogue, using the pronunciation guide. If you are working with a tape-recording, speak the dialogue quietly while listening to the tape-recording. By degrees increase the volume of your own voice, and decrease the volume of the recording. After two or three times, it should be possible to pronounce the dialogue accurately and with good expression. When you are beginning to establish a correct pronunciation of the sentences, it will probably help to stop the tape-recording after each sentence, and to repeat it aloud several times before continuing to the next sentence. Probably all students will be able to derive some benefit from working with the dialogues in this way.

2. **For students with little language learning experience**

(a) Having worked through the dialogues in the way described above, go on to the section labelled *Structures to learn*. With the help of the pronunciation key, speak the sentences aloud, noting carefully which uses of language they help you to master.

(b) For those with little linguistic experience it is probably advisable to omit the study of the grammatical section, and go straight to those exercises which are based on the objectives stated at the beginning of the chapter. Do the exercises as best you can without referring to the answers at the back of the book. Only when you have really thought about what you want to say, and tried hard to get it right, should you check with the answers.

(c) Beginners may well find the best way of using *Mastering German 1* is to work their way through the book as indicated above, concentrating on:
   (i) The Dialogues,
   (ii) The Structures to learn,
   (iii) The Exercises (Section A).
When the whole book has been worked through in this way, it would be appropriate to return to Chapter 1, and go through the book again as indicated below.

3. **Intermediate students**
   Intermediate students who have already mastered the rudiments of German should work first through the dialogues as indicated above, and run through the *Structures to learn* and the communicative exercises as indicated for beginners. In this way, intermediate students will derive considerable benefit from putting to practical use elements of the language which they may previously have learned.
   Intermediate students would then be well advised to proceed directly to the grammar section, in order to give the language of the dialogues and the structures to learn a firm grammatical foundation.
   The structural exercises (Section B) based on the grammar section should then be gone through carefully, checking answers with the answer key at the back of the book.

## STUDENTS WISHING TO USE MASTERING GERMAN TO REVISE FOR PUBLIC EXAMINATIONS

These students should consult the table of contents, looking particularly at the second entry for each chapter, in order to find the particular point of grammar which they wish to study. These students should read and study very carefully the grammar section, and should not forget that there are exercises on it, which can be checked by referring to the answer key at the back.

## VOCABULARY LEARNING

Section 2 of each chapter contains a list of the most important words which have occurred in the chapter. It is not a complete list of all the new words which have occurred, since these are given by the translation of the dialogues. The word list gives a basic vocabulary which you should be able to use actively.

Here are some suggestions, intended to help you to learn new vocabulary items:

1.  Cover up the English translation, and try to use your existing knowledge and your increasing knowledge of German to guess the meaning of the German word. Then check whether you are right or wrong by uncovering the English version. Continue in this way until you can recognise all the new words.

2.  Then go on to the more difficult way of learning vocabulary, and cover up the German version and try to remember the equivalent for each English word. You should try to remember whether nouns are masculine, feminine or neuter, and how they make their plurals. If possible, work with a friend who can ask you the English words and check whether you have succeeded in remembering the German equivalent.

## REVISION TESTS

Chapter 10 and Chapter 20 consist of tests on the earlier chapters in the book and are intended to help you gauge your own progress.

Alles Gute!!

# I TEACHING UNITS

# CHAPTER 1

# GREETINGS AND INTRODUCTIONS

## 1.1 DIALOGUES 📼

**Dialogue 1**

Professor Hecht has called to return a catalogue which he borrowed from a business acquaintance, Herr Kirchhof.

1 *Sekretärin*: Ach, Herr Professor. Guten Tag!
  *Prof. Hecht*: Guten Tag, Frau Hausmann.
    Ist Herr Kirchhof da?
  *Sekretärin*: Ja, Moment bitte.
5 Herr Kirchhof . . .
  Professor Hecht ist da.

. . .

  *Herr Kirchhof*: (at door) Guten Tag, Herr Professor!
  *Prof. Hecht*: Guten Tag, Herr Kirchhof!
  *Herr Kirchhof*: Bitte, kommen Sie herein.
10 *Prof. Hecht*: Danke.
  Wie geht es Ihnen?
  *Herr Kirchhof*: Sehr gut, danke.
  Bitte, nehmen Sie Platz.
  *Prof. Hecht*: Danke.
15 *Herr Kirchhof*: Eine Tasse Kaffee?
  *Prof. Hecht*: Oh ja, bitte sehr.
  *Herr Kirchhof*: Frau Hausmann, zwei Tassen
  Kaffee, bitte.
  *Frau Hausmann*: Ja, gern.
20 *Herr Kirchhof*: Nun, wie geht es Ihrer Frau?
  *Prof. Hecht*: Ausgezeichnet!
  *Herr Kirchhof*: Und Andreas und Daniella?

4

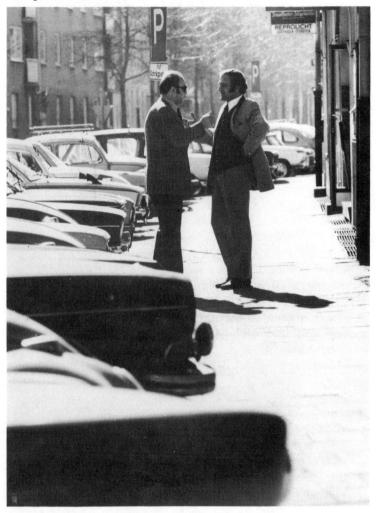

*Photograph: Bavaria-Verlag/Oscar Poss*

|  | *Prof. Hecht*: | Auch sehr gut. |
|---|---|---|
| 25 | *Herr Kirchhof*: | Und hier ist der Katalog. |
|  | *Prof. Hecht*: | Ja, der Katalog. |

**Dialogue 2**

Elke Kustmann is having a party at her flat in the Fürstenstraße in Munich. She works at a smart dress shop in Munich and is celebrating having sold a very expensive fur coat to the wife of a businessman. She has been rewarded with a handsome commission. Amongst her guests is her current admirer, Fritz Löb.

(Front door bell rings)

1 *Elke*: Herr Doktor! Guten Abend!
   *Doktor Neumann*: Elke! Guten Abend!
   *Elke*: Wie schön.
   Kommen Sie herein.
5 *Doktor Neumann*: Danke.
   Darf ich meine Frau vorstellen?
   *Elke*: Guten Abend, Frau Neumann.
   Willkommen!
   *Frau Neumann*: Guten Abend!
10 Danke schön für die Einladung.
   *Elke*: Bitte, bitte.
   Das ist Fritz.
   *Fritz*: Guten Abend!
   Löb ist mein Name.
(Front door bell rings again)
15 *Elke*: Eckhard!
   *Eckhard*: Elke!
   *Elke*: Du hier!
   Das ist fantastisch!
   *Eckhard*: Elke, du bist noch immer so schön.
20 *Elke*: Ach, nein.
   *Eckhard*: Doch. Doch.
   *Fritz*: (Clears his throat)
   *Elke*: Ach, ja.
   Das ist Fritz.
   *Eckhard*: Becker.
25 *Fritz*: Angenehm.
   *Fritz*: Löb.
   *Eckhard*: Angenehm.
(Front door bell rings again)
   *Elke*: Entschuldigen Sie!

. . .

(Some hours later)
   *Prof. Hecht*: Auf Wiedersehen!
30 Vielen Dank.
   *Elke*: Nichts zu danken.
   Auf Wiedersehen!

## 1.2 INFORMATION

### (a) Notes on Dialogue 1

| | |
|---|---|
| 1. Herr Professor | When you speak to a person with a title, such as 'Professor' or 'Doctor', you address them in German as Herr Professor or Herr Doktor. Other titles are: Herr: 'Mr', Frau: 'Mrs', Fräulein: 'Miss' |
| 1. Guten Tag | The greeting Guten Tag applies to the whole day, where in English we would say 'Good morning' or 'Good afternoon'. |
| 15. Eine Tasse Kaffee? | This is short for '(Would you like) a cup of coffee?' |

### (b) Notes on Dialogue 2

| | |
|---|---|
| 1. Guten Abend | This greeting is used from about 6 pm onwards. |
| 11. Bitte, bitte | This emphatic repetition of the word bitte is best translated as 'don't mention it'. |
| 14. Löb ist mein Name | If you wish to state your name, you can begin by stating it in order to give it emphasis, but it would also be quite possible to say Mein Name ist Löb. |
| 18. Fantastisch | Here are some other words which you might find useful for expressing enthusiasm: wunderbar großartig klasse Note that you can use the first two in any society, but klasse is slightly more colloquial. |
| 21. Doch | This word means 'yes' when spoken emphatically, because |

the previous sentence has been in the negative. If, therefore, the previous speaker says e.g. 'no it isn't' and you wish to reply emphatically 'oh yes it is', you would use the word doch.

24. Becker — Adults who introduce themselves to other adults do so by stating their family name.

25. Angenehm — This word literally means 'pleasant' and is best translated by the conventional English phrase 'pleased to meet you'.

31. Nichts zu danken — 'Don't mention it' is clearly not a literal translation, but is a good rendering of the meaning.

**(c) Word list**

Here is a list of the most important words in this chapter. They should be learnt by heart. They are given here in the order in which they occur in the chapter. After each noun, the plural ending is given in brackets. For more information on the plural of nouns, see the Grammar section of Chapter 14. In German, certain syllables of words are stressed. This is shown in bold type.

| | |
|---|---|
| die Sekretärin (-nen) | secretary |
| der Herr (-en) | man; husband |
| Frau | Mrs |
| da | there |
| bitte | please |
| kommen | to come |
| danke | thank you |
| sehr | very |
| gut | good |
| nehmen | to take |
| der Kaffee | coffee |
| die Tasse (-n) | cup |
| ausgezeichnet | splendid |
| und | and |
| auch | also/too |
| hier | here |
| der Katalog (-e) | catalogue |

| | |
|---|---|
| die Frau (-en) | wife; woman |
| **vor**stellen | to introduce |
| will**kom**men | welcome |
| **danke** schön | thank you very much |
| die **Ein**ladung (-en) | invitation |
| fan**tas**tisch | fabulous |
| der **Name** (-n) | name |
| noch **imm**er | still |
| schön | beautiful |
| doch | yes (after a negative) |
| der Mann (¨er) | husband; man |
| das **Aut**o (-s) | car |
| der Schuh (-e) | shoe |

**(d) Some phrases**

| | |
|---|---|
| M**om**ent **bitt**e | Just a moment, please |
| **Komm**en Sie her**ein** | Do come in |
| Wie geht es **Ihn**en? | How are you? |
| **Bitt**e, **neh**men Sie Platz | Please sit down |
| **Bitt**e sehr | yes please |
| Wie schön! | How nice! |
| Noch **imm**er | Still |
| Ent**schuld**igen Sie | Excuse me |
| Auf **Wied**ersehen | Goodbye |
| **Viel**en Dank | Thank you very much |

## 1.3 STRUCTURAL EXPLANATIONS

**(a) Structures to learn**

  (i) **How to greet people**

| Guten | $\begin{cases} \text{Tag} \\ \text{Morgen} \\ \text{Abend} \end{cases}$ | Good | $\begin{cases} \text{morning; afternoon} \\ \text{morning} \\ \text{evening} \end{cases}$ |
|---|---|---|---|
| Gute | $\begin{cases} \text{Nacht} \\ \text{Besserung} \\ \text{Reise} \end{cases}$ | | Goodnight<br>Get better soon<br>Have a good journey |

  (ii) **Other frequently used greetings**

| | |
|---|---|
| Guten Appetit! | Enjoy your meal. (Nearly always said by people sitting at the same table, before they begin to eat.) |

| | |
|---|---|
| Alles Gute! | All the best |
| Prost! <br> Prosit! <br> Zum Wohl! | Cheers! Good health! |
| Viel Glück | Good luck! |
| Viel Spaß! <br> Viel Vergnügen! | Have a good time! |

(iii) **How to be polite**

| | |
|---|---|
| Bitte <br> Bitte schön <br> Bitte sehr | These phrases are used when you offer somebody something, e.g. when you tender a salesperson some money, or when you hand somebody an object, or when a waiter places a dish of food on the table. It is a rather more polite equivalent of 'Here you are'. |
| Bitte <br> Bitte schön <br> Bitte sehr | The same expression means 'please'. Bitte schön and Bitte sehr are slightly more emphatic. |
| Danke <br> Danke schön <br> Danke vielmals | All these expressions mean 'thank you'. They are arranged in order of degree of emphasis. |
| Bitte | Bitte can also mean 'don't mention it'. It is used when somebody has thanked you for something. Here is a possible exchange: <br> Er: (offering something) <br>      Bitte sehr! <br> Sie: (thanking him emphatically) <br>      Danke vielmals. <br> Er: Bitte, bitte (don't mention it). |
| Grüß Gott | This means the same as Guten Tag, but is used in the south of Germany and Austria. |

N.B. The letter ß is pronounced as if it were 'ss'.

(iv) **How to introduce yourself**
1. State your family name e.g. Freeman!
   Hardy!
   Willis!
   If somebody introduces himself to you by stating his or her family name, shake hands and say Angenehm.

2. Johnson ⎱
   Peterson ⎬ ist mein Name
   Davidson ⎰

3. Mein Name ist ⎰ Jones
   ⎨ Smith
   ⎱ Robinson

(v) **How to introduce somebody else**
1. Hier ist ⎰ Mr Smith
   ⎨ Dr Jones
   ⎱ Prof. Pike

2. Darf ich ⎰ meinen Mann ⎱
   ⎨ meine Frau ⎬ vorstellen?
   ⎨ Herrn Schmidt ⎬
   ⎱ Dr Jones ⎰

3. If you wish to make it known that you are about to introduce people to each other, you can use the phrase Darf ich vorstellen? to indicate your intention, and then continue with:

   Hier ist ⎰ Mr Jones
   ⎱ Herr Schmidt

(vi) **How to take your leave**

Auf Wiedersehen     This can be used on most occasions.

Auf Wiederhören     Reserved exclusively for ending a telephone conversation.

Kommen Sie gut heim ⎱ An expression of the wish that the
Kommen Sie gut nach ⎬ person concerned will reach
Hause ⎰ home safely.

**(b) Grammar**
(i) **Verbs and pronouns**
*Verbs* are words, or combinations of words, which express states,

actions or events. In the following sentences, the verbs are printed in italics.

| | |
|---|---|
| He *is* ill | They both *jumped* for the ball |
| She *lives* in Manchester | She *gets* a cheque every month |
| I *like* beer | They *are going* on holiday soon |
| He *has* a bad cold | I *buy* my shirts at Harrods |

Each verb in German has six forms, three in the singular and three in the plural. These forms tell you who performs the action or event of the verb, or to whom or to what the state expressed by the verb refers.
Here is a table showing corresponding English forms.

**Singular**          **Plural**
ich  I                wir  we
du   you (familiar form)   ihr  you (familiar form)
⎧ er   he              ⎧ Sie  you (formal or polite form)
⎨ sie  she             ⎨ sie  they
⎩ es   it

The above forms are called *pronouns*. They are words used instead of nouns. All the above pronouns are known as *personal pronouns* because they refer to people. Here, you see them together with the verb 'to be'.

The verb SEIN — to be

| | |
|---|---|
| ich bin | I am |
| du bist | you are (familiar form) |
| er ist | he is |
| sie ist | she is |
| es ist | it is |
| wir sind | we are |
| ihr seid | you are (familiar form) |
| Sie sind | you are (formal or polite form) |
| sie sind | they are |

N.B. The familiar forms du bist and ihr seid are used amongst members of the family, and when addressing children up to the age of about 12 or 13.

## (ii) Adjectives
An *adjective* is a word which *describes* someone or something. In the following sentences, the adjectives are printed in italics.

| | |
|---|---|
| That is a *fat* man | *My* son is thirteen |
| This car is *old* | Beer is *best* |

*Possessive adjectives* indicate to whom something belongs. They correspond to the *personal pronouns* given above.

Mein Name   –   my name
Meine Frau   –   my wife

You will find a complete list of *possessive adjectives* in the appendix.

### (iii) Nouns

The names of people, things and places are *nouns*. In the following sentences, the nouns are printed in italics. Note that some nouns can be abstract.

| | |
|---|---|
| The *man* was drowning | We're going to *town* |
| She made some *coffee* | He felt great *happiness* |

### (iv) Gender

All nouns in German are categorised in three genders: masculine, feminine, neuter. Gender only *partly* corresponds to male and female, and you should consequently learn the gender of each noun as you meet it.

Mann (man or husband) is masculine, shown in the vocabulary list thus: der Mann.

Frau ('Mrs' as a title, or wife) is feminine, shown in the vocabulary list thus: die Frau.

Auto (car) is neuter, shown in the vocabulary list thus: das Auto.

### (v) Singular and plural

A singular noun is *one* person, thing or place. A plural noun is *more than one* person, thing or place.

### (vi) Agreement

Agreement means that two words, e.g. a noun and an adjective, are both masculine, or both plural.

Possessive adjectives, as all adjectives, must agree with the noun they describe.

| | | | |
|---|---|---|---|
| mein Mann | my husband | dein Mann | your husband |
| meine Frau | my wife | deine Frau | your wife |
| mein Auto | my car | dein Auto | your car |
| meine Schuhe | my shoes | deine Schuhe | your shoes |

You will find a complete list of *adjective agreements* in the appendix.

(vii) **Capital letters**
a) Capital letters are used at the beginning of sentences.
b) They are also used for all nouns.
c) They are used for 'you' in the polite form and also for possessive adjectives in the polite form.

## 1.4 EXERCISES

### Exercise 1
1. What would you say to somebody who is just going to bed?
2. What would you say to somebody who is just going to take her driving test?
3. What would you say to somebody for whom you have just poured out a drink?
4. What would you say to your secretary first thing in the morning?
5. What would you say to your aged mother as she gets into the train to go home?
6. What would you say to your friend when you visit him in hospital?
7. What would you say to the head waiter as you go into a restaurant one evening?
8. What would you say to a friend who is just going off on holiday?
9. What would you say to an acquaintance you met on the street during the lunch hour?

### Exercise 2
You are giving a party to celebrate your birthday. The frontdoor bell rings, Dr Schmidt and his wife are there.
1. What do you say to him?
2. He introduces his wife to you. What does he say?
3. You are very pleased to meet her.
4. Ask them to come in.
5. Ask them to sit down.
6. Frau Schmidt wants to thank you for the invitation. What does she say?
7. Ask them if they would like a cup of coffee.
8. He would like a cup. What does he say?
9. She doesn't like coffee.
10. The frontdoor bell rings again.

### Exercise 3
You have been corresponding with Herr Kunze of Siemens for some time. You have an appointment to see him in Düsseldorf, and he has

invited you to his home for dinner. How would you reply to the things
he says to you?
1. Guten Abend!
2. Kommen Sie herein.
3. Wie geht es Ihnen?
4. Darf ich meine Frau vorstellen?
5. Bitte, nehmen Sie Platz.
6. Whisky?

# CHAPTER 2

# GETTING ABOUT

## 2.1 DIALOGUES 📼

**Dialogue 1**

Frau Meyer is a widowed lady of 75. She has gone on a special cheap day-return train journey to Regensburg. She wants to revisit the house where she was born. She is looking for the post office in the Amalienstraße, where her parents used to have a flat on the third floor. However, everything has changed since she was a girl.

1   *Frau Meyer*:  Entschuldigen Sie!
                Wie komme ich zur Amalienstraße, bitte?
    *Fußgänger*:  Wie bitte?
    *Frau Meyer*:  Die Amalienstraße.
5          Wie komme ich zur Amalienstraße?
    *Fußgänger*:  Ja ... die Amalienstraße ...
    *Frau Meyer*:  (interrupting) Furchtbar!
                Ganz furchtbar!
    *Fußgänger*:  Wie bitte?
10  *Frau Meyer*:  Hier ist alles neu.
    *Fußgänger*:  Ja, das stimmt.
                Zur Adriastraße, nicht wahr?
    *Frau Meyer*:  Nein, nicht zur Adriastraße, zur Amalienstraße.
                Wie komme ich zur Amalienstraße?
15  *Fußgänger*:  Ach, ja.
                Gehen Sie hier geradeaus, nehmen Sie dann die erste Straße links.
    *Frau Meyer*:  Die erste Straße links.
    *Fußgänger*:  Das ist die Marktstraße.
20         Gehen Sie die Marktstraße hoch, dann kommen Sie zur Amalienstraße.

*Regensburg – hier ist alles neu . . .*

Photograph: J. Allan Cash Ltd

*Frau Meyer*:   Danke.
*Fußgänger*:   Bitte.

## Dialogue 2

Fritz Löb teaches English at a Munich school. He is an expert on
romanesque churches. He is separated from his wife, but has no
children. He is friendly with Elke but can't really afford her
tastes. Elke is driving Fritz to see a very beautiful baroque
church in a small Alpine town called Mittenwald.

(Elke hoots her horn)
1 *Elke*:   Entschuldigen Sie!
    Wie kommen wir nach Mittenwald?
  *Junge*:   Wie bitte?
  *Elke*:   Nach Mittenwald
5 *Junge*:   Ich weiß es nicht.
  *Elke*:   Danke.
  (Under breath)
    Blöder Kerl!
    Du Fritz, frag' doch das Mädchen dort drüben.
  *Fritz*:   Entschuldigen Sie!
10   Wie kommen wir nach Mittenwald?
  *Mädchen*:   Nach Mittenwald?
    Fahren Sie hier geradeaus.

*Fritz*: Geradeaus.
*Mädchen*: Nach Garmisch.
15 Dort biegen Sie nach links ab.
Das ist die B28.
*Fritz*: Ist das weit?
*Mädchen*: Nein.
Zwanzig Kilometer ungefähr.
20 *Fritz*: Danke.
*Mädchen*: Fahren Sie Richtung Innsbruck.
*Fritz*: Richtung Innsbruck.
Danke.
*Mädchen*: Bitte.

## 2.2 INFORMATION

**(a) Notes on Dialogue 1**

4. Wie bitte?

You can say wie bitte? or just bitte? if you do not understand what somebody says and you want them to repeat it.

7. Ja ... die Amalienstraße

Note that it is very typically German, when people ask you a direct question, to begin the answer with the word ja. It is really just a way of getting time to think, but if you learn to use it, you will sound immensely typical.

12. Das stimmt

This is a very useful phrase for conveying your agreement with what somebody else has just said.

**(b) Notes on Dialogue 2**

7. Blöder Kerl!

We know it's nice to know how to be rude to people, but beware! In Germany you may have to pay a fine for saying something like this.

16. Die B28         The letter 'B' stands for Bundesstraße. This is the equivalent of an 'A' road.

**(c) Word list**

Here is a list of the most important words in this chapter. They should be learnt by heart. They are given here in the order in which they occur in the chapter.

| | |
|---|---|
| der Fußgänger | pedestrian |
| wie? | how? |
| kommen | to come |
| furchtbar | terrible |
| ganz | quite |
| hier | here |
| alles | everything |
| neu | new |
| nein | no |
| nicht | not |
| gehen | to go |
| geradeaus | straight on |
| nehmen | to take |
| dann | then |
| die Straße (-n) | street |
| links | left |
| rechts | right |
| fragen | to ask |
| das Mädchen (-) | girl |
| dort drüben | over there |
| fahren | to go (by car) |
| biegen | to turn |
| weit | far |
| zwanzig | twenty |
| ungefähr | approximately |
| die Richtung (-en) | direction |
| das Krankenhaus (¨er) | hospital |
| das Kurhotel (-s) | spa hotel |
| der Bahnhof (¨e) | station |
| der Sportplatz (-e) | sports ground |
| die Sparkasse (-n) | savings bank |
| nächst- | next |
| erst- | first |
| zweit- | second |
| dritt- | third |
| das Hallenbad (¨er) | indoor swimming pool |
| das Freibad (¨er) | open-air swimming pool |

| | |
|---|---|
| die **Grund**schule (-n) | primary school |
| der **Camp**ingplatz (¨e) | camping ground |
| der **Kind**ergarten (¨) | nursery school |
| die **Reit**halle (-n) | riding hall |
| das **Restaur**ant (-s) | restaurant |
| der **Markt**platz (¨e) | market place |
| die **Post** | post office |
| das **Rat**haus | town hall |
| der **Dom** | cathedral |
| der **Park**platz (¨e) | car park |
| die **Werk**statt (¨e) | service station |

**(d) Some phrases**

| | |
|---|---|
| Nicht wahr? | Isn't it? etc. |
| **Geh**en Sie die **Markt**straße hoch | Go up Market Street |
| Ich weiß es nicht | I don't know |

## 2.3 STRUCTURAL EXPLANATIONS

**(a) Structures to learn**
  **(i) How to find your way in town**

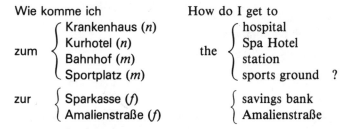

Note that you use zum with all masculine and neuter words, and zur with all feminine words.

**(ii) How to understand some of the directions which people may give**

| (a) Gehen Sie (hier): | (a) You go: |
|---|---|
| geradeaus | straight on |
| links | to the left |
| rechts | to the right |
| die Marktstraße { hoch / entlang | up / along } Market Street |

(b) Nehmen Sie die:

$$\left.\begin{array}{l}\text{nächste}\\\text{erste}\\\text{zweite}\\\text{dritte}\end{array}\right\}\text{Straße}\left\{\begin{array}{l}\text{rechts}\\\\\text{links}\end{array}\right.$$

(b) You take the:

$$\left.\begin{array}{l}\text{next}\\\text{first}\\\text{second}\\\text{third}\end{array}\right\}\text{street}\left\{\begin{array}{l}\text{on the right}\\\\\text{on the left}\end{array}\right.$$

(iii) **How to find your way when driving**

When you are driving the places you want to get to are usually some distance away, and you must use the word nach.

Wie $\left\{\begin{array}{l}\text{komme ich}\\\text{kommen wir}\end{array}\right.$ How do I/we get to

nach $\left\{\begin{array}{l}\text{Perlach}\\\text{Rothenburg} \quad ?\\\text{Dasburg}\end{array}\right.$ 
Perlach
Rothenburg ?
Dasburg

(iv) **How to understand some of the directions you may hear**

Fahren Sie (hier) $\left\{\begin{array}{l}\text{links}\\\text{geradeaus}\\\text{rechts}\end{array}\right.$ Go $\left\{\begin{array}{l}\text{left}\\\text{straight on}\\\text{right}\end{array}\right.$

Biegen Sie nach $\left.\begin{array}{l}\text{rechts}\\\text{links}\end{array}\right\}$ ab Turn $\left\{\begin{array}{l}\text{right}\\\text{left}\end{array}\right.$

**(b) Grammar**

(i) **Cardinal numbers**

The numbers 1 – 30 are as follows:

| | | | | | |
|---|---|---|---|---|---|
| 1 | eins | 11 | elf | 21 | einundzwanzig |
| 2 | zwei | 12 | zwölf | 22 | zweiundzwanzig |
| 3 | drei | 13 | dreizehn | 23 | dreiundzwanzig |
| 4 | vier | 14 | vierzehn | 24 | vierundzwanzig |
| 5 | fünf | 15 | fünfzehn | 25 | fünfundzwanzig |
| 6 | sechs | 16 | sechzehn | 26 | sechsundzwanzig |
| 7 | sieben | 17 | siebzehn | 27 | siebenundzwanzig |
| 8 | acht | 18 | achtzehn | 28 | achtundzwanzig |
| 9 | neun | 19 | neunzehn | 29 | neunundzwanzig |
| 10 | zehn | 20 | zwanzig | 30 | dreißig |

N.B. There is no 's' in 16. There is no 'en' in 17.

You will find further numbers in the appendix.

(ii) **Ordinal numbers**
Numbers indicating the chronological order in which things occur.

| | |
|---|---|
| 1st (first) | der, die, das erste |
| 2nd (second) | der, die, das zweite |
| 3rd (third) | der, die, das dritte |
| 4th (fourth) | der, die, das vierte |
| 5th (fifth) | der, die, das fünfte |

You will find further such numbers in the appendix.

(iii) **Fahren and gehen**
The words fahren and gehen both mean 'to go'. You use fahren when
you are mobile with a car or a motorbicycle, and you use gehen when
you are on foot.

(iv) **Zu and nach**
You use zu for the names of streets, or places or buildings in town
which are a comparatively short distance away. You use nach for
greater distances, for the names of suburbs of towns, e.g. Perlach, or
when asking how to get to other towns, e.g. Mittenwald.

(v) **Verbs**
The most frequently used parts of verbs are:

| | | | |
|---|---|---|---|
| I | — | e.g. | I go, I have |
| he | — | e.g. | he goes, he has |
| she | — | e.g. | she goes, she has |
| we | — | e.g. | we go, we have |
| you | — | e.g. | you go, you have |

In German, verb forms have endings which agree with the personal
pronouns they accompany.

*Regular verbs* follow a regular pattern of agreement which, once
learned, can be applied to other regular verbs of the same type.

Here are two examples of *regular* verbs:

The verb GEHEN – to go

| Personal pronoun | Stem | Ending |
|---|---|---|
| ich (I) | | e |
| er (he) | | t |
| sie (she) | GEH- | t |
| wir (we) | | en |
| Sie (you) | | en |

The verb KOMMEN – to come

| Personal pronoun | Stem | Ending |
|---|---|---|
| ich (I) | | e |
| er (he) | | t |
| sie (she) | KOMM- | t |
| wir (we) | | en |
| Sie (you) | | en |

| ich | gehe | I go | ich | komme | I come |
|-----|------|------|-----|-------|--------|
| er | geht | he goes | er | kommt | he comes |
| sie | geht | she goes | sie | kommt | she comes |
| wir | gehen | we go | wir | kommen | we come |
| Sie | gehen | you go | Sie | kommen | you come |
| | | (formal or | | | (formal or |
| | | polite) | | | polite) |

The verbs GEHEN and KOMMEN are *regular* in the sense that:
a) the stem is unchanged for each part of the verb,
b) the endings are identical for each verb.

Note that the *polite* or *formal* 'you' has a personal pronoun Sie with a capital 'S'.

The verb FAHREN – to go, or to travel (by car or public transport).

This verb is *irregular*, because the spelling and pronunciation of its stem changes from one person to another.

| | | ich | fahre | I go |
|-----|-----|-----|-------|------|
| Vowel | ⟶ | er | fährt | he goes |
| changes here | ⟶ | sie | fährt | she goes |
| | | wir | fahren | we go |
| | | Sie | fahren | you go (formal or polite) |

You will find tables of the most common German verbs in the appendix.

(vi) **Accents**
The only accent in German is called the Umlaut. It is written with two small dots. They occur from time to time above the letters 'a', 'o' and 'u'. The Umlaut has the effect of changing the sound of the vowel beneath it. Whenever you see a word with an Umlaut in one of the dialogues, you should pay particular attention to the pronunciation.


## 2.4 EXERCISES

**Exercise 1**
Imagine that you are in the small town of Brakel and really want to find out what it has to offer. How would you ask the way to the following places?

1. The hospital       Krankenhaus (*n*)
2. Savings bank       Sparkasse (*f*)
3. Station       Bahnhof (*m*)

| | |
|---|---|
| 4. The sports ground | Sportplatz (*m*) |
| 5. The indoor swimming-pool | Hallenbad (*n*) |
| 6. The open-air swimming-pool | Freibad (*n*) |
| 7. The primary school | Grundschule (*f*) |
| 8. The old-people's home | Altenheim (*n*) |
| 9. The Capuchin church | Kapuzinerkirche (*f*) |
| 10. The camping ground | Campingplatz (*m*) |
| 11. The nursery school | Kindergarten (*m*) |
| 12. The riding hall | Reithalle (*f*) |
| 13. The mini golf course | Minigolfplatz (*m*) |
| 14. The Forest restaurant | Waldrestaurant (*n*) |
| 15. The market place | Marktplatz (*m*) |
| 16. The post office | Post (*f*) |
| 17. The town hall | Rathaus (*n*) |
| 18. The cathedral | Dom (*m*) |
| 19. The car park | Parkplatz (*m*) |

*m* – masculine
*f* – feminine
*n* – neuter

**Exercise 2**
Suppose your exhaust-pipe has gone while you have been bombing down the Autobahn. How are you going to find your way to the following service stations?

| | |
|---|---|
| 1. The Audi service station | Audi-Werkstatt (*f*) |
| 2. The Volkswagen service station | Volkswagen-Werkstatt (*f*) |
| 3. The Opel service station | Opel-Werkstatt (*f*) |
| 4. The Ford service station | Ford-Werkstatt (*f*) |
| 5. The Rolls-Royce service station | Rolls-Royce-Werkstatt (*f*) |

**Exercise 3**
You are on holiday travelling by car in Germany (possibly in your Rolls-Royce). You are by yourself and you want to find the way to the following places:
1. Warburg
2. Brakel
3. Eissen
4. Manrode
5. Offendorf

By now you've picked up a hitch-hiker.

6. Paderborn
7. Detmold
8. Peckelsheim
9. Steinheim
10. Holzminden

## Exercise 4

Learn the following dialogue. Take it in turns to play the parts, if you are learning with a partner.

| SALZBURG 6km |

A: Wie weit ist es nach
Salzburg, bitte?

B: Sechs Kilometer ungefähr.

How far is it to Salzburg,
please?

About 6 km.

1. | DESSAU 21 km |

2. | HALLE 52 km |

3. | JENA 101 km |

4. | LINZ 23 km |

5. | KITZBÜHEL 39 km |

6. | KUFSTEIN 9 km |

7. | ZÜRICH 56 km |

8. | TÜBINGEN 71 km |

9. | ANSBACH 56 km |

10. | FULDA 45 km |

# CHAPTER 3

# STAYING IN HOTELS

## 3.1 DIALOGUES 📼

**Dialogue 1**

Antonio Santos came from Naples when he was 5 years old, went to school in Germany, and consequently speaks perfect German. He studies at a fashion school in Munich and is currently doing some practical work in the business where Elke works. Antonio's Uncle and Aunt have written from Naples to say that they want to come and see him in Munich. They have asked him to book a room for them.

1 *Antonio*: Guten Abend!
  *Empfang*: Guten Abend!
  *Antonio*: Ich möchte ein Zimmer reservieren.
  *Empfang*: Ja, für wie lange?
5 *Antonio*: Für fünf Nächte.
    Von Montag bis Samstag.
  *Empfang*: Ja. Ein Einzelzimmer oder ein Doppelzimmer?
  *Antonio*: Ein Doppelzimmer.
  *Empfang*: Mit Bad oder Dusche?
10 *Antonio*: Mit Dusche.
    Ein ruhiges Zimmer bitte.
  *Empfang*: Ja, ja. Das Zimmer ist schön ruhig.
  *Antonio*: Gut.
  *Empfang*: Auf welchen Namen bitte?
15 *Antonio*: Santos. S-A-N-T-O-S.
  *Empfang*: Vielen Dank.
  *Antonio*: Was kostet das Zimmer?
  *Empfang*: Es kostet 60 Mark.
  *Antonio*: Ist das mit Frühstück?

20 *Empfang*: Ja, das ist mit Frühstück und Mehrwertsteuer.
   *Antonio*: Danke.
   *Empfang*: Bitte.

**Dialogue 2**

Elke has decided to go north to Hamburg for the weekend, and try to see an old boyfriend of hers. She hopes that if she sees him again, it may help her to get her emotions sorted out with respect to Fritz.

1 *Elke*: Guten Tag!
  *Empfang*: Guten Tag?
  *Elke*: Haben Sie ein Zimmer frei bitte?
  *Empfang*: Jawohl.
5  Was für ein Zimmer?
  *Elke*: Ein Einzelzimmer.
  Mit Bad.
  *Empfang*: Für wieviele Nächte, bitte schön?
  *Elke*: Ich bleibe zwei Nächte.
10 *Empfang*: Ein Einzelzimmer mit Bad.
  Ja, das ist möglich.
  *Elke*: Was kostet das Zimmer?

*Ihr Zimmer ist im fünften Stock . . .*

*Photograph: Bavaria-Verlag/Ulrike Kment*

*Empfang*: Das kostet pro Nacht 95 Mark mit Frühstück.
*Elke*: Ich nehme es.
15 *Empfang*: Bitte, tragen Sie sich ein.
. . .
Ihr Zimmer ist im fünften Stock.
*Elke*: Hat das Zimmer einen Ausblick?
*Empfang*: Jawohl, es hat einen schönen Ausblick.
Über die Alster.
20 *Elke*: Wie schön.
*Empfang*: Haben Sie Gepäck?
*Elke*: Ja, mein Gepäck ist hier.
*Empfang*: Portier!

**Dialogue 3**
Fritz has been wanting to see the Petrikirche in Bad Reichenhall
for ages. Elke won't be in Munich next weekend, so that will give
him just the opportunity he needs. Anyway, Elke is not so
interested in churches.
(On the telephone)
1 *Empfang*: Hotel Bayerischer Hof.
*Fritz*: Guten Tag!
Haben Sie ein Zimmer für nächsten Samstag, bitte?
*Empfang*: Für den zwölften?
5 *Fritz*: Ja, für Samstag den zwölften.
*Empfang*: Nein, es tut mir leid, wir sind völlig ausgebucht.
*Fritz*: Danke schön.
*Empfang*: Bitte sehr.

**3.2 INFORMATION**

**(a) Notes on Dialogue 1**

6. Samstag — There are two words for 'Saturday' in German, Samstag, which is used predominantly in the south of Germany, that is to say south of the river Main. The other word is Sonnabend, which is used more frequently in the north.

20. Mehrwertsteuer — You have to pay VAT in Germany, just as you do in

England. Usually, however, the VAT is already included in the price.

**(b) Notes on Dialogue 2**

7. Mit Bad

Although only a bath is mentioned, this nearly always means that you have a private bathroom.

15. Bitte, tragen Sie sich ein

'Please sign the register' is naturally not a word-for-word translation of the German, but it does give the meaning.

20. Die Alster

The Alster is a lake in the centre of Hamburg, which is one of the main attractions of the city. There are several steamer routes which criss-cross the lake, and which many workers use to travel to and from work. In the winter the Alster often freezes over, and becomes a vast skating rink.

**(c) Word list**

Here is a list of the most important words in this chapter. They should be learnt by heart. They are given here in the order in which they occur in the chapter.

| | |
|---|---|
| gut | good |
| der **A**bend (-e) | evening |
| das **Zimm**er (-) | room |
| reser**vier**en | to reserve |
| die Nacht (-̈e) | night |
| von | from |
| bis | to |
| **Mon**tag | Monday |
| **Sam**stag | Saturday |
| das **Einz**elzimmer (-) | single room |
| oder | or |
| das **Doppe**lzimmer (-) | double room |
| mit | with |

| | |
|---|---|
| das Bad (¨er) | bath |
| die **Dusche** (-n) | shower |
| **ruh**ig | quiet |
| das **Früh**stück | breakfast |
| **kos**ten | to cost |
| frei | free; available |
| wie**viel**? | how many? |
| **blei**ben | to stay |
| **mög**lich | possible |
| was? | what? |
| **neh**men | to take |
| der Stock (¨e) | floor (of a building) |
| der **Aus**blick (-e) | view |
| schön | beautiful |
| das Ge**päck** | luggage |
| **völl**ig | completely |
| **aus**gebucht | booked up |
| **lei**der | unfortunately |
| mit | with |
| **oh**ne | without |
| das **Zwei**bettzimmer (-) | twin bedroom |
| die **Wo**che (-n) | week |
| **heu**te | today |
| von | from |
| bis | until |
| wann? | when? |
| **mor**gen | tomorrow |
| ein **biß**chen | a bit |

**(d) Some phrases**

| | |
|---|---|
| Für wie **lange**? | For how long? |
| Schön **ruh**ig | Nice and quiet |
| Auf **wel**chen **Na**men, bitte? | What name, please? |
| **Vie**len Dank | Thank you very much |
| Was **kos**tet . . . ? | What does . . . cost? |
| Was für ein . . . ? | What sort of a . . . ? |
| Im **fünf**ten Stock | On the fifth floor |
| Es tut mir leid | I'm sorry |
| Das geht in **Ord**nung | That's all right |

## 3.3 STRUCTURAL EXPLANATIONS

### (a) Structures to learn
#### (i) How to establish whether there is a room available

What you need to *say*

Ich möchte ein Zimmer reservieren
I should like to reserve a room

Haben Sie ein Zimmer frei?
Have you got a room available?

Haben Sie ein Zimmer für heute abend?
Have you got a room for tonight?

What you need to *understand*

1. Ja, das ist möglich
Ja, das geht
Ja, ein Zimmer habe ich noch
There is a room available

2. Nein, leider, alles ist ausgebucht
Nein, wir sind völlig ausgebucht
Nein, es tut mir leid
There is no room available

#### (ii) How to describe the sort of room you want

What you need to *say*

|  |  |  |
|---|---|---|
| (Ich möchte) | ein Einzelzimmer | a single room |
|  | ein Doppelzimmer | a double room |
|  | ein Zweibettzimmer | a twin bedroom |
|  | mit/ohne Dusche | with/without shower |
|  | mit/ohne Bad | with/without bath |

#### (iii) How to say how long you want it for

What you need to *understand*

| Für wie lange, bitte? | For how long? |
|---|---|
| Für wieviele Nächte? | For how many nights? |
| Von wann bis wann? | From when to when? |

What you need to *say*

| Für eine Nacht | For one night |
|---|---|
| Für zwei Nächte | For two nights |
| Für eine Woche | For a week |

| | |
|---|---|
| Von heute bis Montag | From today until Monday |
| Von Montag bis Samstag | From Monday until Saturday |

What you need to *understand*

1. Ja, das ist möglich
   Ja, das geht in Ordnung
   You're in luck

2. Nein, es tut mir leid
   Nein, das ist nicht möglich
   You'd better try somewhere else!

### (iv) How to confirm the booking

| | |
|---|---|
| Gut, ich nehme das Zimmer | Bitte, tragen Sie sich ein |
| Good, I'll take the room | Please sign the register |

## (b) Grammar

### (i) Days of the week
You will find a complete list in the appendix.

### (ii) Months of the year
These are in the appendix, too.

### (iii) Dates
When you want to say 'On a certain date', the ordinal number for the date ends in -en. The English word 'of' is not translated.

| | |
|---|---|
| Am ersten Januar | On the first of January |
| Am zweiten Februar | On the second of February |
| Am dritten März | On the third of March |
| Am vierten April | On the fourth of April |

See Chapter 2 for information on ordinal numbers.

When you want to say 'For the (a certain date)', the ordinal number for the date ends in -en.

Haben Sie ein Zimmer {
für den ersten Januar
für den zweiten Februar
für den dritten März ?
für den vierten April
für den fünften Mai
}

$$\text{Have you got a room} \begin{cases} \text{for the 1st January} \\ \text{for the 2nd February} \\ \text{for the 3rd March} \\ \text{for the 4th April} \\ \text{for the 5th May} \end{cases} ?$$

### (iv) Dates continued

Der wievielte ist heute?　　　　What is the date today?

When you want to say '*It is* (a certain date)', the ordinal number for the date ends in -e.

$$\text{Es ist} \begin{cases} \text{der erste Januar} \\ \text{der zweite Februar} \\ \text{der dritte März} \\ \text{der vierte April} \\ \text{der fünfte Mai} \end{cases} \quad \text{It is} \begin{cases} \text{the 1st of January} \\ \text{the 2nd of February} \\ \text{the 3rd of March} \\ \text{the 4th of April} \\ \text{the 5th of May} \end{cases}$$

### (v) More verbs
The verb BLEIBEN – to stay or remain

This is a *regular* verb. Its stem is unchanged throughout and its endings are also regular.

| | | | | |
|---|---|---|---|---|
| ich | e | ich | bleibe | I stay |
| er | t | er | bleibt | he stays |
| sie　BLEIB- | t | sie | bleibt | she stays |
| wir | en | wir | bleiben | we stay |
| Sie | en | Sie | bleiben | you stay (formal or polite) |

The verb HABEN – to have

This is unfortunately *irregular*, but it is one of the most important and frequent verbs in the whole language, so you had better learn it.

| | | |
|---|---|---|
| ich | habe | I have |
| er | hat | he has |
| sie | hat | she has |
| wir | haben | we have |
| Sie | haben | you have (formal or polite) |

The verb NEHMEN – to take

This is *irregular*, too. Notice how the spelling of the stem changes.

| ich | NEHM- | e | | ich | nehme | I take |
|-----|-------|---|---|-----|-------|--------|
| er | NIMM- | t | | er | nimmt | he takes |
| sie | | | | sie | nimmt | she takes |
| wir | NEHM- | en | | wir | nehmen | we take |
| Sie | | | | Sie | nehmen | you take (formal or polite) |

You will find a table of the most common verbs in the appendix.

### (vi) How to express duration

Questions about duration
Wie lange? – How long?
Für wie lange? – For how long?
Wie lange bleiben Sie? – How long will you be staying?

Statements about duration
O lange! – For a long time
Nicht lange – Not for long

Von Dienstag bis Freitag – From Tuesday until Friday
Bis morgen – Until tomorrow
Bis Dienstag – Until Tuesday
Nur bis Mittwoch – Only until Wednesday
Ein bißchen – For a little while
Noch ein bißchen – For a little while longer

## 3.4 EXERCISES

### Section A

**Exercise 1**
Ask for the following types of hotel room for the length of time indicated. The first one is done for you. If you are studying with a partner, take it in turns to provide both roles.

*Guest*: Haben Sie ein Zimmer frei?
*Hotel*: Jawohl. Was für ein Zimmer?
*Guest*: Ein Einzelzimmer.
*Hotel*: Für wie lange?
*Guest*: Für eine Nacht.

1.
2.
3.
4.
5.
6.
7.
8.
9.
10.

**Exercise 2**
Provide the role of Herr Schmidt. If you are studying with a partner, take it in turns to provide both roles. You will find the complete dialogue with the answers to the exercises in the appendix.

*Schmidt*

1. Greet the receptionist.

3. Ask if there is a room available.

5. Ask whether there is a single room available.

7. Say you want it for one night.

9. Say you'll take the room.

*Empfang*

2. Guten Tag, der Herr!

4. Ja, ein Zimmer habe ich.

6. Für wie lange, bitte?

8. Für eine Nacht. Das geht in Ordnung.

10. Tragen Sie sich bitte ein!


**Exercise 3**
Provide the role of Herr Müller. If you are studying with a partner, take turns to provide both roles. You will find the complete dialogue with the answers to the exercises.

*Müller*

1. Greet the receptionist.

3. Ask whether there is a room available.

5. Ask whether there is a double room available with a private bathroom.

7. Say you want it from today till Sunday.

9. Say you'll take the room.

*Rezeption*

2. Grüß Gott!

4. Ja, das ist möglich.

6. Ja, ein Doppelzimmer habe ich noch. Für wieviele Nächte bitte?

8. Ja, das geht.

10. Bitte, tragen Sie sich ein.

**Section B**

**Exercise 4**

Note the endings of the verb BLEIBEN. Most German verbs in the present tense have the same endings.

| ich | bleibe | -e |
|-----|--------|-----|
| du | bleibst | -st |
| er | bleibt | -t |
| sie | bleibt | -t |
| wir | bleiben | -en |
| ihr | bleibt | -t |
| Sie | bleiben | -en |
| sie | bleiben | -en |

Complete the verbs with the correct endings:
1. Hab– Sie ein Einzelzimmer?
2. Wie lange bleib– Sie?
3. Ich nehm– das Zimmer.
4. Entschuldig– Sie, bitte.
5. Wie komm– ich nach Stauting?
6. Fahr– Sie hier geradeaus.
7. Er bieg– hier nach links ab.
8. Nehm– Sie dann die erste Straße links.
9. Geh– Sie die Marktstraße hoch.
10. Hab– Sie einen Tisch für zwei?
11. Ich hab– einen Tisch um 8 Uhr.
12. Sie bleib– eine Nacht.
13. Sie komm– zur Adriastraße.

**Exercise 5**

This is how to express the year

1933 – neunzehnhundertdreiunddreißig
1956 – neunzehnhundertsechsundfünfzig
1981 – neunzehnhunderteinundachtzig

Now state the following dates (c.f. ordinal numbers in Chapter 2):
1. 2.5.1978.
2. 16.6.1982.
3. 31.12.1979.
4. 11.8.1982.
5. 27.3.1983.
6. 17.5.1985.

# CHAPTER 4

# TRAVELLING BY TRAIN

## 4.1 DIALOGUES 📼

### Dialogue 1

Frau Meyer is going to see her great friend Mitzi, who lives in Augsburg, about 50 km from Munich.

1   *Frau Meyer*:   Grüß Gott!
    *Angestellte*:   Grüß Gott!
    *Frau Meyer*:   Einmal zweiter Klasse nach Augsburg, bitte.
    *Angestellte*:   Einfach oder hin und zurück?
5   *Frau Meyer*:   Hin und zurück , bitte.
    Was kostet das?
    *Angestellte*:   Zweiunddreißig Mark, bitte sehr.
    *Frau Meyer*:   Was? So viel?
    *Angestellte*:   Tut mir leid.
10  *Frau Meyer*:   Das ist ja unerhört!
    *Angestellte*:   Ich kann nichts dafür.
    *Frau Meyer*:   Vierzig Mark.
    *Angestellte*:   (counts) 33, 34, 35, 40, bitte.
    Frau Meyer:   Danke.
15  (still grumbling) Zweiunddreißig Mark.
    Das ist ja unerhört.

    *Frau Meyer*:   Entschuldigen Sie, bitte!
    *Information*:   Ja, bitte?
    *Frau Meyer*:   Wann fährt der Zug nach Augsburg?
20  *Information*:   Augsburg ... Augsburg ....
    Der Zug fährt um 9 Uhr 27.
    Und kommt um 10 Uhr 13 an.
    *Frau Meyer*:   Danke.
    Muß ich umsteigen?

*Einmal zweiter Klasse, bitte*

Photograph: J. Allan Cash Ltd

25  *Information*:  Nein. Der Zug fährt direkt.
   *Frau Me‚eı*.  Danke.
   *Information*:  Bitte.


## Dialogue 2

Antonio wants to go with his uncle and aunt as far as Innsbruck.
They will go on to Rome, and he will return alone to Munich.

1  *Antonio*:  Guten Tag!
   *Angestellte*:  Guten Tag!
   *Antonio*:  Zweimal zweiter Klasse nach Innsbruck, bitte.
   *Angestellte*:  Einfach oder hin und zurück?
5  *Antonio*:  Einfach, bitte.

*Angestellte*: Zweimal einfach nach Innsbruck.
Achtundneunzig Mark, bitte schön.
*Antonio*: Moment.
Dann auch einmal nach Innsbruck.
10 *Angestellte*: Einfach?
*Antonio*: Nein.
Hin und zurück.
*Angestellte*: Zweimal einfach.
Einmal hin und zurück.
15 Stimmt's?
*Antonio*: Ja, das stimmt.
*Angestellte*: Das macht 196 Mark, bitte schön.
*Antonio*: Um wieviel Uhr fährt der Zug nach Innsbruck?
*Information*: Um neun Uhr einunddreißig.
20 *Antonio*: Danke.
Auf welchem Gleis?
*Information*: Auf Gleis 3.
*Antonio*: Danke.
*Information*: Bitte.

## 4.2 INFORMATION

### (a) Notes on Dialogue 1

3. Einmal

In German you draw attention linguistically to the fact that there is only one person travelling. Compare with line 3 of Dialogue 2.

4. Einfach

Literally this means 'simple', but in this context means 'a single'.

5. Hin und zurück

This means literally 'there and back'.

9. Tut mir leid
(Es) tut mir leid

Es tut mir leid is the fuller form of this expression, and is slightly more formal.

19. Wann fährt der Zug ...?

Note that the word 'does' does not exist in German. The question form is made by

| | making the subject and the verb change places in the sentence. |
|---|---|
| 22. Und kommt ... an | The English verb 'to arrive' is rendered in this sentence in German by a verb which has two parts to it. |

**(b) Notes on Dialogue 2**

| 3. Zweimal | This indicates that there are two people travelling. |
|---|---|
| 15. Stimmt's? | Literally stimmt es?. This more colloquial form is usually used. |

**(c) Word list**

Here is a list of the most important words in this chapter. They should be learnt by heart. They are given here in the order in which they occur in the chapter. N.B. Verbs with separable affixes are shown thus: an_kommen.

| | |
|---|---|
| einfach | single |
| oder | or |
| hin und zurück | return |
| was? | what? |
| unerhört | terrible |
| der Zug (-e) | train |
| um_steigen | to change (trains) |
| direkt | straight through |
| einmal | one (i.e. person travelling) |
| zweimal | two (i.e. people travelling) |
| dann | then |
| auch | also/too |
| der Gleis (-e) | platform |
| an_kommen | to arrive |
| ab_fahren | to leave |
| ab_waschen | to wash up |
| ab_trocknen | to dry up |
| auf_räumen | to tidy up |
| an_rufen | to ring up (i.e. telephone) |
| ein_kaufen | to do the shopping |
| ab_schließen | to lock up |

| auf-ab_geben | to give up |
|---|---|
| aus_gehen | to go out |
| der **Tell**er (-) | plate |
| das **Spiel**zeug (-e) | toy |
| die **Le**bens**mitt**el (plural only) | provisions |
| der **Lad**en (ː) | shop |
| die **Ar**beit | work |
| wieder**hol**en | to repeat |
| der Chef | boss |
| die **Mutt**er (ː) | mother |
| das Kind (-er) | child |

## (d) Some phrases

| So viel? | As much as that? |
|---|---|
| Ich kann nichts da**für** | There's nothing I can do about it |
| Das stimmt | That's right |
| Um **wie**viel Uhr? | At what time? |
| Muß ich ... ? | Must I ... ? |
| Um 9 Uhr | At nine o'clock |

## Special note

| Eine Angestellte | A female employee |
|---|---|
| Ein Angestellter | A male employee |
| Eine Reisende | A female traveller |
| Ein Reisender | A male traveller |

## 4.3 STRUCTURAL EXPLANATIONS

### (a) Structures to learn

#### (i) How to state how many tickets you want
(in other words how many people are travelling)

| Einmal | — | one person is travelling |
|---|---|---|
| Zweimal | — | two people are travelling |
| Dreimal | — | three people are travelling |

#### (ii) How to state the class you are travelling

| Erster Klasse | — | 1st class |
|---|---|---|
| Zweiter Klasse | — | 2nd class |

### (iii) How to state your destination
nach Augsburg
nach Innsbruck

### (iv) Single or return?
Einfach
Hin und zurück

Note the similar construction of the following sentences:
1. Einmal erster Klasse nach München, hin und zurück.
2. Zweimal zweiter Klasse nach Bremen, einfach.
3. Dreimal erster Klasse nach Regensburg, hin und zurück.
4. Einmal zweiter Klasse nach Reutlingen, einfach.
5. Zweimal erster Klasse nach Fürth, hin und zurück.
6. Zweimal erster Klasse nach Feuchtwangen, einfach.

If you miss out any of these elements when you ask for your ticket, you will be asked about it.

Einmal zweiter Klasse   This phrase is really an abbreviation of: 'a ticket of the second class'. The idea of a ticket belonging to such a category is conveyed by using the genitive case. See grammatical summary page 310.

### (v) How to ask what time a train leaves

Wann fährt der Zug nach ⎰ Hamm / Münster / Höxter / Bielefeld / München ⎱ ?

### (vi) How to ask what time the train arrives

Wann kommt der Zug in ⎰ Hamm / Münster / Höxter / Bielefeld / München ⎱ an?

### (vi) How to ask if and where you have to change trains

(Wo) muß ich umsteigen?
(Where) do I have to change?

## (b) Grammar

(i) Observe how these sentences are formed:

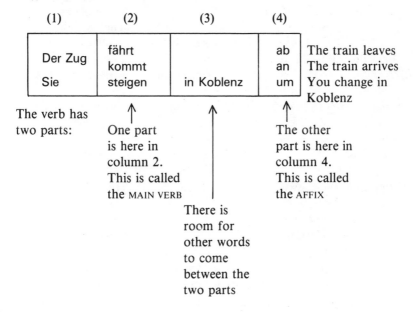

(ii) Observe how these sentences are similar:

| | | |
|---|---|---|
| What do all good husbands do? | Sie waschen ab. | They do the washing up. |
| What do wives do afterwards? | Sie trocknen ab. | They do the drying up. |
| What do (some) children do before they go to bed? | Sie räumen auf. | They tidy up. |
| What does grandma do on Sunday? | Sie ruft an. | She rings up. |
| What does mother do on Friday afternoon? | Sie kauft ein. | She goes shopping. |
| What does the boss do before going home? | Er schließt ab. | He locks up. |
| What does Peter do if he is very discouraged? | Er gibt auf. | He gives up. |
| What does Mary do every Saturday night? | Sie geht aus. | She goes out. |

PERSONAL PRONOUN + MAIN VERB + AFFIX

(iii) And these:

| What does the good husband wash up first? | Er wäscht die Teller ab. | He washes up the plates. |
| What do wives dry up first? | Sie trocknen die Teller ab. | They dry the plates. |
| What do children tidy up? | Sie räumen ihre Spielsachen auf. | They tidy up their toys. |
| When does grandma ring up? | Sie ruft am Sonntag an. | She rings on Sundays. |
| What does mother buy on Fridays? | Sie kauft Lebensmittel ein. | She buys provisions. |
| What does the boss lock up? | Er schließt den Laden ab. | He locks the shop up. |
| What does Peter give up when he is discouraged? | Er gibt seine Arbeit auf. | He gives his work up. |
| When does Mary go out? | Sie geht am Samstag aus. | She goes out on Saturdays. |

PERSONAL PRONOUN + MAIN VERB + another word/expression + AFFIX

Note how these verbs are formed:

| 1 | 2 geh | 2a | 3 aus |
|---|---|---|---|
| ich | | e | |
| er | räum- | t | auf |
| Sie | ruf- | t | an |
| wir | kauf- | en | ein |
| Sie | geh- | en | aus |

← Column 3 contains the verb affixes

↑ These are regular endings to add to the stem of verbs

The most common affixes are: an, auf, aus, bei, ein, her, hin, mit, nach, vor and zu. The affix is put last in the sentence.

Note the formation of the verbs, used in the sentences below:

| ich trockne ab | wasche ab | schließe ab | gebe auf |
| er trocknet ab | wäscht ab | schließt ab | gibt auf |
| sie trocknet ab | wäscht ab | schließt ab | gibt auf |
| wir trocknen ab | waschen ab | schließen ab | geben auf |
| Sie trocknen ab | waschen ab | schließen ab | geben auf |

**Looking up verbs with separable affixes in the dictionary**
If you want to look up one of these verbs in the dictionary, or a vocabulary list, you must look up the right form of the verb. For example, you will not find wäscht ... ab, or trocknet ... ab; you must look up abwaschen or abtrocknen; these forms are called the *infinitive*. Here are some more examples:

| steht auf | aufstehen | ⎫ | infinitive |
|-----------|-----------|---|------------|
| macht ... zu | zumachen | ⎬ | (When the infinitive form |
| fährt ... ab | abfahren | ⎬ | of the verb is used, the |
| kommt ... an | ankommen | ⎭ | affix is stressed) |

## 4.4 EXERCISES

### Section A

**Exercise 1**
Ask the times of trains to the following places:

| | |
|---|---|
| Nürnberg | Erlangen |
| Würzburg | Ansbach |
| Innsbruck | Großhabersdorf |
| Frankfurt | Forchheim |
| Treuchtlingen | Schwabach |

**Exercise 2**
Look at the symbol. You'll see that it is intended to indicate that one person wishes to travel to Berlin, 2nd class; the double-headed arrow indicates that the person wishes to make a return journey, there and back.

*Reisender*:   Einmal zweiter Klasse nach Berlin, bitte.
*Angestellte*:   Einfach oder hin und zurück?
*Reisender*:   Hin und zurück, bitte.

Make up similar dialogues to match the following symbols. If you can work with a partner, take it in turns to play the part of the Reisender and the Angestellte.

1.                               2.

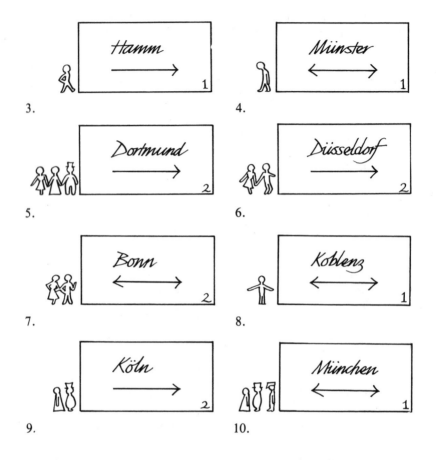

3. Hamm →  1

4. Münster ←→  1

5. Dortmund →  2

6. Düsseldorf →  2

7. Bonn ←→  2

8. Koblenz ←→  1

9. Köln →  2

10. München ←→  1

## Section B

### Exercise 3

Put into German:

1. Grandma (Oma) rings up on Saturday.
2. Ingrid goes out on Tuesday.
3. The children (die Kinder) tidy up the shop.
4. Mother (Mutter) clears up the toys.
5. Peter washes up the plates.
6. Inge buys provisions.
7. Helmut washes up on Sunday.
8. The boss (der Chef) gives up his work.
9. Mary (Maria) closes the shop.
10. Grandma goes out on Saturday.

**Exercise 4**

The words in these sentences are jumbled up. Sort them out so that they are in the correct order.

1. Wann ab fährt der Zug nach Bonn?
2. Wir ab Laden den schließen.
3. Geht Dienstag aus am Oma.
4. Am an Mittwoch Peter ruft.
5. Lebensmittel ein Chef kauft der.
6. Wäscht Teller Mutter ab die.
7. Kinder Teller ab trocknen die die.
8. Er ein Lebensmittel kauft.
9. Gibt Arbeit der seine auf Chef.
10. Ich auf Spielsachen räume die.

# CHAPTER 5

# TRAVELLING BY TAXI, BUS OR TRAM

## 5.1 DIALOGUES 📼

**Dialogue 1**

Elke is late for her appointment with Fritz, and in order to avoid having another row with him about punctuality, she decides to take a taxi.

1  *Elke*:   (dials taxi number) Ich möchte ein Taxi bitte.
   *Angestellte*:   Ihr Name?
   *Elke*:   Kustmann.
5  *Angestellte*:   Adresse?
   *Elke*:   Fürstenstraße 15.
   *Angestellte*:   Wohin?
   *Elke*:   Zur Nietzschestraße.
   *Angestellte*:   Das Taxi ist in 10 Minuten da.
10  *Elke*:   Danke.

   *Taxifahrer*:   (rings frontdoor bell) Frau Kustmann?
   *Elke*:   Ja.
   *Taxifahrer*:   Ihr Taxi ist hier.

15  *Elke*:   (gets in) Zur Nietzschestraße, bitte. Nummer 30.
   *Taxifahrer*:   Ja, ist in Ordnung.
   *Taxifahrer*:   (arriving in Nietzschestraße) So, bitte schön.
20  *Elke*:   Was macht das?
   *Taxifahrer*:   Das macht 6 Mark 50.
   *Elke*:   (giving him 7 Marks) Danke. Das stimmt so.

*Ihr Taxi ist hier!*

*Photograph: Bavaria-Verlag/Ludwig Windstosser*

25  *Taxifahrer*:  Danke schön.
    Auf Wiedersehen.

**Dialogue 2**

Frau Meyer wants to go to the centre of Munich for her annual visit to the Christkindl Markt during the week before Christmas.

The Christkindl Markt takes place on the Marienplatz in front of the town hall. There are many stalls selling fried sausages, hot punch, sweets, nuts, and Christmas delicacies of all sorts. There are also many stalls selling Christmas decorations and presents.

1 *Frau Meyer*: Entschuldigung!
Fährt die Nummer 23 zum Rathaus?
*Mann*: Nein, nicht die Nummer 23.
*Frau Meyer*: Ach du lieber Himmel!
5 Welche Straßenbahn fährt denn zum Rathaus?
*Mann*: Sie brauchen die Nummer 18.
Sie fährt zum Rathaus.
*Frau Meyer*: Ach, vielen Dank.
Die Nummer 18.
10 *Mann*: Ja, sie fährt zum Rathaus.
*Frau Meyer*: (to herself)
Das ist ja unerhört!!
Das war immer die 23!!

## 5.2 INFORMATION

### (a) Notes on Dialogue 1

6. Fürstenstraße 15 — Note that in German you say the name of the street first and the number afterwards.

9. Das Taxi ist in 10 Minuten da — Note that here German uses the present tense to indicate future time.

24. Das stimmt so — The customer indicates that he or she requires no change with the phrase Das stimmt so. It is common practice to round up bills to the next highest mark.

### (b) Word list

Here is a list of the most important words in this chapter. They should be learnt by heart. They are given here in the order in which they occur in the chapter.

| | |
|---|---|
| das **Tax**i (-s) | taxi |
| der **Na**me | name |
| die **Adresse** (-n) | address |
| **wohin?** | where to? |

| | |
|---|---|
| die Minute (-n) | minute |
| da | there |
| hier | here |
| Entschuldigung | excuse me |
| die Nummer (-n) | number |
| welch-? | which? |
| die Straßenbahn (-en) | tram |
| brauchen | to need |
| fahren (fährt) | to go (of transport) |
| immer | always |
| der Hauptbahnhof | main station |
| der Flughafen (⁻) | airport |
| das Zentrum | centre |
| das Rathaus (⁻er) | town hall |
| nicht | not |
| die Stadt (⁻e) | town |
| das Schloß (⁻er) | castle or palace |
| die Stadtmitte (-n) | town centre |
| die Oper (-n) | opera or opera house |
| die Quittung (-en) | receipt |
| der Bus (-se) | bus |
| das Freibad (⁻er) | open-air swimming pool |
| die Sekretärin (-nen) | secretary |
| der Freund (-e) | friend |
| das Geld | money |
| das Zimmer (-) | room |
| der Zug (⁻e) | train |

**Some phrases**

| | |
|---|---|
| Ach, du lieber Himmel! | Good Heavens! |

## 5.3 STRUCTURAL EXPLANATIONS

### (a) Structures to learn

(i) **Ordering a taxi** (how to state your address)

| | |
|---|---|
| Hindenburgstraße 17 | The name of the street is stated |
| Mozartstraße 25 | first. The number comes after. |
| Nietzschestraße 30 | |
| Oskar von Müller Ring 129 | |
| Neue Straße 6 | |
| Kennedy Allee 43 | |

## (ii) How to state your destination

zum
- Hauptbahnhof
- Flughafen
- Rathaus
- Stadtzentrum
- Schloß Nymphenburg

(all these words are masculine or neuter)

zur
- Hindenburgstraße
- Kennedy Allee
- Stadtmitte
- Oper

(all these words are feminine)

Zum is used with masculine and neuter nouns, zur is used with feminine nouns. These expressions are used in the directions which the customer gives when streets or buildings are named, particularly when they are within the town where one takes the taxi.

nach
- Perlach
- Wedding
- Wellingsbüttel
- Zirndorf

Nach is used when the customer names an area or district or when the taxi has to go to another town.

## (iii) How to pay the taxi driver

Was macht das?     How much is that?

## (iv) How to get a receipt for the taxi fare

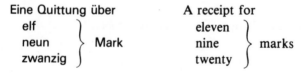

Eine Quittung über
- elf
- neun
- zwanzig
Mark

A receipt for
- eleven
- nine
- twenty
marks

## (v) How to enquire where a bus or tram goes to

Fährt
- diese Straßenbahn
- dieser Bus

- zum Rathaus
- zur Stadtmitte
- nach Fürth
?

Welcher Bus / Welche Straßenbahn fährt
- zum Freibad
- zur Oper
- nach Neustadt
?

## (b) Grammar

### (i) The indefinite article

As we saw in Chapter 1, all German nouns can be categorised in one of three genders: masculine, feminine or neuter. When you want to say, for instance, *a* boy, or *an* apple, these words, which are called *indefinite articles*, vary according to the gender of the noun they accompany. Here are some examples:

| Masc. | Fem. | Neut. |
|---|---|---|
| ein Professor | eine Sekretärin | ein Zimmer |
| ein Zug | eine Straße | ein Taxi |

We can summarise this rule by tabulating the *indefinite articles* alone.

| Masc. | Fem. | Neut. |
|---|---|---|
| ein | eine | ein |

N.B. If you think about it, there can be no plural of 'a', or 'an'.

### (ii) The negative

If you want to say 'not a', or 'not an', then the word is kein. It behaves just like the *indefinite article*.

| Masc. | Fem. | Neut. |
|---|---|---|
| Der ist kein | Sie ist keine | Das ist kein Taxi! |
| Professor! | Sekretärin! | |

We can summarise this rule thus:

| Masc. | Fem. | Neut. | Plur. |
|---|---|---|---|
| kein | keine | kein | keine |

N.B. The play *St Joan* begins with the memorable phrase 'No eggs! No eggs!', from which you see that there can be a plural form of the German word kein. Keine Eier! 'No eggs!'

The word for 'not' is nicht. Nicht die Nummer 13. 'Not the number 13.'

### (iii) Subjects and direct objects

a) The subject of a sentence is the person or thing which *does* the action or event indicated by the verb. All the forms of the indefinite and negative article, described above, are the subjects of sentences. In German, the subjects of sentences are said to be in the 'nominative case'. We can summarise this rule thus:

| | Masc. | Fem. | Neut. |
|---|---|---|---|
| | ein | eine | ein |
| NOMINATIVE | kein | keine | kein |

b) Consider the sentence 'The dog bit the postman'. We know who did the biting. It was the dog; the subject of the sentence. We also know who shouted 'Ouch!' It was the postman! We can say therefore, that whatever is bitten, bought, kicked, liked, etc., is the *direct object* of a verb. In the following sentences, the *direct objects* are printed in italics. Note that verbs describing states, as well as actions, have direct objects.

Peter kicked *a ball*
We bought *a house*
I have *a room*
He likes *beer*
She has not got *a cheque book*

Here are some German sentences with the *direct objects* underlined.

Der Professor hat eine Sekretärin
Sie hat keinen Freund
Ich habe kein Geld
Frau Meyer braucht eine Tasse Kaffee

In German, the direct objects of sentences are said to be in the 'accusative case'. We can summarise this rule thus:

|  | **Masc.** | **Fem.** | **Neut.** |
|---|---|---|---|
|  | einen | eine | ein |
| ACCUSATIVE | keinen | keine | kein |

N.B. It is the *masculine* form of the *indefinite article* which is different in the *accusative case*. The difference is the letter n.

N.B. There is no direct object after the verb sein: 'to be'.

(iv) **The definite article**

a) When you want to say *the* professor, *the* street, or *the* house, these words, which are called *definite articles* vary according to the gender of the noun they accompany. Here are some examples:

| **Masc.** | **Fem.** | **Neut.** |
|---|---|---|
| der Professor | die Straße | das Haus |
| der Zug | die Sekretärin | das Taxi |

We can summarise this rule by tabulating the definite article alone:

|  | **Masc.** | **Fem.** | **Neut.** |
|---|---|---|---|
| NOMINATIVE | der | die | das |

b) If you think back to that postman who got bitten a little while ago, you will remember what *direct objects* are. They are said to be in the 'accusative case'. Now, we can summarise the rule about the *definite article* as we did for the *indefinite article*:

|  | **Masc.** | **Fem.** | **Neut.** | **Plur.** |
|---|---|---|---|---|
| NOMINATIVE | der | die | das | die |
| ACCUSATIVE | den | die | das | die |

Notice the definite article has a *plural form*, because we can talk about 'the dogs', or even 'the postmen'. Notice, too, that the difference between the nominative and the accusative case is again the letter n.

You will find a full list of definite and indefinite articles in the appendix.

(v) **'Some' or 'any'**

These words which are so important in English are generally not required in German:

| Haben Sie Geld? | Have you any money? |
|---|---|
| Nein, ich habe kein Geld | No, I haven't got any money |
| (at a party): | |
| Herr Müller, Sie haben kein Bier | Herr Müller, you haven't got any beer |

(vi) **Prepositions**

Consider the following sentences, taken from the dialogues:

| Zur Nietzschestraße | To Nietzsche Street |
|---|---|
| Die Nummer 18 fährt zum Rathaus | The number 18 goes to the town hall |

As we saw earlier, zum is used with *masculine* and *neuter* nouns, zur is used with *feminine* nouns.

Now, we must understand that each of these two words is a contraction of two other words:

zum = zu dem
zur = zu der

The two words dem and der are examples of our old friends, the definite articles. Here, where they accompany the *preposition* zu, they are said to be in the *dative case*. Another case!! There will be more about this in Chapter 9.

(vii) Some prepositions accompany the *accusative case*, and others accompany the *dative case*. (Some prepositions may be used with both cases!) You will find a complete list in the appendix.

## 5.4 EXERCISES

### Section A

### Exercise 1
See how many sentences you can make.

$$\text{Fährt}\left\{\begin{array}{l}\text{dieser Bus}\\\text{diese Straßenbahn}\\\text{dieser Zug}\\\text{die Nummer 15}\end{array}\right\}\left\{\begin{array}{l}\text{nach}\\\\\text{zum}\\\\\text{zur}\end{array}\right.\left\{\begin{array}{l}\text{Egersdorf}\\\text{Steinach}\\\text{Stadttheater}\\\text{Rathaus}\\\text{Flughafen}\\\text{Stadtmitte}\\\text{Goethestraße}\end{array}\right.\quad?$$

### Exercise 2
1. You're at the Number 17 tram stop and you want to go to the town hall. What do you say to the lady who is already waiting there?
2. Perhaps you're an opera singer visiting the town for the first time.
3. Perhaps you want to go to the district of Munich called Perlach.
4. You think you want the Number 23, but does it go to the town centre?
5. Was it the 31 that goes to the airport?
6. You're pretty certain that it's the Number 1, but does it go to the open-air swimming pool?
7. Which tram is it that goes to the station?
8. And which bus goes to the Heidenstraße?
9. You know there's a bus to Egersdorf, but which one?
10. Which bus goes to Göttingen?

### Section B

### Exercise 3
Convert the following sentences into the negative. The first one is done for you:

e.g. Ich habe ein Buch.
　　 Ich habe kein Buch.

1. Er hat ein Auto.
2. Sie möchte einen Kaffee.
3. Er ist Professor.
4. Sie hat eine Einladung.
5. Wir haben einen Hund.

6. Das ist der Bahnhof.
7. Der Garten ist groß.
8. Der Vater ist alt.
9. Frau Meier ist jung.
10. Santos ist in Hamburg.

# CHAPTER 6

# ILLNESS

## 6.1 DIALOGUES 📼

**Dialogue 1**

Frau Meyer has had another very bad night, so she decides to go and see her doctor. She rings for an appointment.

1  *Assistentin*:  Praxis Doktor Storm.
Guten Morgen.
*Frau Meyer*:  Guten Morgen.
Ich möchte den Arzt sehen.
5  *Assistentin*:  Haben Sie einen Termin?
*Frau Meyer*:  Nein.
Geht es heute vormittag?
*Assistentin*:  Nein.
Es tut mir leid.
10  Heute vormittag ist nichts mehr frei.
*Frau Meyer*:  Donnerwetter!
Ist nichts mehr frei?
*Assistentin*:  Nein.
Es tut mir leid.
15  *Frau Meyer*:  Geht es heute nachmittag?
*Assistentin*:  Ja. Kommen Sie um 16 Uhr.
*Frau Meyer*:  Gott sei Dank!
Um 16 Uhr.
Ja, das geht.
20  Danke schön.
*Assistentin*:  Auf Wiederhören!
*Frau Meyer*:  Auf Wiederhören!

**Dialogue 2**

Fritz Löb went out to his Stammtisch at the Gasthaus Adler last night. It was his regular Wednesday night out and as sometimes

*Patienten – Wartezimmer*

Photograph: Bavaria-Verlag/Laurinpress

happens he had too much to drink. The following morning he finds himself in Dr Storm's surgery explaining his symptoms.

1 *Doktor Storm*: Nun, was fehlt Ihnen denn?
  *Fritz*: Ich habe Kopfschmerzen.
  *Doktor Storm*: Ist das alles?
  *Fritz*: Nein, Herr Doktor.
5   Mein Bauch tut weh, und ich habe Durchfall.
  *Doktor Storm*: Seit wann haben Sie Durchfall?
  *Fritz*: Seit gestern.
  *Doktor Storm*: Ich verschreibe Ihnen etwas für den Durchfall.
  *Fritz*: Vielen Dank, Herr Doktor.

**Dialogue 3**
Antonio once entertained ambitions of playing for Inter Milan. He has had to settle for something less exalted, however, and he plays for a Munich club called TSV 1886. On Sunday afternoon he had a difference of opinion with an opposing goalkeeper and on this Monday morning he finds himself in Dr Storm's surgery.

1 *Doktor Storm*: Nun, wo tut es weh?
  *Antonio*: Hier.
    Es ist mein Rücken.

*Doktor Storm*: Hier?
(He pokes Antonio's back)
5 *Antonio*: Au!! Ja!
*Doktor Storm*: Ist das ein stechender Schmerz?
*Antonio*: Ja! Stichartig.
*Doktor Storm*: Ist der Schmerz immer stichartig?
*Antonio*: Nein.
10 In der Nacht war es ein dumpfer Schmerz.
*Doktor Storm*: So, so.
Kein Fußball für Sie.
*Antonio*: O weh.

## 6.2 INFORMATION

### (a) Notes on Dialogue 1

| | |
|---|---|
| 5. Termin | der Termin means a date or a fixed time for an appointment. |
| 7. Geht es | The expressions Geht es? or Es geht are very useful expressions which can be used in many situations. It is the equivalent, in English, of expressions such as 'It's all right' or 'It's OK' or 'It's working'. |
| 11. Donnerwetter | This is a fairly acute expression of impatience or irritation but one which can be used in society without giving offence. |
| 16. 16 Uhr | Note that the 24-hour clock is used in any sort of formal situation. |

### (b) Notes on Dialogue 2

| | |
|---|---|
| Stammtisch | A Stammtisch is a table in a Gasthaus which is reserved for certain regular customers on a particular day each week. Nearly every Gasthaus has its Stammtisch and there is often a notice on it indicating that it is reserved on a particular day. |

The Stammtisch customers sometimes meet in order to talk about matters of mutual interest but they may also often play cards and in particular the very popular German card game Skat.

6. Seit wann?  Note that the English expression 'How long?' is rendered in German by the expression 'Since when?' It is, therefore, quite logical, as in the next line, to have the expression Seit gestern.

**(c) Notes on Dialogue 3**

TSV 1886  The letters TSV stand for Turn- und Sportverein and the date indicates the year in which the club was founded.

**(d) Word list**

Here is a list of the most important words in this chapter. They should be learnt by heart. They are given here in the order in which they occur in the chapter.

N.B. Parts of the body are given in the appendix.

| | |
|---|---|
| die **Prax**is | practice (of a doctor) |
| der Arzt (ᴗə) | doctor |
| **seh**en | to see |
| **heu**te | today |
| der **Vor**mittag (-e) | morning |
| nichts | nothing |
| der **Nach**mittag (-e) | afternoon |
| nun | now |
| die **Kopf**schmerzen (plural) | headache |
| **all**es | everything |
| der Bauch | stomach |
| der **Durch**fall | diarrhoea |
| seit | since |
| **ges**tern | yesterday |
| ver**schrei**ben | to prescribe |
| **et**was | something |

| der **Rücken** (-) | back |
| der **Schmerz** (-en) | pain |
| **stech**end | sharp (of a pain) |
| **stich**artig | shooting (of a pain) |
| **im**mer | always |
| die **Nacht** (¨e) | night |
| **dumpf** | dull |
| der **Fuß**ball (-) | football |
| der **Zahn**arzt (¨e) | dentist |
| das **Fie**ber | fever or high temperature |
| die **Stun**de (-n) | hour |
| der **Tag** (-e) | day |
| **leicht** | slight |
| **stark** | strong or severe |
| **tro**cken | dry |
| ge**broch**en | broken |
| die **Reise** (-n) | journey |
| **nett** | nice |

**(e) Some phrases**

| **Heu**te **Vor**mittag | this morning |
| **Heu**te **Nach**mittag | this afternoon |
| Es tut mir leid | I'm sorry |
| Gott sei Dank! | Thank Goodness! |
| Das geht | That's all right |
| Auf **Wie**dersehen | Goodbye |
| Was fehlt **Ih**nen? | What's the matter? |
| ... tut weh | ... hurts |
| O weh! | Oh dear! |

## 6.3 STRUCTURAL EXPLANATIONS

**(a) Structures to learn**

(i) **How to make an appointment to see the doctor**

Ich möchte
den Arzt
den Zahnarzt } sehen

I'd like to see the
{ doctor
{ dentist

Geht es
heute vormittag
heute nachmittag ?
morgen

Is
this morning
this afternoon } possible?
tomorrow

| Kommen Sie um | Come at |
|---|---|
| 10 Uhr | ten o'clock |
| 14 Uhr | two o'clock |
| 16 Uhr 30 | four thirty |

## (ii) How to describe symptoms of illness

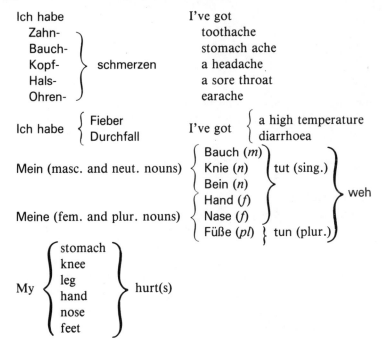

| Ich habe | I've got |
|---|---|
| Zahn- | toothache |
| Bauch- | stomach ache |
| Kopf- ⟩ schmerzen | a headache |
| Hals- | a sore throat |
| Ohren- | earache |

Ich habe { Fieber / Durchfall }   I've got { a high temperature / diarrhoea }

Mein (masc. and neut. nouns) { Bauch (*m*) / Knie (*n*) / Bein (*n*) } tut (sing.)

Meine (fem. and plur. nouns) { Hand (*f*) / Nase (*f*) / Füße (*pl*) } tun (plur.) } weh

My { stomach / knee / leg / hand / nose / feet } hurt(s)

## (iii) How to express how long symptoms have lasted

| Seit | gestern | Since yesterday |
|---|---|---|
| | mehreren Stunden | For several hours |
| | drei Tagen | For three days |

## (iv) How to describe the type of pain

| Es tut weh | It hurts or aches |
|---|---|
| Wo tut es weh? | Where does it hurt? |

| Ist es | Is it |
|---|---|
| Es ist | It's |

ein { stechender / dumpfer / stichartiger / leichter / starker } Schmerz   a { sharp / dull / shooting / slight / severe } pain

## (b) Grammar

### (i) Parts of the body
You will find a list of parts of the body in the appendix.

### (ii) Adjectives
The following words appeared in the dialogues. They are *adjectives*. They *describe* nouns.

| stechend | – | sharp (of pain) |
| stichartig | – | shooting (of pain) |
| dumpf | – | dull (of pain) |
| trocken | – | dry |

When adjectives occur in speech, they sometimes come *before* the noun they describe, and they sometimes come *after* it. Here are some examples.

Das ist ein stechend*er* Schmerz
Der Schmerz ist stechend

You will have noticed that when the adjective *precedes* the noun, it has an ending and when it comes *after* the noun, it doesn't have one.

The problem is to know which ending to give the adjective, and when. Here is part of the rule:

> When one of the following words comes in front of the adjective, certain endings, shown below, are required. It is important to point out that these endings, while being important in *written* German, will, if got wrong, hardly ever prevent you from being understood. So take heart!

| ein | – | a; an | unser | – | our |
| kein | – | not a | euer | – | your (familiar plural) |
| mein | – | my | | | |
| dein | – | your (familiar) | Ihr | – | your (polite) |
| sein | – | his | ihr | – | their |
| ihr | – | her | | | |
| sein | – | its | | | |

Note the endings of the adjectives after ein, kein, mein, etc.

| | **Sing.** | |
| | **Masc.** | **Fem.** |
| | a dull pain | a sore or chapped lip |
| NOMINATIVE | ein dumpf*er* Schmerz | eine trocken*e* Lippe |
| ACCUSATIVE | einen dumpf*en* Schmerz | eine trocken*e* Lippe |

**Neut.**

a broken leg

NOMINATIVE ein gebrochenes Bein
ACCUSATIVE ein gebrochenes Bein

**Plur.** (all genders)

|  | Masc. | Fem. | Neut. |
|---|---|---|---|
| NOMINATIVE | keine gebrochenen Arme | Rippen | Beine |
| ACCUSATIVE | keine gebrochenen Arme | Rippen | Beine |

(iii) **The 24-hour clock**

In German-speaking countries the 24-hour clock is used for all formal expressions of time and in particular for travelling in order to express times of arrival and departure, etc. As long as you know the cardinal numbers up to 60, it is very easy (see Chapter 2).

1. 13:00 dreizehn Uhr
2. 12:00 zwölf Uhr
3. 09:05 neun Uhr fünf
4. 18:15 achtzehn Uhr fünfzehn
5. 16:25 sechzehn Uhr fünfundzwanzig
6. 21:30 einundzwanzig Uhr dreißig
7. 11:10 elf Uhr zehn
8. 06:20 sechs Uhr zwanzig
9. 21:30 einundzwanzig Uhr dreißig
10. 14:45 vierzehn Uhr fünfundvierzig

## 6.4 EXERCISES

**Section A**

**Exercise 1**

What would you say if:

1. The filling in your wisdom tooth has come out.
2. You have eaten too many cherries.
3. You drank too much wine last night.
4. You have been coughing all night.
5. Your neuralgia has returned.
6. You have a fever.
7. Your shoes are too tight.
8. That meat you had yesterday wasn't fresh.
9. You have tripped up and fallen on your knee.
10. Your temperature is 103°.

N.B. *Normal* body temperature is 98.4° Fahrenheit, but 36.6° Celsius, the system used in Germany.

**Exercise 2**

Play the role of the patient in the following dialogue. Make up the part of the patient and read aloud the part of the doctor. If you are working with a partner, take it in turns to play the role of the doctor and the patient.

| Patient | Arzt |
|---|---|
| 1. Greet the doctor | |
| | 2. Guten Tag. Was fehlt Ihnen? |
| 3. Say you have a sore throat. | |
| | 4. Seit wann haben Sie Halsschmerzen? |
| 5. Say you've had it for three days. | |
| | 6. Ich verschreibe Ihnen etwas für die Halsschmerzen. |

**Exercise 3**

Say the following parts of your body hurt:

| Your | head | Your | arm |
|---|---|---|---|
| | leg | | stomach |
| | foot | | ear |
| | hand | | knee |
| | back | | tooth |

**Section B**

**Exercise 4**

You are feeling very negative about life. Answer all the following questions in the negative.
1. Ist das ein gutes Buch?
2. Ist das eine schöne Frau?
3. Ist das eine ruhige Straße?
4. Ist das ein ruhiges Zimmer?
5. War das ein schöner Abend?
6. War das eine gute Reise?
7. War das eine ruhige Nacht?
8. War das ein schöner Ausblick?

**Exercise 5**

You are still feeling very negative.
1. Haben Sie eine ruhige Frau?
2. Haben Sie ein gutes Zimmer?

3. Haben Sie einen schönen Ausblick?
4. Haben Sie ein neues Buch?
5. Haben Sie einen neuen Fußball?
6. Haben Sie einen guten Doktor?
7. Haben Sie eine nette Schwester?
8. Haben Sie eine ruhige Straße?

# CHAPTER 7

# SHOPPING

## 7.1 DIALOGUES 📼

**Dialogue 1**

It will soon be Elke's birthday, and Fritz Löb wants to buy her a pullover. However, he is rather unused to buying ladies' clothes.

1  *Verkäuferin*:  Was darf es sein?

   *Fritz*:  (speaking by instinct)

   Ich schaue mich nur um.

   *Verkäuferin*:  Ja, bitte schön.

   Fritz:  (clears his throat)

   Fräulein!

5  *Verkäuferin*:  Ja? Was darf es sein, bitte?

*Ich möchte einen Damenpullover*

*Photograph: Bavaria-Verlag / Rudolf Holtappel*

*Fritz*: Ich möchte einen Pullover.
*Verkäuferin*: Ja. Herren- oder Damenpullover?
*Fritz*: Einen Damenpullover suche ich.
*Verkäuferin*: Ja. Welche Größe trägt die Dame?
10 *Fritz*: O, ich weiß es nicht genau.
Mittelgröße, glaube ich.
*Verkäuferin*: So wie ich?
*Fritz*: (embarrassed and trying not to look too closely)
Ja, so ungefähr.
*Verkäuferin*: Ja, Größe vierzig.
15 An welches Material hatten Sie gedacht?
*Fritz*: Ach ja. Das Material. Natürlich.
*Verkäuferin*: Wolle? Baumwolle? Oder eine Kunstfaser?
*Fritz*: Wolle! Ja, aus Wolle.
*Verkäuferin*: Ich habe hier einen schönen roten Pullover.
20 Der ist aus Wolle.
*Fritz*: Nein. Sie hat schon einen roten Pullover.
Haben Sie diese Art in blau?
*Verkäuferin*: Hat die Dame blaue Augen?
*Fritz*: Eigentlich ja.
25 *Verkäuferin*: Ich habe hier einen blauen Pullover.
*Fritz*: Ja. Der blaue Pullover ist bestimmt schön.
Was kostet er?
*Verkäuferin*: 65 Mark.
*Fritz*: Ich nehme ihn.

**Dialogue 2**
Frau Meyer has been needing a pair of new shoes for ages.
1 *Verkäufer*: Kann ich Ihnen helfen?
*Frau Meyer*: Ich brauche neue Schuhe.
*Verkäufer*: Ja, bitte schön.
(looking at Frau Meyer's shoes)
Sie tragen Größe 37, glaube ich.
5 *Frau Meyer*: Nein. Ich trage immer Größe 36.
*Verkäufer*: (sceptically)
Ach so.
*Frau Meyer*: Was kosten die braunen Schuhe im
Schaufenster?
*Verkäufer*: Die sind Größe 37.
10 *Frau Meyer*: Haben Sie die braunen Schuhe eine Nummer
kleiner?
*Verkäufer*: Ja, die gleichen Schuhe habe ich hier.
Sie sind aber schwarz.

*Kann ich sie anprobieren?*

Photograph: Bavaria-Verlag/Rudolph Holtappel

  *Frau Meyer*: Kann ich sie anprobieren?
15 *Verkäufer*: Selbstverständlich können Sie sie anprobieren.
  *Frau Meyer*: (taking a few steps)
  Au!!! Das tut weh!
  Sie sind zu klein.
  *Verkäufer*: Möchten Sie die braunen Schuhe anprobieren?
  *Frau Meyer*: Sind die Sohlen aus Leder?
20 *Verkäufer*: Nein. Die braunen Schuhe haben
  Kunststoffsohlen.
  *Frau Meyer*: Kunststoffsohlen! Furchtbar!
  Das gefällt mir überhaupt nicht.
  Haben Sie keine Schuhe mit Ledersohlen.
25 *Verkäufer*: Na, freilich.
  Schauen Sie.
  Diese blauen Schuhe sind sehr elegant.
  Sie sind hundertprozentig aus Leder.
  *Frau Meyer*: Welche Größe?
30 *Verkäufer*: Größe 37.
  *Frau Meyer*: Was kosten sie?
  *Verkäufer*: Sie kosten 145 Mark.
  *Frau Meyer*: Was? Das ist mir zu teuer!
  Auf Wiedersehen!
35 *Verkäufer*: Auf Wiedersehen!
  *Frau Meyer*: (grumbling to herself) Allerhand! Allerhand ist
  das! 145 Mark!!

## 7.2 INFORMATION

### (a) Notes on Dialogue 1

| | |
|---|---|
| 4. Fräulein! | This word is used, regardless of age, to summon the attention of a salesgirl or saleslady. |
| 8. Einen Damenpullover | Note how the positions of the subject and the object in this sentence have been reversed. In German the object quite often comes at the beginning of a sentence, so that it can be emphasised. German is able to do this quite easily because the masculine object of a sentence is 'marked', in this case by the letters -en, which are added to the word ein. |
| 10. Ich weiß es | Note how German has to say Ich weiß es – 'I know it', where English would normally just say 'I know'. |
| 15. An welches Material . . . ? | Note that where English says 'I think of', German says denken an. |
| 18. aus Wolle | English says 'made of wool'. German says aus Wolle. |
| 20. Der ist . . . | The subject pronoun is normally er, or sie. However, to give the pronoun emphasis the words der or die are frequently used. |

### (b) Notes on Dialogue 2

| | |
|---|---|
| 6. Ach so | This is one of the most useful expressions you can learn in German because it allows you to express polite interest in what other people are saying, even if you don't feel up to uttering a word yourself. By using it |

judiciously, and with a good pronunciation, you can probably establish a reputation for vast intelligence and language mastery. It means 'really', 'is that what you mean?', 'how interesting!', 'indeed'. Whichever of these meanings you intend the phrase to have, the one constant underlying significance of the phrase is that you are being told something which you did not know before. If you say nothing else, you will probably get full marks for diplomacy.

| | | |
|---|---|---|
| 8. | im Schaufenster | The word im is a contraction of in dem. |
| 9. | Die sind . . . | See note to line 20 on Dialogue 1. |
| 12. | Die gleichen Schuhe | See note to line 8 on Dialogue 1. |
| 26. | Überhaupt nicht | This phrase or gar nicht are very useful idioms meaning 'not at all'. |
| 29. | Schauen Sie | In the north of Germany you may hear an alternative version of this expression: Sehen Sie. |
| 31. | Hundertprozentig | This useful word can be used for expressions such as 'absolutely' or 'completely'. |

**(c) Word list**

Here is a list of the most important words in this chapter. They should be learnt by heart. They are given here in the order in which they occur in the chapter.

der Pull**over** (-)            pullover

| | |
|---|---|
| der **Herr**enpullover (-) | gentlemen's pullover |
| **su**chen | to look for |
| die **Größ**e (-n) | size |
| **tra**gen | to wear |
| die **Da**me (-n) | lady |
| **wiss**en | to know |
| gen**au** | exactly |
| die **Mittelgröß**e | medium size |
| unge**fähr** | approximately |
| das **Mat**erial | material |
| na**tür**lich | of course |
| die **Wo**lle | wool |
| die **Baum**wolle | cotton |
| rot | red |
| schon | already |
| die Art | sort or kind |
| blau | blue |
| das **Au**ge (-n) | eye |
| **ei**gentlich | actually |
| be**stimmt** | really or certainly |
| **kos**ten | to cost |
| **neh**men | to take |
| **hel**fen (hilft) | to help |
| **brau**chen | to need |
| neu | new |
| der Schuh (-e) | shoe |
| **glau**ben | to believe |
| braun | brown |
| das **Schau**fenster (-) | window (of a shop) |
| klein | small |
| groß | large |
| gleich | the same |
| aber | but |
| schwarz | black |
| anpro**bier**en | to try on |
| selbstver**ständ**lich | of course |
| **kö**nnen | to be able to or to be allowed to |
| die **Soh**le (-n) | sole |
| das **Le**der | leather |
| der **Kunst**stoff | artificial material |
| **furcht**bar | terrible |
| **frei**lich | certainly |
| **schau**en | to look |

| hundertprozentig | entirely |
|---|---|
| teuer | dear or expensive |
| der Rock (¨e) | skirt |
| die Hose | trousers |
| das Nachthemd (-en) | nightshirt |
| die Bluse (-n) | blouse |
| die Weste (-n) | sleeveless jacket |
| das Kleid (-er) | dress |
| der Mantel (¨) | coat |
| die Jacke (-n) | jacket |
| der Anzug (¨e) | suit |
| das Bluson (-s) | light jacket |
| der Sakko (-s) | sports jacket |
| der Regenmantel (¨) | raincoat |
| die Farbe (-n) | colour |
| der Wein (-e) | wine |
| die Milch | milk |
| das Bier | beer |

**Some phrases**

| Ich schaue mich nur um | I'm just looking round |
|---|---|
| Was darf es sein? | Can I help you? |

## 7.3 STRUCTURAL EXPLANATIONS

### (a) Structures to learn
(i) Here are some phrases to use when you go shopping:

| Ich schaue mich nur um | I'm just looking |
|---|---|
| Ich weiß es nicht genau | I don't know exactly |
| Das ist mir zu teuer | That's too expensive |

(ii) Here are some phrases which you may hear when you go shopping, and which it will help you to understand:

| Kann ich Ihnen helfen? | Can I help you? |
|---|---|
| Was darf es sein? | What would you like? |
| Welche Größe? | Which size? |
| Welche Farbe? | Which colour? |
| Welches Material? | Which material? |
| Sonst noch etwas? | Anything else? |
| Darf es noch etwas sein? | Anything else? |

| Haben Sie sonst noch einen Wunsch? | Anything else? |
|---|---|
| Zahlen Sie an der Kasse, bitte | Please pay at the counter. |

(iii) How to ask if you can try on an article of clothing (ladies'):

| Kann ich | den Rock | | skirt |
|---|---|---|---|
| | die Hose | | trousers |
| | das Nachthemd | | nightshirt |
| | die Bluse | | blouse |
| | die Weste | anprobieren? | sleeveless jacket |
| | das Kleid | | dress |
| | den Mantel | | coat |
| | die Jacke | | jacket |
| | den Sonnenanzug | | sunsuit |

(iv) Gentlemen, of course, may wish to have the same privileges:

| Kann ich | das Hemd | | shirt |
|---|---|---|---|
| | das Bluson | | light jacket with zip-front |
| | die Jacke | anprobieren? | jacket |
| | die Hose | | trousers |
| | den Anzug | | suit |
| | den Sakko | | sports jacket |
| | den Regenmantel | | raincoat |

(v) This is how you ask for something a little bit different from what you have been shown. The diagrams below allow you to make up lots of different sentences, so that you can ask for something different.

| Haben Sie | diese Art diese Farbe diese Größe dieses Material | eine Nummer | größer kleiner | ? |
|---|---|---|---|---|
| | | in | blau rot weiß | |
| | | aus | Wolle Leder Nylon | |

| Have you got | something like this | a size | bigger smaller |
|---|---|---|---|
| | this colour this size this material | in | blue red white |
| | | in | wool leather nylon |

?

(vi) How to ask the price:

The diagram below will cover most things you are likely to want to buy:

Was
  kostet
    der Anzug
    die Bluse
    das Hemd
    er
    sie
    es
  kosten
    sie
    die Schuhe
?

What
  does
    the suit
    the blouse
    the shirt
    it
  do
    they
    the shoes
  cost?

## (b) Grammar

### (i) Verbs

In Chapter 2, we looked at some common *regular* and *irregular* verbs. Here are some more; the regular ones first. Regular verbs, you will remember, keep their stem unchanged and use the standard set of endings. Once again, you will find the most frequently used parts of the verbs given here. The full table is in the appendix.

The verb SUCHEN – to seek/look for

| ich | (I) | | e |
|---|---|---|---|
| er | (he) | | t |
| sie | (she) | SUCH- | t |
| wir | (we) | | en |
| Sie | (you) | | en |

The verb GLAUBEN – to believe

| ich | | e |
|---|---|---|
| er | | t |
| sie | GLAUB- | t |
| wir | | en |
| Sie | | en |

The verb BRAUCHEN – to need

| ich | | e |
| er | | t |
| sie | BRAUCH- | t |
| wir | | en |
| Sie | | en |

Now for the *irregular* verbs!

The verb TRAGEN – to wear

Note how the vowel sounds change with the addition of an Umlaut.

| ich | trage |
| er | trägt |
| sie | trägt |
| wir | tragen |
| Sie | tragen |

The verb NEHMEN – to take

Here, not only does the vowel change, the stem changes too!

| ich | nehme |
| er | nimmt |
| sie | nimmt |
| wir | nehmen |
| Sie | nehmen |

Here is part of the verb MÖGEN – to like. It enables you to say what you *would like*, as in the sentence: Ich möchte einen Pullover – 'I would like a pullover'.

| ich | möchte | – | I would like |
| er | möchte | – | he would like |
| sie | möchte | – | she would like |
| wir | möchten | – | we would like |
| Sie | möchten | – | you would like |

einen Pullover

This part of the verb is slightly irregular, in that the er form and the sie form end in -e instead of the more usual -t.

(ii) **Adjectives**
a) In the previous chapter, we looked at the endings of adjectives when they are preceded by words like ein, kein, mein, unser, and so on. In this chapter, we look at the endings of adjectives, when they are preceded by words like der (the), dieser (this), and so on.

| *Der blaue Pullover* ist sehr elegant | The blue pullover is very elegant |
| *Die elegante Dame* heißt Frau Müller | The elegant woman is called Mrs Müller |
| *Das alte Taxi* fährt schnell | The old taxi goes fast |
| *Diese braunen Schuhe* sind aus Leder | These brown shoes are made of leather |

The above adjectives all form part of the *subject* of their respective sentences, and so, as we saw in Chapter 5, they are said to be in the 'nominative case'. We can summarise this rule thus:

|  |  | Masc. | Fem. | Neut. | Plur. (all genders) |
|---|---|---|---|---|---|
| Adjectives after der, dieser | NOMINATIVE | -e | -e | -e | -en |

Consider the following sentences.

| | |
|---|---|
| Fritz kauft den blauen Pullover | Fritz buys the blue pullover |
| Elke braucht die weiße Bluse | Elke needs the white blouse |
| Wir sitzen um den runden Tisch | We are sitting around the round table |
| Konrad hat das rote Hemd | Konrad has the red shirt |
| Haben Sie die blauen Schuhe? | Have you got the blue shoes? |

In each of these sentences, the adjectives are part of the *direct object* of their respective sentences, and they are consequently in the 'accusative case', as we saw in Chapter 5. The third sentence contains a phrase with a preposition governing the 'accusative case'. We can summarise the rule about adjectives when they occur in the 'accusative case' thus:

|  |  | Masc. | Fem. | Neut. | Plur. (all genders) |
|---|---|---|---|---|---|
| Adjectives after der, dieser | ACCUSATIVE | -en | -e | -e | -en |

It is the *masculine* form of the adjective which has a different spelling in the accusative case. The difference is the letter n.

You will find a full account of the endings of adjectives in the appendix. It is worth pointing out, however, that although it is very *easy* to explain how the adjectives make their endings, it is very *hard* to remember the rules well enough to get the endings right when you are speaking. Take heart from the thought that mistakes will seldom prevent you from communicating your meaning to a German speaker. Come back to the adjective endings again and again, and you will gradually begin to get them right as you practise them.

## 7.4 EXERCISES

### Section A

Get ready to go shopping in Germany and be ready to get exactly what you want. Here are some more useful words.

**Colours**

| | |
|---|---|
| pastellgrün | pastel green |
| rosa | pink |
| mittelbraun | medium brown |
| gold | gold coloured |
| beige | beige |
| hellblau | light blue |
| dunkelrot | dark red |
| gelb | yellow |
| natur | natural colour |

**Materials**

| | |
|---|---|
| Tweed | tweed |
| Seide | silk |
| Krepp | crepe |
| Leinen | linen |
| Cord | corduroy |
| Velours | velvet |
| Gabardine | gabardine |

**Trade names for artificial materials**

| | |
|---|---|
| Popeline | poplin |
| Diolen | (trade name of a lightweight man-made fibre) |
| Polyester | polyester |
| Trevira | trevira |
| Acryl | acrylic |

Some of these are easily washed in a washing machine. They are then marked:

Vollwaschbar

### Exercise 1
Study this model conversation carefully.
*Verkäuferin*:  Was darf es sein?
*Kunde*:  (Ich möchte einen Pullover.)
*Verkäuferin*:  Welche Größe brauchen Sie?
*Kunde*:  (Größe 40.)

*Verkäuferin*:  An welches Material hatten Sie gedacht?
*Kunde*:  (Wolle.)
*Verkäuferin*:  Welche Farbe möchten Sie?
*Kunde*:  (Ich möchte hellblau.)
*Verkäuferin*:  Der ist sehr elegant.
*Kunde*:  (Ja, der gefällt mir.)
 (Was kostet er?)

Here are some clothes that you want to buy. Don't forget to look up the equivalent sizes in the appendix, page 309.
1. You fancy a skirt made of poplin. It ought to be dark red. Your size is 14. Don't forget to ask the price.
2. You've been thinking about a crepe blouse for some time. Your size is 16. How about a delicate shade of pink?
3. You've been meaning to treat yourself to a silk shirt for ages. You want a white one, size 12.
4. Those leather jackets in Germany are really good value. A dark brown one would just suit you, size 20.

## Exercise 2
You are shopping in Hamburg in Karstadt, a well-known shop in the Mönckebergstraße. The salesgirl offers you a number of things and you like them all. Ask what they cost.
1. Hier habe ich einen Rock.
2. Diese Hose ist schön.
3. Hier ist ein schönes Nachthemd.
4. Die Bluse ist elegant.
5. Und hier habe ich eine schöne Weste.
6. Der Regenmantel ist nicht teuer.
7. Dieser Anzug ist aus Wolle.
8. Hier habe ich eine Hose aus Cord.
9. Eine schöne Lederjacke.
10. Hier habe ich ein schönes Hemd.

## Section B

### Exercise 3
Check that you know what the following German sentences mean.
1. Ich schaue mich nur um.
2. Ich möchte einen Pullover.
3. Ich weiß es nicht genau.
4. An welches Material hatten Sie gedacht?
5. Der blaue Pullover ist bestimmt schön.

6. Ich brauche neue Schuhe.
7. Ich trage immer Größe 40.
8. Kann ich sie anprobieren?
9. Haben Sie keine Schuhe mit Ledersohlen?
10. Das ist mir zu teuer.

**Exercise 4**
Translate the following sentences into German.
1. What do they cost?
2. I don't like the shoes at all.
3. Are the soles made of leather?
4. Have you got the same sort of thing a size smaller?
5. How much are the brown shoes in the window?
6. I would like a nightdress.
7. I'm just looking.
8. The shirt is made of silk.
9. How much are the shoes?
10. The pullover is too expensive.

**Exercise 5**
Put the following expressions into German.
1. The white skirt.
2. The red trousers.
3. The black shoes.
4. The long dress.
5. The brown jacket.
6. The light blue shirt.
7. The brown suit.
8. The short raincoat.
9. The green blouse.
10. The little black dress.

# CHAPTER 8

# FAMILIES

# AND NATIONALITIES

## 8.1 DIALOGUES 📼

### Dialogue 1

Antonio Santos is always short of money. He notices this fact particularly when Elke wears her fur coat when coming to work. He has decided to try and get a week-end job in an Italian restaurant. He goes off to see the manager of the Pizzeria Giovanni.

```
 1  Antonio:  Guten Tag!
    Inhaber:  Guten Tag!
    Antonio:  Ich komme wegen der Stelle als Kellner.
    Inhaber:  Ach ja.
 5            Haben Sie Erfahrung als Kellner?
    Antonio:  Nein, leider nicht.
    Inhaber:  Hmm. Sprechen Sie Italienisch?
    Antonio:  Natürlich.
              Ich bin Italiener.
10  Inhaber:  Ah, Sie sind Italiener.
              Von wo kommen Sie?
    Antonio:  Ich komme aus Napoli.
    Inhaber:  Napoli! Na ja, Napoli!
              Ich komme aus Benevento.
15  Antonio:  Na. Wunderbar!
              Meine Tante Concetta kommt aus Benevento.
    Inhaber:  Nein.
    Antonio:  Doch, doch.
    Inhaber:  Fantastico, fantastico!
20            Wann können Sie anfangen?
```

**Dialogue 2**

Fritz Löb is visiting a lovely church near Landshut. He has come especially to see it (Elke is just not interested in seeing yet another church). The parson is showing him round.

1  *Pfarrer*:  Die Kirche ist sehr alt, Herr Löb.
   *Fritz*:  Ja, das sieht man.
   *Pfarrer*:  Über drei hundert Jahre alt.
   *Fritz*:  Tatsächlich?
5  *Pfarrer*:  Ja.
   Schauen Sie.
   Der Altar ist schön, nicht wahr?
   *Fritz*:  Das stimmt, wirklich.
   Er ist wunderschön.
10  *Pfarrer*:  Riemenschneider.
   *Fritz*:  Ach so.
   Tilman Riemenschneider.
   *Pfarrer*:  Ja.
   Sagen Sie, Herr Löb.
15  Was sind Sie von Beruf, wenn ich fragen darf?
   *Fritz*:  Ich bin Hauptschullehrer.
   In München.
   *Pfarrer*:  Ach so.
   Sind Sie verheiratet?
20  *Fritz*:  Ja. Das heißt, wir leben getrennt.
   *Pfarrer*:  Das tut mir leid.
   *Fritz*:  Danke.
   *Pfarrer*:  Haben Sie Kinder?
   *Fritz*:  Nein, ich habe keine Kinder.
25  *Pfarrer*:  Es ist vielleicht besser so.
   *Fritz*:  Ja, es ist besser so.
   Kleine Kinder brauchen einen Vater.
   *Pfarrer*:  Das stimmt.

## 8.2 INFORMATION

### (a) Notes on Dialogue 1

3.  wegen    This word means 'on account of'. It is very useful when you want to explain a reason. It is followed by a noun in the genitive case. See grammatical summary page 310.

| | Compare with Italiener (l.9), which is a noun and therefore written with a capital letter. |
|---|---|
| 8. Natürlich | Other words meaning the same could be: selbstverständlich, sicher or freilich. |
| 13. Napoli | The German form of the name of the town Naples is Neapel. Antonio is here speaking in Italian. |
| 18. Doch, doch | Note that this word means 'yes' when it is used emphatically, after somebody else has used a negative. |

### (b) Notes on Dialogue 2

| 2. Das sieht man | Each verb can have the subject man. It means 'one'. In English we quite often use the 'you' form of the verb, when we mean 'everybody'. We say, for instance 'you mustn't drive fast in a built-up area', when we really mean 'no-one' must do it. We say, for instance, in English 'You can go into a pub after 6 o'clock in the evening'. What we really mean is everyone can, or 'one' can. German always uses man in order to show that the idea is general to many people. The form of the verb is the same as the er form or sie form. |
|---|---|
| 4. Tatsächlich | Another word meaning the same thing would be wirklich. |
| 6. Schauen Sie | The verb schauen meaning 'to look' tends to be used more in the south of Germany. In the north it would be more normal to use the verb sehen. |

| | |
|---|---|
| 7. Nicht wahr? | In this sentence the expression nicht wahr? means 'isn't it?' The same expression, however, will do for 'don't they? can't I? mustn't we?' etc. It is consequently a very useful phrase which doesn't change, and can be used for turning any statement into a question. |
| 10. Riemenschneider | Tilman Riemenschneider was a famous sculptor, who worked principally in wood. He worked during the fifteenth and sixteenth centuries, and there are many fine altars carved by him to be seen in churches, especially in the south of Germany. |
| 14. Sagen Sie | This is a very useful phrase, which indicates to the person you are talking to that you now wish to say something. |
| 15. Wenn ich fragen darf | Do not attempt to analyse this phrase at this time. Simply use it in order to mean 'if you don't mind my asking'. You will find a brief discussion of word order in subordinate clauses in the grammatical summary on page 290. |
| 16. Hauptschullehrer | In Germany all children go to the Grundschule at the age of 6. When they reach 10+ they transfer to the Hauptschule, where many of them stay until they leave to go into paid employment. Some children leave, however, at the age of 10, as a result of tests and teachers' assessment, in order to go to a |

Gymnasium, which is
approximately the equivalent of
a grammar school.

20. Wir leben getrennt

This literally means 'we live
separated'.

23. Haben Sie Kinder?

Note that where English would
need the word 'any', this does
not occur in German.

**(c) Word list**

Here is a list of the most important words in this chapter. They should
be learnt by heart. They are given here in the order in which they occur
in the chapter.

| | |
|---|---|
| kommen | to come |
| wegen | on account of |
| die Stelle (-n) | job or position |
| der Kellner (-) | waiter |
| die Erfahrung | experience |
| leider | unfortunately |
| sprechen | to speak |
| natürlich | naturally |
| der Italiener (-) | Italian |
| wunderbar | wonderful |
| die Tante (-n) | aunt |
| wann? | when? |
| können | to be able |
| anfangen | to begin |
| die Kirche (-n) | church |
| sehr | very |
| alt | old |
| sehen | to see |
| hundert | a hundred |
| tatsächlich? | really? |
| das Jahr (-e) | year |
| der Altar (-e) | altar |
| wirklich | really |
| wunderschön | very beautiful |
| sagen | to say |
| der Beruf | job/profession |
| fragen | to ask |
| der Lehrer (-) | teacher |
| verheiratet | married |
| leben | to live |

| getrennt | separated |
|---|---|
| das Kind (-er) | child |
| vielleicht | perhaps |
| besser | better |
| brauchen | to need |
| der Vater (̈) | father |
| klein | small |
| ein wenig | a little |
| verlobt | engaged |
| ledig | single |
| geschieden | divorced |
| verwitwet | widowed |
| Geschwister | brothers or sisters |
| der Sohn (̈e) | son |
| die Tochter (̈) | daughter |
| der Bruder (̈) | brother |
| die Schwester (-n) | sister |

## Some phrases

| Das stimmt | That's right |
|---|---|
| Was sind Sie von Beruf? | What is your job? |
| Das heißt | That is to say |
| Das tut mir leid | I'm sorry |

## 8.3 STRUCTURAL EXPLANATIONS

### (a) Structures to learn

(i) **How to ask somebody their nationality and how to state your own**

| | Men | Women | |
|---|---|---|---|
| Sind Sie | Deutscher | Deutsche | |
| Ich bin | Engländer | Engländerin | |
| | Franzose | Französin | (?) |
| | Spanier | Spanierin | |
| | Däne | Dänin | |

(ii) **How to ask where people come from, and how to say where you come from yourself**

| | | England |
|---|---|---|
| Woher sind Sie? | | Schottland |
| Von wo kommen Sie? | Ich komme aus | Frankreich |
| | | Spanien |
| | | Dänemark |

N.B. Since Germany is divided into two independent countries, Germans very often give the full name of their state when they say where they come from: Thus, Ich komme aus der Bundesrepublik (Deutschland)'. Or, 'Ich komme aus der DDR' (DDR stands for die Deutsche Demokratische Republik. The first two words are adjectives and agree with the word Republik).

(iii) **How to ask whether somebody speaks a particular language**

Sprechen Sie
{
Deutsch
Englisch    Ja
Französisch ?    Nein
Spanisch    Ein wenig
Dänisch    Ein bißchen
} − a little

(iv) **How to ask if someone is married, and how to refer to your own status**

Sind Sie verheiratet?

Ich bin
{
verheiratet
nicht verheiratet
verlobt    engaged
ledig    single
geschieden    divorced
verwitwet    widowed
}

(v) **How to ask about a person's family**

Haben Sie
{
Geschwister    brothers or sisters
Kinder    children
Söhne ?    sons
Töchter    daughters
}

Ja, ich habe
Ja, wir haben
{
ein Baby    a baby
ein Kind    a child
einen Sohn    a son
eine Tochter    a daughter
einen Bruder    a brother
eine Schwester    a sister
}

Ich habe
Wir haben
}
{ zwei
drei }
{
Kinder    children
Söhne    sons
Töchter    daughters
Brüder    brothers
Schwestern    sisters
}

Nein, $\left\{\begin{array}{l}\text{ich habe}\\\text{wir haben}\end{array}\right\}$ $\left\{\begin{array}{l}\text{kein Baby}\\\text{kein Kind}\\\text{keinen Sohn}\\\text{keine Tochter}\\\text{keinen Bruder}\\\text{keine Schwester}\end{array}\right.$

$\left.\begin{array}{l}\text{Ich bin}\\\text{Wir sind}\end{array}\right\}$ kinderlos     (We haven't any children/We have no children/We are childless)

### (vi) How to ask about someone's job or profession

Was sind Sie von Beruf?

|  | Men | Women |  |
|---|---|---|---|
|  | Architekt | Architektin | architect |
|  | Student | Studentin | student |
| Ich bin | Arzt | Ärztin | doctor |
|  | Lehrer | Lehrerin | teacher |
|  | Polizist | Polizistin | policeman/woman |
|  | Verkäufer | Verkäuferin | salesman/woman |

### (b) Grammar
(i) You will find a list of nouns of nationality in the appendix.
(ii) There is also a list of European languages there.

(iii) **More about adjectives**
Sometimes adjectives occur by themselves, as in the sentence:

Kleine Kinder brauchen     Young children need a father
einen Vater

When it is said that adjectives 'occur by themselves', this means that they do not follow words such as ein, mein, unser, or der, dieser, etc.
You will find the endings of such 'unaccompanied' adjectives in the appendix.

## 8.4 EXERCISES

### Section A

**Exercise 1**
Read the following dialogue.
*Pfarrer*: Sagen Sie, Herr Schmidt.
Sind Sie verheiratet?

*Herr Schmidt*: Ja.
*Pfarrer*: Und haben Sie Kinder?
*Herr Schmidt*: Ja, ich habe zwei Kinder.
*Pfarrer*: Ach so!

Play out the above scene, imagining that the circumstances are different. If possible, take parts with a partner, each taking a role.
1. Herr Schmidt is divorced and has no children (don't forget what the parson said in the dialogue!).
2. He is widowed and has three children.
3. He is separated and has one child.
4. He is not married (this will be a shorter conversation).

**Exercise 2**
You are getting to know people and they are all very inquisitive about your family circumstances. What would you say? Here is an example:
*Question*: Sind Sie verheiratet?
*Answer*: Ja.
*Question*: Und haben Sie Kinder?
*Answer*: Ja, wir haben ein Kind.
1. You are still being woken up at 3 o'clock in the morning.
2. You have one of each.
3. You have two girls.
4. You have three boys.
5. You had to wait to have four boys before you had a girl.

**Section B**

**Exercise 3**
State your job as one of the following:
1. Male architect
2. Lady teacher
3. Policewoman
4. Doctor (male)
5. Student (female)
6. Teacher
7. Salesman
8. Saleswoman

# CHAPTER 9

# PLACES AND WEATHER

## 9.1 DIALOGUES 📼

**Dialogue 1**

Elke has taken herself to the Alte Pinakothek, a famous art gallery in Munich. She finds it quite refreshing not to have Fritz trailing about with her for once. Poor Fritz! He'd better watch out!

1   *Mann*:   Entschuldigen Sie!
      *Elke*:   Ja?
      *Mann*:   Ich wollte nur sagen . . . das ist ein sehr elegantes
      Kleid.
5   *Elke*:   Oh, vielen Dank.
      Das ist sehr nett von Ihnen.
      *Mann*:   Sie haben einen norddeutschen Akzent.
      *Elke*:   Ja. Ich komme aus Mölln.
      *Mann*:   Mölln? Wo ist denn Mölln?
10   *Elke*:   In Norddeutschland.
      Nicht weit von Hamburg.
      *Mann*:   Ach so! In der Nähe von Hamburg.
      *Elke*:   Ja. Zwischen Hamburg und Lübeck.
      *Mann*:   Wie ist die Landschaft dort?
15   *Elke*:   Es gibt einen großen See dort, und eine sehr schöne
      Kirche.
      *Mann*:   Haben Sie noch Verwandtschaft dort?
      *Elke*:   Ja. Mein Bruder wohnt in Mölln, bei meinen Eltern.
      *Mann*:   Ach, Sie haben einen Bruder.
20   *Elke*:   Ja. Er kommt nächste Woche nach München.
      Er ist begeisterter Skiläufer.
      *Mann*:   Gibt es denn keinen Schnee in Mölln?

*In der Alten Pinakothek*

Photograph: Bavaria-Verlag/Hans Schmied

*Elke*:   Nein. Im Winter regnet es sehr viel.
          Aber es gibt nicht viel Schnee.
25 *Mann*:  So, so, so.


## Dialogue 2

Antonio is enjoying the Oktoberfest, a famous beer festival
which is held every year in Munich. He is sitting in a Bierzelt,

where he has been listening to the brass band playing. He has just
got talking to a girl sitting opposite him. She is dressed in a very
nice Dirndl.

1 *Antonio*: Prost!
  *Mädchen*: Prost!
  *Antonio*: Sind Sie Münchnerin?
  *Mädchen*: Nein. Ich komme aus Bad Reichenhall.
5 *Antonio*: Wo ist denn Bad Reichenhall?
  *Mädchen*: Nicht weit von Salzburg.
    Und Sie?
  *Antonio*: Ich komme aus Neapel.
    Aber jetzt bin ich Münchener.

*Prost!*

*Photograph: Bavaria-Verlag/Hans Schmied*

10 *Mädchen*:  So.
     *Antonio*:  Was gibt es dort zu sehen, in Bad Reichenhall?
     *Mädchen*:  Es gibt ein schönes Kurhaus und gute Geschäfte.
     *Antonio*:  Und die Landschaft?
     Wie ist dort die Landschaft?
15 *Mädchen*:  Ach, die Landschaft ist wunderbar!
     Es gibt hohe Berge.
     *Antonio*:  Das ist schön.
     *Mädchen*:  Ja. Der Predigtstuhl zum Beispiel.
     Das ist ein sehr hoher Berg.
20 *Antonio*:  Wie ist das Wetter dort?
     *Mädchen*:  Meistens schön.
     Es gibt viel Schnee im Winter.
     *Antonio*:  Und im Sommer?
     *Mädchen*:  Im Sommer regnet es manchmal.
25 Leider.

## 9.2 INFORMATION

### (a) Notes on Dialogue 1

| | |
|---|---|
| Alte Pinakothek | This is a famous art gallery in Munich containing a very important collection of oil paintings from all over the world. |
| 7. Akzent | Most Germans speak with a regional accent. It is fairly easy to hear whether somebody comes from northern Germany or Bavaria for instance. The practised ear can identify quite easily the different regions of Germany just by listening to a few sentences. This regional accent does not, however, provide any information about social class. |
| 12. in der Nähe von | This expression means 'near'. You can think of it as an abbreviated form of 'in the neighbourhood of'. |

13. Hamburg und Lübeck

Hamburg is Germany's most important port. It stands on the river Elbe, with access to the North Sea. Lübeck is about 30 or 40 miles away, standing just back from the Baltic Sea. Hamburg is still an independent city state in the German Federation.

17. Verwandtschaft

This is a very general word which stands for any form of blood relationship.

20. er kommt

Note that German, like English, can use the present tense with an expression of future time, to indicate the future.

23. Im Winter

Notice that the expression im Winter has been brought to the beginning of the sentence in order to emphasise it. The subject consequently follows the verb.

**(b) Notes on Dialogue 2**

Oktoberfest

This is a festival which attracts many tourists from all over Germany and abroad. It takes place on a large area of ground, specially reserved for this and other festivals. The attractions include a funfair, with lots of roundabouts, shooting booths and stalls selling food and drink. The centre-piece, however, consists of the large tents (Bierzelte) where brass bands play and where large 1 litre tankards of beer (Biersteine) are served by waitresses who manage to carry five in each hand.

| | |
|---|---|
| Dirndl | This is a traditional costume still frequently worn in the southern part of Bavaria. It consists of a blouse with a deep décolletage, and short, puffy sleeves. The waist is drawn in tightly to accentuate the hips, and a small apron is worn on top of the skirt. Most women and girls in the south of Bavaria possess a Dirndl and wear it quite frequently. |
| 3. Münchenerin | This is the feminine form of Münchener and means somebody who lives in Munich. |
| 4. Bad Reichenhall | This is a well-known spa in the south-eastern tip of Germany, standing on the frontier with Austria. |
| 12. Kurhaus | This is where guests go to take the waters: the pump room. |
| 18. Der Predigtstuhl | This is a mountain standing just to the south of Bad Reichenhall which reaches the height of 1617 metres. |

**(c) Word list**

Here is a list of the most important words in this chapter. They should be learnt by heart. They are given here in the order in which they occur in the chapter.

| | |
|---|---|
| nur | just/only |
| sagen | to say |
| sehr | very |
| elegant | elegant |
| das Kleid (-er) | dress |
| nett | nice |
| der Akzent | accent |
| wo? | where? |
| weit | far |
| von | from |
| zwischen | between |

| | |
|---|---|
| die **Land**schaft (-en) | countryside |
| dort | there |
| schön | beautiful |
| die **Kir**che (-n) | church |
| der See (-n) | lake |
| groß | large |
| noch | still |
| die Ver**wandt**schaft | relationship |
| der **Bru**der (⁻) | brother |
| **woh**nen | to live |
| die **El**tern | parents |
| die **Wo**che (-n) | week |
| be**gei**stert | enthusiastic |
| der **Schi**läufer (-) | skier |
| der Schnee | snow |
| der **Win**ter | winter |
| es **reg**net | it is raining |
| viel | much |
| Prost! | Cheers! |
| **a**ber | but |
| jetzt | now |
| dort | there |
| **seh**en | to see |
| gut | good |
| das Ge**schäft** (-e) | shop; business |
| der Berg (-e) | mountain |
| das **Wet**ter | weather |
| **mei**stens | usually |
| **man**chmal | sometimes |
| der **Som**mer | summer |
| **lei**der | unfortunately |
| mit | with |
| von | of; from |
| zu | to; at |
| gegen**ü**ber | opposite |
| die **Fahr**karte (-n) | ticket |

## (d) Some phrases

| | |
|---|---|
| Ent**schul**digen Sie | Excuse me; I beg your pardon |
| Das ist sehr nett von **Ih**nen | That is very nice of you |
| Nicht weit von | Not far from |
| In der **Nä**he von | Near |
| Es gibt | There is; there are |

| Bei meinen **El**tern | With my parents |
|---|---|
| Was gibt es dort zu **seh**en? | What is there to see there? |
| Zum **Bei**spiel | For example |

## 9.3 STRUCTURAL EXPLANATION

### (a) Structures to learn

(i)

Wo ist { Mölln / Bad Reichenhall / Zirndorf } ?  Where is { Mölln / Bad Reichenhall / Zirndorf } ?

### (ii) How to say that one place is near another place

Mölln / Bad Reichenhall / Zirndorf } ist { nicht weit von / in der Nähe von / bei } { Hamburg / Salzburg / Nürnberg }

Mölln / Bad Reichenhall / Zirndorf } is { not far from / near / near } { Hamburg / Salzburg / Nuremburg }

### (iii) How to ask for information about a place

| Wie ist die Landschaft dort? | What is the countryside like there? |
|---|---|
| Was gibt es dort zu sehen? | What is there to see there? |

### (iv) How to describe a place

Es gibt { eine sehr schöne Kirche / einen großen See / ein schönes Kurhaus / gute Geschäfte }

a very beautiful church
a large lake
a fine kurhaús
good shops

### (v) How to ask what the weather is like

Wie ist das Wetter?

### (vi) How to describe the weather

| (Das Wetter ist) meistens schön | The weather is usually nice |
|---|---|

Im Winter / Im Sommer } regnet es { sehr viel / manchmal }

N.B. The subject of this sentence is es. However, the sentence begins with the phrases: Im Winter/Im Sommer for emphasis, and the subject comes after the verb.

| Es gibt | $\begin{Bmatrix} \text{nicht viel} \\ \text{viel} \end{Bmatrix}$ | Schnee | (im Winter) |
|---|---|---|---|
| In winter<br>In summer | $\begin{Bmatrix} \text{it rains} \end{Bmatrix}$ | a lot<br>sometimes | |
| There is | $\begin{Bmatrix} \text{not much} \\ \text{a lot of} \end{Bmatrix}$ | snow | (in winter) |

**(b) Grammar**

(i) You will find a list of expressions about the seasons of the year in the appendix.

(ii) There is a list of the months there too.

(iii) **The indirect object**
a)  Do you remember how we defined the direct object of a verb in Chapter 5, with the story of the dog biting the postman? Now we have to turn our attention to another concept called the *indirect object*.

Let us imagine that the postman is determined to make friends with the dog. Consider the sentence: *The postman gives the dog a bone*. We know that *the postman* does the giving, and that phrase is consequently the subject of the sentence. The thing that is given is *a bone*, and that is therefore the direct object of the sentence.

The person, or thing, to whom or for whom things are given, bought, sent, taken, etc. – in other words, the recipients – are *indirect objects*. Here are some examples:

I bought (my wife) some flowers
She sent (the man) a letter
We took (him) some chocolate
He threw (her) a kiss
She gave (the car) a good kick

Note that these sentences still make good sense if the *indirect object*, in brackets, is deleted. This would *not* be the case if the *direct objects* were to be deleted.

In German, the *indirect object* is marked or signalled by special forms of the definite and indefinite articles, the personal pronouns and possessive adjectives. They are said to be in the *'dative case'*.

b) **Definite articles**

| | |
|---|---|
| Er gibt *dem Mann* den Brief | He gives the man the letter |
| | (He gives the letter to the man) |
| Er gibt *der Frau* das Geld | He gives the woman the money |
| | (He gives the money to the woman) |
| Er gibt *dem Mädchen* (das Mädchen) einen Kuß | He gives the girl a kiss |
| | (He gives a kiss to the girl) |

N.B. The gender of the word Mädchen is neuter in German, despite its meaning.

| | |
|---|---|
| Er gibt *den Kindern* Geschenke | He gives the children presents |
| | (He gives presents to the children) |

We can summarise the rule for *definite articles* in the *dative case*, thus:

| | Masc. | Fem. | Neut. | Plur. (all genders) |
|---|---|---|---|---|
| DATIVE CASE | dem | der | dem | den |

c) **Indefinite articles and possessive adjectives**

| | |
|---|---|
| Er gibt *seinem Vater* den Brief | He gives his father the letter |
| | (He gives the letter to his father |
| Er gibt *seiner Frau* das Geld | He gives his wife the money |
| | (He gives the money to his wife) |
| Er gibt *einem Mädchen* seinen Mantel | He gives a girl his coat |
| | (He gives his coat to a girl) |
| Er gibt *ihren Kindern* Geschenke | He gives her children presents |
| | (He gives presents to her children) |

We can summarise the rule for *indefinite articles* and *possessive adjectives* in the *dative case*, thus:

| | | Masc. | Fem. | Neut. | Plur. |
|---|---|---|---|---|---|
| DATIVE CASE | (a, an) | einem | einer | einem | — |
| | (not a) | keinem | keiner | keinem | keinen |
| | (my) | meinem | meiner | meinem | meinen |
| | (his) | seinem | seiner | seinem | seinen |
| | (her) | ihrem | ihrer | ihrem | ihren |
| | (our) | unserem | unserer | unserem | unseren |
| | (your) | Ihrem | Ihrer | Ihrem | Ihren |

You will find a full list of possessive adjectives in the dative case in the appendix.

## d) Key letters

For definite and indefinite articles, as well as for possessive adjectives, the key letters, signalling the dative case, are as follows:

|  | Masc. | Fem. | Neut. | Plur. |
|---|---|---|---|---|
| DATIVE CASE | m | r | m | n |

## e) Personal Pronouns

| | |
|---|---|
| Er gibt mir einen Brief | He gives me a letter |
| Er gibt ihm einen Mantel | He gives him a coat |
| Er gibt ihr das Geld | He gives her the money |
| Er gibt uns unsere Fahrkarten | He gives us our tickets |
| Er gibt Ihnen den Schlüssel | He gives you the key |

We can summarise the rule for *personal pronouns* in the *dative case*, thus:

| Nominative | Dative |
|---|---|
| ich | mir |
| er | ihm |
| sie | ihr |
| wir | uns |
| Sie | Ihnen (polite form) |

Note that the polite form has a capital letter. You will find a complete list of personal pronouns in the dative case in the appendix. You will also find there notes on the order of objects in a sentence.

## f) Prepositions

Certain *prepositions* accompany the *dative case*. Here are some example sentences from the dialogues of this chapter.

Das ist sehr nett von Ihnen
Mein Bruder wohnt bei meinen Eltern
Zum (zu dem) Beispiel

The commonest of the prepositions which always accompany the dative case are: mit (with), von (from, of) and zu (to, at).

| | |
|---|---|
| Er fährt mit einem Freund nach Deutschland | mit einem Freund – with a friend |
| Er schreibt mit dem Bleistift | mit dem Bleistift – with the pencil |
| Sie kommt mit mir | mit mir – with me |

| | |
|---|---|
| Er kommt von meinem Haus | von meinem Haus – from my house |
| Er wohnt nicht weit von dem Berg | nich weit von dem Berg – not far from the mountain |
| Ich spreche von ihm | von ihm – of him |
| Er geht zu meiner Frau | zu meiner Frau – to my wife |
| Sie geht zur (zu der) Haltestelle | zur Haltestelle – to the bus stop |

In the appendix you will find a list of the *prepositions* which always accompany the *dative case*.

N.B. When a noun occurs in the dative case in the plural, it always ends in -n.

## 9.4 EXERCISES

### Section A

**Exercise 1**
Say where the following towns are.
Example: Wo ist Fürth?
Nicht weit von Nürnberg.

1. Wo ist Oldenburg?
2. Wo ist Braunschweig?
3. Wo ist Paderborn?
4. Wo ist Limburg?
5. Wo ist Wiesbaden?
6. Wo ist Heidelberg?
7. Wo ist Cadolzburg?
8. Wo ist Augsburg?
9. Wo ist Pforzheim?
10. Wo ist Bad Reichenhall?

1. • Oldenburg   Bremen •
2. • Hannover   Braunschweig •
3. Bielefeld •   Paderborn •
4. • Koblenz   Limburg •
5. Wiesbaden •   • Frankfurt
6. • Mannheim   • Heidelberg
7. • Cadolzburg   Nürnberg •
8. • Augsburg   München •
9. • Pforzheim   Stuttgart •
10. • Bad Reichenhall   Salzburg •

**Exercise 2**
Say where the following places are.
Example: Wo ist Lübeck?
Lübeck ist in Norddeutschland.
1. Wo ist Kiel?
2. Wo ist Passau?

3. Wo ist Lübeck?
4. Wo ist München?
5. Wo ist Hamburg?
6. Wo ist Augsburg?
7. Wo ist Oldenburg?
8. Wo ist Ulm?
9. Wo ist Bremen?
10. Wo ist Freiburg?

## Section B

### Exercise 3
Translate into German (*c.f.* appendix).
1. At Christmas. (zu)
2. With my parents. (bei)
3. For this reason. (aus)
4. By mistake. (aus)
5. In this weather. (bei)
6. By train. (mit)
7. On foot. (zu)
8. In my opinion (nach)
9. At work. (bei)
10. After half an hour. (nach)

### Exercise 4
Complete the following sentences.
1. Sie kommt mit ein . . . elegant . . . Kleid.
2. Er hat ein . . . süddeutsch . . . Akzent.
3. Es gibt ein . . . schön . . . Kirche dort.
4. Mein klein . . . Bruder wohnt in Hamburg.
5. Bad Reichenhall ist nicht weit von ein . . . hoh . . . Berg.
6. Dort gibt ein groß . . . Kurhaus.
7. Bei Schaffhausen ist ein groß . . . See.
8. Die Zugspitze ist ein hoh . . . Berg.
9. Er hat ein weiß . . . Hemd.
10. Sie trägt ein . . . blau . . . Pullover.

# CHAPTER 10

# REVISION TESTS

In this chapter you will have an opportunity to consolidate the language you have learned in the previous nine chapters. Each test indicates whereabouts in the earlier part of the book you ought to search if you have forgotten a particular point.

**Test 1 – How to introduce somebody** (Chapter 1)
You live in an old-fashioned family, where all your brothers and your cousins and your aunts live in the same house. You bring a colleague home for a meal and introduce all the members of the family to him one by one. There are some new words in this exercise, and so you ought to consult the pronunciation key before you do it. When you have tried the exercise yourself, check your pronunciation with the tape-recording.
First introduce your wife.
Then your father – Vater (*m*)
Then your mother – Mutter (*f*)
Then your son – Sohn (*m*)
Then your daughter – Tochter (*f*)
Then your uncle – Onkel (*m*)
Then your aunt – Tante (*f*)

**Test 2 – Possessive adjectives** (Chapter 1)
Like everybody else, you are houseproud about your own house and inquisitive about other people's houses. Together with your husband (or wife), you take your guest round the house and show off its special features.
You show the guests your garden – Garten (*m*)
Your kitchen – Küche (*f*)
Your bedroom – Schlafzimmer (*n*)
Your garage – Garage (*f*)

Your dog – Hund (*m*)
Your cat – Katze (*f*)

**Test 3 – Greetings** (Chapter 1)
1. What would you say to somebody you met at 8 o'clock in the morning?
2. What would you say to somebody who had just poured you out a drink?
3. What would you say if the telephone rang while you were talking to somebody?
4. What would you say to your son if he was just going off on holiday?
5. What would you say if your boss asked you out to dinner and you spilt your wine all over the best tablecloth?
6. What would you say as you left a friend who was ill in hospital?
7. What would you say to your husband just before you turned the light out at night?
8. What would you say if you stood on somebody's toe?
9. What would you say if you arrived late at the theatre, and had to reach your seat in the middle of the row after the play had started?
10. What would you say to your girlfriend as you prepared to tackle a juicy steak at a restaurant?

**Test 4 – Staying in hotels** (Chapter 3)
Here is a model letter, written to confirm a hotel booking made by telephone.

---

An das Hotel Atlantik            Bristol
An der Alster                   den 2. April
D – 2000 Hamburg

---

Sehr geehrte Herren!
Hiermit bestätige ich meine Reservierung für (ein Einzelzimmer mit Dusche) für die Zeit vom (27. Juni) bis zum (30. Juni) einschließlich.

          Hochachtungsvoll

---

Notes:
1. The address of the hotel you are writing to goes in the top left-hand corner of the writing paper. Note that the name of the town,

together with its postal code, is underlined. The name of the street comes before.

2. When writing your own address on writing paper you only write the name of the town.
3. The date is written as shown. The number is always followed by a full stop.
4. When writing to a hotel, the greeting is as shown. All letter greetings are followed by an exclamation mark.
5. The standard greeting at the end of a letter, written to somebody you do not know is Hochachtungsvoll. A good, standard farewell greeting for somebody you know moderately well would be Mit herzlichen Grüßen.

Translations of key terms in the model letter:

| | |
|---|---|
| Sehr geehrte Herren! | Dear Sir |
| Hiermit bestätige ich ... | This is to confirm |
| Einschließlich | Inclusive |
| Hochachtungsvoll | Yours faithfully |

Note that those parts of the letter in brackets can be changed to fit in with your particular requirements. Practise writing the following letters, each of which is intended to confirm a hotel booking made earlier by telephone.

Note the letter D in the address indicates a town in Germany (D is Deutschland). The letter A in the address indicates Austria.

1. Hotel Sonnenhof
   Wagnerstraße 10
   D – 8352 Grafenau

2. Hotel Bergland
   Unterstraße 4
   A – 6416 Obsteig
   Tirol

108

3. Hotel Wachtelhof
   Mittelstraße 1
   A – 5761 Hinterthal

4. Sporthotel Fellhoist
   Teichstraße 12
   D – 2443 Großenbrode

5. Frühstückspension ,,Olga"
   Hauptstraße 91
   A – 5600 St. Johann
   Salzburger Land

**Test 5 – Greetings and making hotel bookings** (Chapter 3)
Can you complete your part of the conversation. You will find the complete text on p. 239.

*Empfang*: Grüß Gott!
*You*: Greet her.
   Ask if there is a room available.
*Empfang*: Möchten Sie ein Einzelzimmer oder ein Doppelzimmer?
*You*: Say you want a double room.
*Empfang*: Ja, das ist möglich.
   Für wieviele Nächte bitte?
*You*: Say you want the room for three nights.
*Empfang*: Möchten Sie das Zimmer mit Bad oder mit Dusche?
*You*: Say you want it with a shower.
*Empfang*: Ja, ein Doppelzimmer mit Dusche habe ich.
   Das geht in Ordnung.

*You*: Ask how much the room is.
*Empfang*: Das Zimmer kostet 55 Mark pro Nacht.
*You*: Ask if that includes breakfast.
*Empfang*: Jawohl.
*You*: Ask if it includes VAT.
*Empfang*: Ja, selbstverständlich.
*You*: Say you'll take the room.
*Empfang*: Tragen Sie sich bitte ein.

**Test 6 – Asking the times of departure and arrival of trains**
(Chapter 4)

Look at these dialogues:

a)

| HAMBURG – FRANKFURT – BASEL | | |
|---|---|---|
| | | IC |
| | | 175 |
| Hamburg – Altona | ab | 9.32 |
| Hamburg Dammtor | an | 9.38 |
| | ab | 9.39 |
| Hamburg Hbf. | an | 9.44 |
| | ab | 9.45 |
| Hamburg – Harburg | an | 9.59 |
| | ab | 10.00 |
| Hannover | an | 11.10 |
| | ab | 11.14 |
| Göttingen | an | 12.09 |
| | ab | 12.10 |
| Fulda | an | 13.36 |
| | ab | 13.37 |
| Frankfurt (M) | an | 14.36 |
| | ab | 14.42 |
| Mannheim | an | 15.26 |
| | ab | 15.34 |
| Karlsruhe | an | 16.02 |
| | ab | 16.03 |
| Freiburg | an | 17.03 |
| | ab | 17.04 |
| Basel | an | 17.46 |

*Reisender*: Wann fährt der Zug nach Hamburg – Dammtor ab?
*Angestellte*: Er fährt um 9 Uhr 32 ab.
*Reisender*: Wann kommt er in Hamburg – Dammtor an?
*Angestellte*: Er kommt um 9 Uhr 38 an.
*Reisender*: Muß ich umsteigen?
*Angestellte*: Nein der Zug fährt direkt.

b)
*Reisender*: Wann fährt der Zug nach Hamburg Hbf (Hauptbahnhof) ab?
*Angestellte*: Er fährt um 9 Uhr 39 ab.
*Reisender*: Wann kommt er in Hamburg Hbf. an?
*Angestellte*: Er kommt um 9 Uhr 44 an.
*Reisender*: Muß ich umsteigen?
*Angestellte*: Nein, der Zug fährt direkt.

Make up dialogues similar to these. If you are studying with a partner, take it in turns to ask the questions.

| This is where you are: | This is where you want to go: |
|---|---|
| 1. Hamburg Hbf | Freiburg |
| 2. Hannover | Fulda |
| 3. Göttingen | Basel |
| 4. Mannheim | Freiburg |
| 5. Fulda | Karlsruhe |
| 6. Freiburg | Basel |
| 7. Frankfurt | Freiburg |
| 8. Hamburg – Harburg | Frankfurt |
| 9. Hannover | Frankfurt |
| 10. Karlsruhe | Basel |

**Test 7 – Verbs with separable affixes** (Chapter 4)
Put into German
1. Grandma (Oma) rings up on Saturday.
2. Ingrid goes out on Tuesday.
3. The children (die Kinder) tidy up the shop.
4. Mother (Mutter) clears up the toys.
5. Peter washes up the plates.
6. Inge buys provisions.
7. Helmut washes up on Sunday.
8. The boss (der Chef) gives up his work.
9. Mary (Maria) closes the shop.
10. Grandma goes out on Saturday.

**Test 8 – Finding your way by bus and tram** (Chapter 5)
Can you complete the following dialogue? If you are working with a partner, take it in turns to play the parts.
**Dialogue A**
*Müller*: ......
*Meier*: Ja, bitte?
*Müller*: ......
*Meier*: Nach Opladen?
  Nein, dieser Bus fährt nach Ludwigshafen.
*Müller*: ......
*Meier*: Sie brauchen die Nummer 14.
**Dialogue B**
*Schmidt*: ......
*Schüth*: Ja. Kann ich Ihnen helfen?
*Schmidt*: ......
*Schüth*: Nein, nicht zum Schauspielhaus.
  Sie fährt zum Hofgarten.

*Schmidt:* ......
*Schüth:* Sie brauchen die Nummer 1.
Sie fährt zum Schauspielhaus.
*Schmidt:* ......

## Test 9 – The definite article (Chapter 5)
Complete the following sentences:
1. ... Professor heißt Doktor Schmidt.
2. Wo ist ... Tasse?
3. Hier ist ... Buch.
4. ... Kaffee ist heiß.
5. Hier ist ... Frau.
6. ... Auto fährt schnell.
7. ... Mann heißt Herr Müller.
8. ... Einladung kommt heute.
9. ... Schlafzimmer ist groß.
10. ... Küche ist klein.

## Test 10 – Describing symptoms of illness (Chapter 6)
Look carefully at the doctor's part of the following dialogue. Then make up the patient's role and speak it aloud. Read aloud the doctor's part (if you are working with a partner, take it in turns to play the role of the doctor and the patient).

| *Arzt* | *Patient* |
|---|---|
| 1. Guten Tag. | |
| | 2. ...... |
| 3. Was fehlt Ihnen denn? | |
| | 4. ...... |
| 5. Ihr Bein? Ist es ein leichter Schmerz? | |
| | 6. ...... |
| 7. Ach so, stichartig. Seit wann tut es weh? | |
| | 8. ...... |
| 9. So, so. Drei Tage schon. Kein Fußball für Sie. | |

## Test 11 – Describing symptoms of illness (Chapter 6)
Poor Sepp Steinbauer has fallen off his bicycle while on his way to a football match. He wanted to see 1.FC Nürnberg versus Bayern München. He's been taken to hospital where the staff nurse is trying to find out how badly he's hurt. From his answers it seems he is only just alive. You play the part of Sepp.

*Note*: Don't try to make up sentences like the nurse's. Just use her questions as clues to the answers. Example:

*Schwester*: Tut der Kopf weh?
*Sepp*: Ja, mein Kopf tut weh.
*Schwester*: Und das Bein?
*Sepp*: Ja, mein Bein tut weh.

Now begin:
*Schwester*: Tut der Kopf weh?
Und das Bein?
Wie geht's Ihrem Knie?
Wie ist mit dem Rücken?
Tut es am Hals weh?
Haben Sie Schmerzen am Ellbogen?
Ist Ihr Ohr wund?
Und die Nase?
Die Schulter ist verletzt, glaube ich.
O, und der Finger auch.

**Test 12 – Finding exactly what you want when shopping** (Chapter 7)
You are in Munich in the Kaufhaus, Oberpollinger. This time you are a difficult customer to please.

1. *Verkäuferin*: Hier habe ich ein schönes Hemd.
   (You want something in the same material, but blue.)
2. *Verkäuferin*: Das ist ein schöner Rock.
   (You want something like this, but a size smaller.)
3. *Verkäuferin*: Dieser Anzug ist sehr schön.
   (You want the same colour, but in wool.)
4. *Verkäuferin*: Diese Schuhe sind sehr elegant.
   (You want this colour a size larger.)
5. *Verkäuferin*: Hier habe ich ein Hemd aus Seide.
   (You want the same material, but in light blue.)
6. *Verkäuferin*: Das ist ein schöner Regenmantel.
   (You want the same sort of thing in cotton.)
7. *Verkäuferin*: Der Pullover hier ist nicht teuer.
   (You want the same colour in Polyester.)
8. *Verkäuferin*: Ein sehr elegantes Nachthemd.
   (You want the same sort of thing in black.)
9. *Verkäuferin*: Mm, die Jacke ist aber schön.
   (You want the same sort of thing in velvet.)
10. *Verkäuferin*: Nehmen Sie dieses Hemd?
    (You want the same size in white.)

**Test 13 – Describing the weather** (Chapter 9)
Expressions

Es ist sehr warm!                    Es ist sehr kalt!

Es gibt viel Schnee.                 Es regnet.

Example: Using the symbols, describe the climate in Munich

Sommer                    Winter

München

Wie ist das Wetter in München?
*A*:   Es ist sehr heiß im Sommer.
       Und es gibt viel Schnee im Winter.

|  | Sommer | Winter |
|---|---|---|
| 1. Wie ist das Wetter in Hamburg? |  |  |
| 2. Wie ist das Wetter in Bad Reichenhall? |  |  |
| 3. Wie ist das Wetter in London? |  |  |
| 4. Wie ist das Wetter in Nürnberg? |  |  |
| 5. Wie ist das Wetter in Kiel? |  |  |

# EATING OUT

## 11.1 DIALOGUES 📼

**Dialogue 1**
Fritz is telephoning the restaurant, in order to reserve a table for himself and Elke.

1 *Besitzer*: Restaurant das Blaue Haus.
   Guten Tag.
   *Fritz*: Guten Tag.
   Ich möchte einen Tisch für heute abend.
5 *Besitzer*: Für wieviele Personen?
   *Fritz*: Für zwei.
   *Besitzer*: Um wieviel Uhr, bitte?
   *Fritz*: Um acht Uhr.
   *Besitzer*: Ja, um acht Uhr.
10    Ich habe einen Tisch um acht Uhr.
   *Fritz*: Sehr gut.
   *Besitzer*: Auf welchen Namen, bitte?
   *Fritz*: Löb. L – O – umlaut – B.
   *Besitzer*: Herr Löb.
15    Ist in Ordnung, Herr Löb.
   *Fritz*: Auf Wiederhören!
   *Besitzer*: Auf Wiederhören!

(Fritz and Elke have arrived at the restaurant)
   *Fritz*: Guten Abend!
   *Empfang*: Guten Abend!
20 *Fritz*: Ich habe einen Tisch reserviert.
   *Empfang*: Für wieviele Personen?
   *Fritz*: Für zwei Personen.
   *Empfang*: Auf welchen Namen, bitte?

*Im Restaurant*

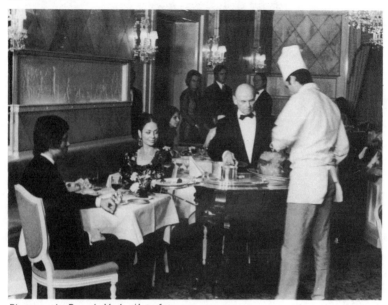

Photograph: Bavaria-Verlag/Interfoto

    *Fritz*: Löb.
25 *Empfang*: Ach ja.
    Herr Löb.
    Kommen Sie, bitte.

## Dialogue 2

Fritz and Elke are considering the menu.

 1 *Fritz*: Möchten Sie eine Vorspeise?
    *Elke*: Ich möchte eine Suppe – eine Zwiebelsuppe.
    *Fritz*: Und dann?
    *Elke*: Ein Texas Steak.
 5 Und Sie?
    Was möchten Sie?
   *Fritz*: Ich glaube, daß ich auch ein Suppe möchte – eine
    Gulaschsuppe.
    Und dann . . . auch ein Texas Steak.
10 *Kellner*: Haben Sie gewählt?
    *Fritz*: Einmal Zwiebelsuppe.
    Einmal Gulaschsuppe.
    *Kellner*: Einmal Zwiebelsuppe.
    Einmal Gulaschsuppe.

15 *Fritz*:  Und dann – zweimal Texas Steak.
   *Elke*:  Ohne Pommes frites, bitte.
   *Kellner*:  Zweimal Texas Steak.
   Einmal mit Pommes frites.
   Einmal ohne.
20  Jawohl.
   *Fritz*:  Möchten Sie etwas trinken?
   *Elke*:  Ja, ich möchte bitte ein Viertel Rotwein.
   *Fritz*:  Zwei Viertel Rotwein, bitte.
   *Kellner*:  Zwei Viertel Rotwein.
25  Danke schön.

## 11.2 INFORMATION

### (a) Notes on Dialogue 1

12.  Auf welchen Namen

Note that German uses auf welchen Namen in order to enquire the name of the guest.

16.  Auf Wiederhören!

This is a special greeting for terminating a telephone conversation.

### (b) Notes on Dialogue 2

1.  Vorspeise

This word can mean either 'a starter' or 'hors d'oeuvre'.

2.  eine Suppe

Note that German uses *eine* Suppe where in English we say '*some* soup'.

7.  daß ich auch eine Suppe möchte

You will find a brief discussion of word order in subordinate clauses in the grammatical summary on page 290.

11.  Einmal

Literally, this word means 'once'. It is the way you indicate how many portions or

118

dishes you want. Zweimal – two
(portions).

22. Viertel      This refers to a quarter of a
litre. The wine would be served
in a small carafe.

## (c) Word list

| | |
|---|---|
| der Besitzer | owner |
| das Restaurant (-s) | restaurant |
| der Tisch (-e) | table |
| heute | today |
| heute abend | this evening |
| wieviel? | how many? |
| die Person (-en) | person |
| sehr | very |
| gut | good |
| der Name (-n) | name |
| reservieren | to reserve |
| kommen | to come |
| die Vorspeise (-n) | hors d'oeuvre |
| die Suppe (-n) | soup |
| die Zwiebelsuppe (-n) | onion soup |
| das Steak | steak |
| dann | then |
| glauben | to believe |
| auch | also, too |
| wählen | to choose |
| die Gulaschsuppe (-n) | goulash soup |
| ohne | without |
| mit | with |
| etwas | something |
| trinken | to drink |
| das Viertel (-) | quarter |
| der Rotwein (-e) | red wine |
| die Speisekarte (-n) | menu |
| die Weinkarte (-n) | wine list |
| sehen | to see |
| das Wasser (-) | water |
| essen | to eat |
| zahlen | to pay |
| die Rechnung (-en) | bill |
| wo? | where? |
| welch-? | which? |

| | |
|---|---|
| wer? | who? |
| warum? | why? |
| was? | what? |
| wohin? | where (to)? |
| was für? | what sort of? |
| wie? | how? |
| heute nachmittag | this afternoon |
| heute morgen | this morning |
| morgen | tomorrow |
| morgen abend | tomorrow evening |
| morgen nachmittag | tomorrow afternoon |
| morgen früh | tomorrow morning |
| gestern | yesterday |
| gestern abend | yesterday evening |
| gestern nachmittag | yesterday afternoon |
| gestern morgen | yesterday morning |
| die Woche (-n) | week |
| das Jahr (-e) | year |
| der Monat (-e) | month |
| der Tag (-e) | day |
| die Minute (-n) | minute |
| die Stunde (-n) | hour |
| vor | ago |

**(d) Some phrases**

| | |
|---|---|
| Um wieviel Uhr? | At what time? |
| Auf welchen Namen? | What name? |
| Auf Wiederhören | Goodbye (phone) |
| Was möchten Sie? | What would you like? |

**(e) Menu vocabulary**

| | |
|---|---|
| garniert | dressed |
| gebacken | baked |
| gebraten | fried |
| gefüllt | stuffed |
| gegrillt | grilled |
| gekocht | boiled |
| geräuchert | smoked |
| in Essig | in vinegar |
| mit Sahne | creamed |
| nach Müllerin Art | meunière |
| pochiert | poached |

\*

| | |
|---|---|
| der **Apfelk**uchen | apple pie |
| der **Apfels**aft | apple juice |
| das bel**eg**te Brot | sandwich |
| das **B**ier | beer |
| die **Bock**wurst | thick, boiled sausage |
| die **Bowl**e | cold punch |
| das **Brath**ähnchen | roast chicken |
| **Bratk**artoffeln | roast potatoes |
| die **Brat**wurst | fried pork sausages |
| das **Bröt**chen | bread roll |
| das gek**och**te Ei | boiled egg |
| das **Rühr**ei | scrambled egg |
| **Spiegel**eier | fried eggs |
| der **Eisb**echer | ice-cream sundae |
| das **Eis**bein | pork shank in jelly |
| die **Ent**e | duck |
| der **Fisch** | fish |
| das **Fleisch** | meat |
| die **Forel**le | trout |
| die **Frank**furter | hot-dog sausage |
| das **Frühs**tück | breakfast |
| das **Geflüg**el | poultry |
| **Getränke** | beverages |
| das **Gul**asch | goulash |
| das **Hack**fleisch | minced meat |
| das **Hähn**chen | chicken |
| der **Hum**mer | lobster |
| der **Kaffee** | coffee |
| das **Kalbf**leisch | veal |
| die **Kalbs**haxe | leg of veal |
| das **Kalbss**chnitzel | veal cutlet |
| der **Kart**offel | potato |
| **Salz**kartoffeln | boiled potatoes |
| der **Käse** | cheese |
| der **Kuch**en | cake, tart or flan |
| der **Lachs** | salmon |
| die **Leb**er | liver |
| der **Leber**käs | hot sliced meat loaf |
| der **Leberkn**ödel | liver dumplings |
| das **Mat**jesfillet | herring fillet |
| die **Milch** | milk |

| | |
|---|---|
| das Mineralwasser | mineral water |
| die Nachspeise | pudding, dessert or sweet |
| das Obst | fruit |
| das Omelett | omelette |
| der Pfannkuchen | pancake |
| das Pfeffersteak | steak spiced with pepper |
| Pommes frites | chips |
| die Portion | portion |
| das Ragout | ragout |
| der Rehbraten | venison steak |
| das Rindfleisch | beef |
| der Rollmops | rollmop herring |
| der Saft | juice |
| die Sahne | cream |
| der Salat | salad |
| der grüne Salat | green salad |
| der Kartoffelsalat | potato salad |
| das Salz | salt |
| das Sauerkraut | sauerkraut |
| der Schinken | ham |
| die Schlagsahne | whipped cream |
| der Schnaps | schnapps |
| das Schnitzel | escalope |
| das Schweinefleisch | pork |
| das Schweineschnitzel | pork chop |
| die Schweinshaxe | leg of pork |
| der Spargel | asparagus |
| die Speisekarte | menu |
| die Suppe | soup |
| die Tagessuppe | soup of the day |
| der Tee | tea |
| eine Tasse Tee | a cup of tea |
| ein Kännchen Tee | a pot of tea |
| die Torte | gateau |
| das Viertel | quarter of a litre |
| der Wein | wine |
| der Weinbrand | brandy |
| das Wienerschnitzel | veal escalope with breadcrumbs |
| die Wurst | sausage |
| der Zucker | sugar |
| die Zwiebel | onion |

## 11.3 STRUCTURAL EXPLANATIONS

### (a) Structures to learn

#### (i) How to ask if there is a table

| | |
|---|---|
| Haben Sie einen Tisch | Have you got a table |
| frei | free |
| für zwei  ? | for two   ? |
| für vier | for four |

#### (ii) How to call the waiter or waitress

| | |
|---|---|
| Herr Ober! | Waiter! |
| Fräulein! | Miss! |
| (even if the lady is no longer in the first bloom of youth) | |

#### (iii) How to ask for the menu or the wine list

| | |
|---|---|
| Die Speisekarte, bitte! | The menu, please |
| Die Weinkarte, bitte! | The wine list, please |
| Ich möchte | I'd like to see the |
| die Weinkarte ⎫ sehen | wine list |
| die Speisekarte ⎰ | menu |

#### (iv) How to ask someone what they would like to eat or drink

(1)  Was möchten Sie?     What would you like?

(2)

| Ich möchte ⎫ | ⎧ einen Cognac |
|---|---|
| Möchten Sie ⎰ | ⎨ eine Vorspeise |
| | ⎩ ein Mineralwasser |

| I'd like ⎫ | ⎧ a Cognac |
|---|---|
| Would you like ⎰ | ⎨ a starter |
| | ⎩ a mineral water |

Note the form of ein

(3)  Möchten Sie/Ich möchte     Would you like/I'd like
    etwas essen/etwas trinken   something to eat/something
                                to drink

#### (v) How to order

| Einmal ⎫ ⎧ Texas Steak | One ⎫ ⎧ Texas steak(s) |
|---|---|
| Zweimal ⎬ ⎨ | Two ⎬ ⎨ |
| Dreimal ⎭ ⎩ Gulaschsuppe | Three ⎭ ⎩ goulash soup(s) |

N.B. Einmal, zweimal, etc., indicate the number of portions required, corresponding to the number of people who require them. In German, the noun remains in the singular after zweimal, dreimal, etc.

### (vi) How to ask for the bill

Zahlen, bitte
Die Rechnung, bitte
Ich möchte zahlen, bitte
Ich möchte die Rechnung, bitte

### (vii) How to express the time by clock
#### (1) *Questions*

| | |
|---|---|
| Wieviel Uhr ist es? | What time is it? |
| Wie spät ist es? | |
| Wann . . . ? | When? |
| Um wieviel Uhr . . . ? | At what time? |

### (viii) Expressions of time
#### 1. *The hours*

Es ist  =  It is
Um  =  At

| | | | | | |
|---|---|---|---|---|---|
| Es ist | drei Uhr | Es ist | ein Uhr | Es is | Mittag |
| Um | | Um | | Um | Mitternacht |
| | | | | | zwölf Uhr |

#### 2. *Time past the hour*

| | | | |
|---|---|---|---|
| Es ist | fünf (Minuten) | Es ist | fünfundzwanzig (Minuten) |
| Um | nach neun | Um | nach sechs |

Es ist ⎱ Viertel nach    Es ist ⎱
Um ⎰    sechs       Um ⎰   halb zehn

N.B.! N.B.! 'Half' TOWARDS the next hour.

### 3. Time TO the hour

Es ist ⎱   zwanzig      Es ist ⎱ Viertel vor      Es ist ⎱ zehn vor
Um ⎰   (Minuten)    Um ⎰   zwölf         Um ⎰   zwölf
       vor elf

### (b) Grammar

(i) Here is part of the verb MÖGEN, which we first met in Chapter 7. The part of this verb which is most frequently used is the part which enables you to say what you *would like*.

| | | |
|---|---|---|
| ich | möchte | I would like |
| er | möchte | he would like |
| sie | möchte | she would like |
| wir | möchten | we would like |
| Sie | möchten | you would like (formal or polite) |

You will find the verb in the appendix.

(ii) Note these two question forms

1. Möchten Sie eine Vorspeise?    The verb comes first
   Möchten Sie etwas trinken?

2. Was möchten Sie?   The sentence begins with a
   Was möchten Sie trinken?   question word

(iii) Further question words, or interrogatives, are:

| | | |
|---|---|---|
| Wo? | – Where? | Wo möchten Sie essen?<br>Where would you like to eat? |
| Welcher? (*m*) | – Which? | Welcher Wein ist billiger?<br>Which wine is cheaper? |
| Welche? (*f*) | – Which? | Welche Vorspeise ist besser?<br>Which hors d'oeuvre is better? |
| Welches? (*n*) | – Which? | Welches Mineralwasser<br>schmeckt gut mit Whisky<br>Which mineral water tastes<br>good with whisky? |
| Wer? | – Who? | Wer ist im Restaurant?<br>Who is in the restaurant? |

N.B. 'false friend': don't confuse wer? with wo?

| | | |
|---|---|---|
| Warum? | – Why? | Warum trinken Sie Pils?<br>Why are you drinking Pils? |
| Was? | – What? | Was trinken Sie?<br>What are you drinking? |
| Wohin? | – Where<br>(to)? | Wohin gehen Sie?<br>Where are you going (to)? |
| Was für? | – What<br>sort of? | Was für Bier trinken Sie?<br>What sort of beer are you<br>drinking? |
| Wie? | – How? | Wie kochen Sie Jägerschnitzel<br>How do you cook<br>Jägerschnitzel? |

(iv) **How to say which day**

a) heute – today
   heute abend – this evening/tonight
   heute nachmittag – this afternoon
   heute morgen – this morning

b) morgen – tomorrow
   morgen abend – tomorrow evening/night
   morgen nachmittag – tomorrow afternoon
   morgen früh – tomorrow morning

c) gestern – yesterday
   gestern abend – yesterday evening/night

gestern nachmittag – yesterday afternoon
gestern morgen – yesterday morning

## (v) How to express relative time

a) diese / nächste / letzte } Woche (*f*) — this / next / last } week

b) dieses / nächstes / letztes } Jahr (*n*) — this / next / last } year

c) diesen / nächsten / letzten } Monat (*m*) — this / next / last } month

d) in drei { Tagen / Wochen / Monaten / Jahren — in three { days / weeks / months / years

e) vor drei { Tagen / Wochen / Monaten / Jahren — three { days / weeks / months / years } ago

f) in fünf { Minuten / Stunden — in five { minutes / hours

## 11.4 EXERCISES

### Section A

### Exercise 1

With reference to the menu on page 127, work out how you would order under the following conditions. (If you are working with a partner, take turns to play the part of the waiter.)

1. You are by yourself and want a quick meal; one meat dish will do. You want to spend as little as possible. Nothing to drink.
2. You are dining with an important friend and you can afford the best. Curiously, you both have exactly the same taste in food. You decide to have the lot: hors d'oeuvres, fish, meat, dessert, and, of course, your favourite Rhine wine.

RESTAURANT ZUM RITTER

SPEISEKARTE

## VORSPEISEN

| | |
|---|---|
| Krabbencocktail | 6.00 |
| Aal in Aspik | 7.00 |
| Austern (12) | 12.00 |

## SUPPEN

| | |
|---|---|
| Hühnerbrühe mit Nudeln | 2.00 |
| Gulaschsuppe | 2.50 |
| Zwiebelsuppe | 3.00 |

## EIERSPEISEN

| | |
|---|---|
| Rührei | 4.50 |
| Spiegeleier mit Schinken | 5.00 |
| Omelett – verschiedener Art | 5.25 |

## FISCHGERICHTE

| | |
|---|---|
| Rollmops | 7.50 |
| Forelle, blau, mit grünem Salat, Salzkartoffeln | 12.00 |
| Seezungenfilet mit grünen Bohnen, Salzkartoffeln | 14.50 |

## GETRÄNKE

| | Glas | Flasche |
|---|---|---|
| Pils | 1.50 | |
| Export | 1.75 | |
| Viertel Moselwein | 4.00 | 14.00 |
| Viertel Rheinwein | 4.00 | 14.00 |
| Rotwein | 4.00 | 14.00 |
| Tasse Kaffee oder Tee | 2.10 | |
| Kännchen | 3.50 | |

UNSERE PREISE SIND ENDPREISE

## FLEISCHGERICHTE

| | |
|---|---|
| Eisbein mit Sauerkraut | 7.20 |
| 'Texas' Steak mit Pommes frites und gemischtem Salat | 13.80 |
| Jägerschnitzel mit Pommes frites | 14.00 |
| Wiener Schnitzel mit Spiegelei, Salat, Röstkartoffeln | 14.30 |
| Zigeuner Steak mit Zwiebeln, Reis und grünem Salat | 15.00 |

## ETWAS FÜR DEN KLEINEN APPETIT

| | |
|---|---|
| Rührei mit Schinken | 4.20 |
| Paar Frankfurter mit Pommes frites | 4.80 |

## KÄSE

| | |
|---|---|
| Emmentaler mit Butter, Brot | 3.20 |
| Käseplatte, Butter, Brot | 3.60 |

## NACHSPEISEN

| | |
|---|---|
| Gemischtes Kompott | 2.50 |
| Pampelmuse | 2.50 |
| Pfannkuchen | 3.70 |
| Ananas flambiert mit Kirschwasser | 6.20 |

| | Glas | Flasche |
|---|---|---|
| Sekt | | 22.50 |
| Cognac | 2.50 | |
| Weinbrand | 2.00 | |
| Mineralwasser | 1.50 | |

3. You are taking the children out for their first meal in a restaurant. Peter can't stand eggs and Paula has an aversion to sausages. You have a weakness for trout yourself. You do like wine, but you want to set the children a good example.
4. You want to have a light lunch with a colleague. Ham and eggs for you and a scrambled egg for him shouldn't have too many calories. Afterwards, you could share a selection of different cheeses, perhaps, and a cup of coffee.

**Exercise 2**
You go into a Gasthaus for lunch with two friends. What do you say?
1. Ask if there's a table for three.
2. Call the waitress.
3. Say you want to order.
4. Order two prawn cocktails and jellied eels.
5. Say you'd like three Texas steaks.
6. Order two quarters of red wine and a Pils.
7. Ask for the bill.
If you are working with a partner, take it in turns to play the part of the waitress.

**Section B**

**Exercise 3**
Ask your guests if they want to have the same dish that you have chosen.

Example: Ich möchte eine Vorspeise.
Möchten Sie auch eine Vorspeise?
Ich möchte ein Mineralwasser.
Möchten Sie auch ein Mineralwasser?

1. Ich möchte eine Vorspeise.
2. Ich möchte ein Mineralwasser.
3. Ich möchte einen Cognac.
4. Ich möchte eine Gulaschsuppe.
5. Ich möchte eine Forelle.
6. Ich möchte Salzkartoffeln.
7. Ich möchte Eisbein.
8. Ich möchte ein Wiener Schnitzel.
9. Ich möchte eine Käseplatte.
10. Ich möchte ein gemischtes Kompott.

**Exercise 4**
Ask and say what time it is.

Example:  08:00  Wieviel Uhr ist es?
                    Es ist acht Uhr.
            10:30  Wieviel Uhr ist es?
                    Es ist halb elf.

1. 13:00
2. 12:00
3. 09:05
4. 18:15
5. 16:25

6. 21:30
7. 11:10
8. 06:20
9. 21:30
10. 14:45

# CHAPTER 12

# ASKING PERMISSION

## 12.1 DIALOGUES 📼

**Dialogue 1**

Parking is always a problem in every town, and Munich is no exception.

1 *Antonio*:  Entschuldigen Sie!
(louder) Entschuldigen Sie!
*Polizist*:  Ja?
*Antonio*:  Kann ich hier parken?

*Fahren Sie zum Parkhaus!*

*Photograph: J. Allan Cash Ltd*

5  *Polizist*:  Nein. Es tut mir leid.
    Hier dürfen Sie nicht parken.
    *Antonio*:  (pointing) Und dort drüben?
    Kann ich dort drüben parken?
    *Polizist*:  Nein.
10  Dort dürfen Sie auch nicht parken.
    *Antonio*:  Herr Gott nochmal!!
    Wo kann ich denn hier parken?
    *Polizist*:  Im Parkhaus.
    Fahren Sie zum Parkhaus.
15  *Antonio*:  Zum Parkhaus! Zum Parkhaus!
    Also zum Parkhaus.
    (sound of squealing tyres)

## Dialogue 2

Fritz Löb's car won't start, so he goes to see Frau Meyer, who
lives in the same block, to see if she can help. Perhaps that
dreadful old bicycle of hers is still in working order.
(Fritz rings the frontdoor bell)

1  *Frau Meyer*:  Ja, bitte?
    Ach, Sie sind es, Herr Löb.
    *Fritz*:  Grüß Gott, Frau Meyer!
    Entschuldigen Sie die Störung.
5  *Frau Meyer*:  Was kann ich für Sie tun?
    *Fritz*:  Frau Meyer, mein Auto startet nicht.
    Die Batterie ist kaputt, glaube ich.
    *Frau Meyer*:  O, das tut mir leid.
    *Fritz*:  Darf ich bitte Ihr Fahrrad borgen?
10  *Frau Meyer*:  Mein Fahrrad?
    Selbstverständlich.
    Es ist unten im Keller.
    *Fritz*:  Herzlichen Dank.
    O, darf ich auch die Pumpe borgen?
15  *Frau Meyer*:  Aber natürlich.
    Sie dürfen die Pumpe auch borgen.
    *Fritz*:  Recht vielen Dank.
    *Frau Meyer*:  Gern geschehen.
    Fahren Sie vorsichtig.
20  *Fritz*:  Ja, ja.

## 12.2 INFORMATION

### (a) Notes on Dialogue 1

5. Es tut mir leid

This expression cannot be translated word for word. It is an expression which should be learned as a whole.

10. auch

The word auch has a number of meanings: 'also', 'too', and in this sentence it means 'either', because it is in a sentence containing a negative. Note in particular the position this word has in the sentence and how it is emphasised by the speaker on the cassette.

11. Herr Gott nochmal

This is an expression of real irritation. It is quite colloquial but can be used in any society where it would be allowed to show one's irritation.

### (b) Notes on Dialogue 2

4. die Störung

'The disturbance'. Note that where German uses a noun, English uses the expression 'for disturbing you'.

7. kaputt

This is a very useful phrase which can be used in a large number of situations. Many things, such as a car battery in this instance, can be kaputt where we would normally use an expression in English which was more tailor-made e.g. run down.

12. im Keller

Nearly all German houses have a cellar. In a large house which is divided up into flats or in a block of flats the cellar is divided up into compartments, each one belonging to one of the families living in the house. Cellars normally contain central-heating boilers and are also used as general storage rooms, especially for bottles of wine.

18. Gern geschehen

This is a very useful phrase with which to respond when somebody thanks you for something. It can represent English expressions such as 'that's quite all right', 'you're welcome' or 'don't mention it'.

(c) **Word list**

| | |
|---|---|
| **par**ken | to park |
| **kön**nen | to be able; to be allowed |
| **dür**fen | to be allowed |
| auch | also |
| das **Park**haus (⁻er) | multi-storey car park |
| tun | to do |
| das **Au**to (-s) | car |
| **star**ten | to start |
| die Batt**erie** (-n) | battery |
| ka**putt** | broken |
| **glau**ben | to believe |
| das **Fahr**rad (⁻er) | bicycle |
| **bor**gen | to borrow |
| selbstver**ständ**lich | of course |
| **un**ten | downstairs |
| der **Kel**ler (-) | cellar |
| die **Pum**pe (-n) | pump |
| na**tür**lich | of course |
| **vor**sichtig | careful; carefully |
| der **Re**genmantel (⁻) | raincoat |
| die **Zei**tung (-en) | newspaper |
| **neh**men | to take |
| **seh**en | to see |
| die **Zahn**bürste (-n) | toothbrush |
| die **Zahn**pasta | toothpaste |
| der **Rasier**apparat (-e) | razor |
| die **Ho**se (singular only) | trousers |
| der **Fern**sehapparat | television set |
| der **Zu**cker | sugar |

| das Buch (¨er) | book |
| der Kamm (¨e) | comb |

**(d) Some phrases**

| Ent**schul**digen Sie! | Excuse me! |
| Es tut mir leid | I'm sorry |
| Dort **drü**ben | Over there |
| **Herz**lichen Dank | Thank you very much |
| Recht **vie**len Dank | Thank you very much |
| Das geht nicht | That won't do |
| Das ist un**mög**lich | That is impossible |
| Auf **kein**en Fall | Under no circumstances |

## 12.3 STRUCTURAL EXPLANATIONS

**(a) Structures to learn**

(i) How to ask permission to do something, using the verb KÖNNEN.

a) How to ask permission to *borrow* things

Kann ich { Ihr Fahrrad / Ihren Regenmantel / Ihre Zeitung } borgen?

das Fahrrad – bicycle
der Regenmantel – raincoat
die Zeitung – newspaper

b) How to ask permission to *do other* things

Kann ich { Ihr Fahrrad / Ihren Regenmantel / Ihre Zeitung } { borgen / nehmen / sehen } ?

borgen – to borrow
nehmen – to take
sehen – to see

(ii) If you want to be particularly polite, possibly because you are talking to someone of higher status than yourself, you can ask for permission by using another verb: DÜRFEN.

It may be that you want to refuse permission to somebody to do something, and express the meaning 'you are not allowed to do something'. In both these cases, you use the verb DÜRFEN.

Dort dürfen Sie nicht parken
Darf ich Ihr Fahrrad borgen?
Darf ich die Pumpe borgen?

Here are some sentences which show you how this verb can be used:

Darf ich { Ihr Fahrrad / Ihren Regenmantel / Ihre Zeitung } borgen?

(v) Here are some phrases you can use if you want to give permission to somebody:

Selbstverständlich ⎤
Aber natürlich ⎬ of course
Sicher ⎟
Bitte ⎦

(vi) Here are some expressions you can use if you want to refuse somebody permission. They range from being quite neutral in tone at the top to being very strong at the bottom.

Nein, es tut mir leid
Nein, das geht nicht
Nein, das ist unmöglich
Nein, auf keinen Fall

**(b) Grammar**

(i) Here are the most frequently used parts of the two verbs we have been looking at in this chapter.

The verb KÖNNEN – to be able to

| ich | kann | I can |
| er | kann | he can |
| sie | kann | she can |
| wir | können | we can |
| Sie | können | you can |

The verb DÜRFEN – to be allowed to

| ich | darf | I may i.e. am allowed to |
| er | darf | he may |
| sie | darf | she may |
| wir | dürfen | we may |
| Sie | dürfen | you may |

Both verbs are *irregular* in that their stems change, and their endings do not conform to the standard pattern.

(ii) The verb KÖNNEN has two meanings. One meaning is associated with asking permission, as we have seen earlier. The primary meaning, however, is connected with *ability*. Thus:

Kann er schwimmen? — Can he (is he able to, does he know how to) swim?

Ich kann schwimmen — I can (am able to) swim

(iii) The two verbs KÖNNEN and DÜRFEN can be used in a number of different sentence patterns. Here are some examples:

The verb has two parts:

One part is here in column 2. This is called the *modal* verb

The other part is here in column 3. This is called the *infinitive*

A *modal* verb defines the mode, or manner in which something is done. It refers to the necessity, possibility or impossibility of e.g. swimming, going, seeing, etc.

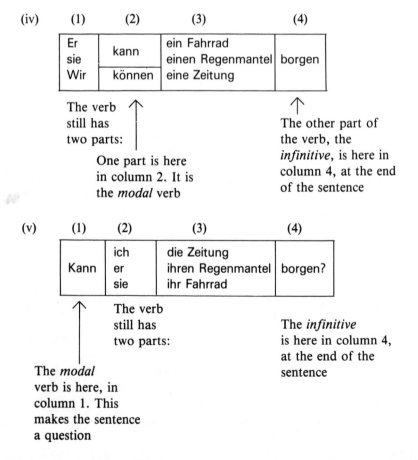

(iv)

| (1) | (2) | (3) | (4) |
|-----|-----|-----|-----|
| Er sie | kann | ein Fahrrad einen Regenmantel | borgen |
| Wir | können | eine Zeitung | |

The verb still has two parts:

One part is here in column 2. It is the *modal* verb

The other part of the verb, the *infinitive*, is here in column 4, at the end of the sentence

(v)

| (1) | (2) | (3) | (4) |
|-----|-----|-----|-----|
| Kann | ich er sie | die Zeitung ihren Regenmantel ihr Fahrrad | borgen? |

The verb still has two parts:

The *modal* verb is here, in column 1. This makes the sentence a question

The *infinitive* is here in column 4, at the end of the sentence

(vi)

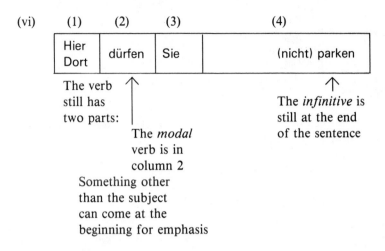

| (1) | (2) | (3) | (4) |
|-----|-----|-----|-----|
| Hier<br>Dort | dürfen | Sie | (nicht) parken |

The verb
still has
two parts:

The *modal*
verb is in
column 2

Something other
than the subject
can come at the
beginning for emphasis

The *infinitive* is
still at the end
of the sentence

(vii) You will find the verbs können and dürfen in the appendix.

## 12.4 EXERCISES

**Exercise 1**
Imagine that you are living with a German family and want to borrow some of their things. This is what you would say:
Example:   Kann ich Ihr Fahrrad borgen bitte?
Now, how would you ask to borrow the following things? Of course, you might not get them.
1. Das Auto.
2. Die Zahnbürste.
3. Die Zahnpasta.
4. Der Rasierapparat.
5. Die Zeitung.

**Exercise 2**
Now it's your turn to practise giving or refusing permission. Here are some things which somebody might – with a stretch of the imagination, of course – ask you if they can borrow. When you check the answers, bear in mind that we have printed the answers we think you may have given. We have no means of telling, of course, how generous you are.
1. Kann ich Ihr Fahrrad borgen, bitte?
2. Kann ich Ihre Hose borgen, bitte?
3. Kann ich Ihre Zeitung borgen, bitte?
4. Kann ich Ihren Rasierapparat borgen, bitte?
5. Kann ich Ihre Zahnpasta borgen, bitte?

6. Kann ich Ihr Auto borgen, bitte?
7. Kann ich Ihren Mann borgen, bitte?
8. Kann ich Ihre Frau borgen, bitte?
9. Kann ich Ihren Regenmantel borgen, bitte?
10. Kann ich Ihren Fernsehapparat borgen, bitte?

**Exercise 3**
Look at the answers which are given below and try and work out what the questions must have been.
1. *Question*: ......?
   *Answer*: Nein, hier dürfen Sie nicht parken.
2. *Question*: ......?
   *Answer*: Aber natürlich. Mein Fahrrad ist dort drüben.
3. *Question*: ......?
   *Answer*: Nein, es tut mir leid. Ich habe keinen Zucker.
4. *Question*: ......?
   *Answer*: Aber sicher. Sie können das Auto nehmen.
5. *Question*: ......?
   *Answer*: Nein, es tut mir leid. Ich habe nur eine Zahnbürste.

**Exercise 4**
Imagine that you are living with a German family called Fiebiger. You have come rather unprepared and you want to borrow a number of things. What do you say?
Example:
You want to borrow Herr Fiebiger's bicycle.
Kann ich Ihr Fahrrad borgen, Herr Fiebiger?
Now continue:
1. You want to see Herr Fiebiger's newspaper.
2. You'd like to borrow his car.
3. You'd like to have Frau Fiebiger's lamp.
4. It would be nice if you could take their television.
5. You'd like to borrow Herr Fiebiger's radio.
6. It's raining and you want to take Frau Fiebiger's raincoat.
7. You've left your razor at home. Can you have his, I wonder.
8. You're quite out of toothpaste. Can you borrow some?
9. That was an interesting book Frau Fiebiger was reading last night. Perhaps you could see it.
10. Your hair is terribly untidy. Can you have Herr Fiebiger's comb, I wonder.

**New words**
    das Auto – the car
    das Buch – the book
    der Kamm – the comb

# CHAPTER 13

# JOBS AND PROFESSIONS

## 13.1 DIALOGUES 📼

**Dialogue 1**

Fritz is bringing back Frau Meyer's bicycle which he borrowed when his car wouldn't start.

(He rings the frontdoor bell)

1 *Frau Meyer*: Ja, bitte?
    Ach, Sie sind es, Herr Löb.
    *Fritz*: Grüß Gott, Frau Meyer!
    Entschuldigen Sie die Störung.
5   Hier ist Ihr Rad.
    *Frau Meyer*: Vielen Dank.
    War alles in Ordnung?
    *Fritz*: Ja, alles war in Ordnung.
    Danke schön.
10 *Frau Meyer*: Sie sind Hauptschullehrer, nicht wahr?
    *Fritz*: Ja, das stimmt.
    *Frau Meyer*: Gefällt Ihnen die Arbeit?
    *Fritz*: O ja, sehr.
    *Frau Meyer*: Wann beginnen Sie am Morgen?
15 *Fritz*: Wir beginnen um acht Uhr.
    *Frau Meyer*: Ach so.
    Und wann kommen Sie normalerweise nach Hause?
    *Fritz*: Ich komme gewöhnlich gegen zwei Uhr nach Hause.
    *Frau Meyer*: Wieviele Tage arbeiten Sie in der Woche?
20 *Fritz*: Nur fünf.
    Gott sei Dank.
    *Frau Meyer*: Als ich Schülerin war, hatten wir auch samstags
    Schule.
    *Fritz*: Ja ja, wir haben es besser.

*Er ist Hauptschullehrer*

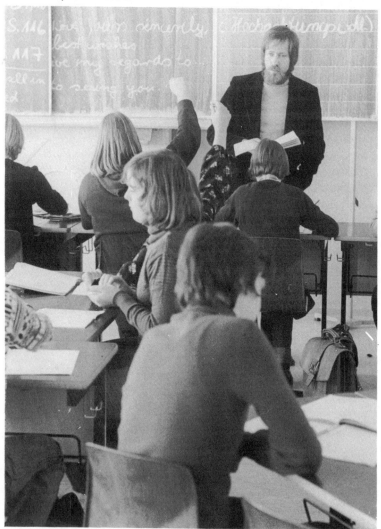

*Photograph: Bavaria-Verlag/Jürgen Gaiser*

25    Nun. Vielen Dank noch einmal für das Rad.
    *Frau Meyer*:   Gern geschehen, Herr Löb.
    Auf Wiedersehen.

## Dialogue 2

You will remember that Elke met a man when she was in the Alte Pinakothek. He has invited her to have a cup of coffee in the museum restaurant.

1   *Mann*:   Was sind Sie von Beruf, wenn ich fragen darf?
     *Elke*:   Ich bin Verkäuferin.
     *Mann*:   Hier in München?
     *Elke*:   Ja, bei Mode Zilling.
5      In der Leopoldstraße.
     *Mann*:   Gefällt Ihnen die Arbeit?
     *Elke*:   O, ja und nein.
     Ich verdiene sehr gut.
     *Mann*:   Wann beginnen Sie mit der Arbeit?
10   *Elke*:   Um acht Uhr.
     *Mann*:   Und haben Sie eine Mittagspause?
     *Elke*:   Ja. Von zwölf bis eins.
     *Mann*:   Zwischen zwölf und eins habe ich auch Mittagspause.
     *Elke*:   (ironically) Schauen Sie mal!
15   *Mann*:   Wann kommen Sie abends nach Hause?
     *Elke*:   Ich habe um fünf Uhr Feierabend.
     *Mann*:   Ich auch.
     Könnte ich Sie an Ihrem Geschäft abholen?
     Ich habe ein Auto.
20      Wir könnten vielleicht aufs Land fahren.
     *Elke*:   Vielen Dank.
     Aber ich habe mein eigenes Auto.
     *Mann*:   Ach so.
     *Elke*:   Und heute kommt mein Freund um fünf Uhr.
25      Wir wollen auf dem Viktualien Markt einkaufen gehen.
     *Mann*:   Schade.
     Ein anderes Mal vielleicht.
     *Elke*:   Vielleicht.

## 13.2 INFORMATION

### (a) Notes on Dialogue 1

7. War — War is the past tense of the verb sein – 'to be'. It is to be translated here as 'was'.

10. Hauptschullehrer — Note that there is no indefinite article in front of the word Hauptschullehrer. In English when we refer to somebody's profession we say, for example, 'He is *a* teacher'. In German the indefinite article is omitted and

Germans say instead Er ist Hauptschullehrer.

10. nicht wahr?

Nicht wahr is a very useful expression for converting a statement into a question. The phrase nicht wahr can be added to any statement in order to turn it into an interrogative.

12. Gefällt Ihnen

No attempt should be made to translate this expression literally. Treat it exactly as if it meant 'Do you like ... ?' Note, however, that in order to say 'I like something', German puts the object of the sentence first, thus: Die Arbeit gefällt mir – 'I like the work'.

17. normalerweise
18. gewöhnlich

These phrases are interchangeable and allow you to refer to what is *usual* or *normal*.

22. Als ich Schülerin war

Students may like to note the position of the verb in this sentence, but they are not required to be able to use it at this stage. Students wishing to inform themselves about the structure of 'subordinate' clauses introduced by als should consult the grammar books listed in the bibliography.

22. hatten

This is the past tense of the verb haben and means 'had'.

22. samstags

Note that by adding an s to the end of the word you make the phrase 'on Saturdays'.

## (b) Notes on Dialogue 2
1. wenn ich fragen darf

Students may like to note the position of the verb in this

phrase but at this stage they are only required to use the sentence as if it were an idiom: 'If you don't mind my asking'.

12. eins     In colloquial German you can say either eins or ein Uhr for one o'clock.

16. Feierabend     This is a very frequent and colloquial expression meaning to finish one's work for the day.

25. Viktualien Markt     Name of a famous food market in Munich.

## (c) Word list

| | |
|---|---|
| das Rad (short for Fahrrad) | bicycle |
| alles | everything |
| der Lehrer | teacher |
| die Arbeit (-en) | work |
| sehr | very much |
| beginnen | to begin |
| wann? | when? |
| der Morgen (-) | morning |
| wieviel? | how many? |
| der Tag (-e) | day |
| arbeiten | to work |
| die Woche (-n) | week |
| der Schüler | school pupil (male) |
| die Schülerin | school pupil (female) |
| die Schule (-n) | school |
| noch einmal | once again |
| besser | better |
| der Beruf (-e) | job; profession |
| fragen | to ask |
| die Verkäuferin (-nen) | sales lady |
| verdienen | to earn |
| zwischen | between |
| abends | in the evening |
| die Mittagspause (-n) | midday break |
| das Geschäft (-e) | shop; business |
| abholen | to call for |
| das Auto (-s) | car |
| vielleicht | perhaps |

| | |
|---|---|
| **fah**ren | to drive |
| **ei**gen | own |
| **heu**te | today |
| der Freund (-e) | (boy) friend |
| **wol**len | to want to |
| **ein**kaufen **geh**en | to go shopping |
| **scha**de | pity |
| die **Buch**handlung (-en) | bookshop |
| das **Büro** (-s) | office |
| die **Fab**rik (-en) | factory |
| die Kondi**tor**ei (-en) | café or cake shop |
| das **Kauf**haus ("er) | store |
| der Pu**llo**ver | pullover |
| das **Wet**ter | weather |
| der Schnee | snow |
| der Schuh (-e) | shoe |
| der Berg (-e) | mountain |

**(d) Some phrases**

| | |
|---|---|
| In **Ord**nung | All right |
| Das stimmt | That's right |
| **Ge**gen | About |
| Gott sei Dank! | Thank God! |
| Gern ge**sch**ehen | You're welcome |
| Aufs Land | Into the country |
| Ein **and**eres Mal | Another time |

## 12.3 STRUCTURAL EXPLANATIONS

**(a) Structures to learn**

(i) How to ask somebody what he or she does for a living

| | |
|---|---|
| Was sind Sie von Beruf? | What do you do? |
| Sie sind (Lehrer), nicht wahr? | You are (a teacher), aren't you? |
| Herr Löb ist Lehrer | Mr Löb is a teacher |

(ii) How to say what you do (for a living)

Ich bin

| | |
|---|---|
| Angestellter | Polizist |
| Bäcker | Schüler |
| Beamter | Student |
| Busfahrer | Taxifahrer |
| Friseur | Techniker |
| Kellner | Verkäufer |
| Lehrer | Verwaltungsangestellter |

|  |  |  |
|---|---|---|
| I am | an employee | a policeman |
|  | a baker | a school-student |
|  | a civil servant | a student |
|  | a bus driver | a taxi-driver |
|  | a hairdresser | a technician |
|  | a waiter | a sales person |
|  | a teacher | a government employee |

An Angestellter is a salaried employee, or white-collar worker.
A Beamter is a civil servant, holding a tenured position.

(iii) The names of jobs held by women frequently end with the letters -in.

Ich bin

| Ärztin | Studentin | lady doctor | girl student |
|---|---|---|---|
| Kellnerin | Sekretärin | waitress | secretary |
| Lehrerin | Taxifahrerin | lady teacher | lady taxi-driver |
| Polizistin | Telephonistin | policewoman | lady telephonist |
| Schülerin | Verkäuferin | girl school-student | sales lady |

(iv) There are some exceptions to the above, normally ending in -e.

|  |  |  |
|---|---|---|
| Ich bin | Angestellte | woman employee |
|  | Empfangsdame | lady receptionist |
|  | Friseuse | lady hairdresser |
|  | Hausfrau | housewife |

(v) How to ask somebody where they work and how to state where you work

Wo arbeiten Sie?    Ich bin bei (name of firm or company)

|  |  |
|---|---|
| Ich bin bei | Siemens |
|  | Grundig |
|  | Ford |
|  | Mode Zilling |
|  | Mercedes |

Ich arbeite in

| einer Buchhandlung | die Buchhandlung – bookshop |
|---|---|
| einem Büro | das Büro – office |
| einer Schule | die Schule – school |
| einer Fabrik | die Fabrik – factory |
| einem Hotel | das Hotel – hotel |
| einer Konditorei | die Konditorei – café or cakeshop |

| einem Kaufhaus | das Kaufhaus – store |
| einem Geschäft | das Geschäft – shop |

(vi) How to ask about somebody's conditions of work

1. Wann beginnen Sie
   { am Morgen?
   { mit der Arbeit?

   When do you begin
   { in the morning?
   { work?

   Ich beginne } um acht Uhr
   Wir beginnen }

   I begin } at eight o'clock
   We begin }

2. Wann kommen Sie (abends) nach Hause?
   When do you come home (in the evening)?

   Um sechs Uhr | At six o'clock
   Ich habe um fünf Uhr | I finish at five o'clock
   Feierabend |

3. Wieviele { Tage
   { Stunden } arbeiten Sie in der Woche?

   How many { days
   { hours } do you work a week?

   Nur fünf Tage | Only five days
   Ich arbeite fünfunddreißig | I work 35 hours (a week)
   Stunden |

4. Haben Sie eine Mittagspause? Do you have a midday break?

   Wann
   Wie lange } haben Sie Mittagspause?

   When
   How long } is your midday break?

   Von zwölf bis eins | From twelve to one

**(b) Grammar**

**(i) Expressions of time (frequency)**

meistens
in der Regel
normalerweise } = usually, as a rule
gewöhnlich

**(ii) Approximate and exact time**

gegen drei Uhr | about or towards three o'clock
gerade drei Uhr | exactly (or just) three o'clock

**(iii) Today, tomorrow, etc.**

| | |
|---|---|
| heute | today |
| morgen | tomorrow |
| übermorgen | the day after tomorrow |
| gestern | yesterday |
| vorgestern | the day before yesterday |

**(iv) Time of day**

| | |
|---|---|
| morgens | in the morning |
| vormittags | in the morning |
| nachmittags | in the afternoon |
| abends | in the evening |
| nachts | in the night |

**(v) Time of day**

| | |
|---|---|
| heute früh | early this morning |
| heute morgen | this morning |
| heute nachmittag | this afternoon |
| heute abend | this evening |
| morgen früh | early tomorrow morning |
| gestern abend | yesterday evening |

**(vi) The use of the accusative**

| | |
|---|---|
| jeden Abend | every evening |
| jeden Freitag | every Friday |
| diesen Abend | this evening |
| heute abend | this evening |
| nächsten Freitag | next Friday |

**(vii) Use of prepositions**

| | |
|---|---|
| heute in acht Tagen | a week today |
| heute in vierzehn Tagen | a fortnight today |
| heute vor acht Tagen | a week ago |

**(viii) Regularity**

| | |
|---|---|
| montags | on Mondays |
| dienstags | on Tuesdays |
| mittwochs | on Wednesdays |
| donnerstags | on Thursdays |
| freitags | on Fridays |
| samstags | on Saturdays |
| sonntags | on Sundays |

N.B. A small letter is used because it is the notion of regularity which is meant, rather than the name of the day.

### (ix) The use of the dative to express liking

Gefällt Ihnen (singular)
{ der Pullover
  das Wetter  ?
  der Schnee

Do you like
{ the pullover
  the weather  ?
  the snow

Gefallen Ihnen (plural)
{ die Schuhe
  die Geschäfte  ?
  die Berge

Do you like
{ the shoes
  the shops  ?
  the mountains

Der Pullover
Das Wetter   } gefällt mir
Der Schnee     (singular)

I like { the pullover
         the weather
         the snow

Die Schuhe
Die Geschäfte } gefallen mir
Die Berge       (plural)

I like { the shoes
         the shops
         the mountains

## 13.4 EXERCISES

### Section A

### Exercise 1
1. Was ist Herr Moezer von Beruf?
2. Was ist Frau Hacker von Beruf?
3. Was ist Fräulein Siegling von Beruf?
4. Was ist Herr Mader von Beruf?
5. Was ist Frau Meyer von Beruf?
6. Was ist Fräulein Bauer von Beruf?
7. Was ist Frau Augustin von Beruf?
8. Was ist Herr Flohr von Beruf?
9. Was ist Herr Kahle von Beruf?
10. Was ist Herr Löb von Beruf?

Herr Kahle is a technician.
Fräulein Augustin is a waitress.
Herr Mader is a taxi-driver.
Herr Löb is a teacher.
Herr Moezer is a baker.

Fräulein Siegling is a student.
Frau Hacker is a hairdresser.
Fräulein Bauer is a secretary.
Frau Meyer is a housewife.
Herr Flohr is a policeman.

**Exercise 2**
Practise this conversation, speaking both the answers and the questions. The first one is done for you.

A: Was sind Sie von Beruf, Herr Flohr?     Herr Flohr (Polizist)
B: Ich bin Polizist.                        0830 – 1600
A: Wann beginnen Sie mit der Arbeit?
B: Um 8.30 Uhr.
A: Wann haben Sie Feierabend?
B: Ich habe um 16 Uhr Feierabend.

Now do these conversations, with a partner, if possible.
1. Herr Löb (Lehrer)
   0800 – 1400
2. Frau Hacker (Friseuse)
   0900 – 1800
3. Frau Augustin (Kellnerin)
   1400 – 2230
4. Herr Mader (Taxifahrer)
   0500 – 1300
5. Herr Moezer (Bäcker)
   0400 – 1100

**Section B**

**Exercise 3**
Give questions which will produce the following answers.
1. Die Farbe gefällt mir.
2. Die Landschaft gefällt mir.
3. Das Auto gefällt mir.
4. Die Schuhe gefallen mir.
5. Der Wind gefällt mir nicht.
6. Das Material gefällt mir.
7. Das Wetter gefällt mir.
8. Der Schnee gefällt mir.
9. Die Geschäfte gefallen mir.
10. Der Regen gefällt mir nicht.

# CHAPTER 14

# ACCOMMODATION

## 14.1 DIALOGUES 📼

**Dialogue 1**

Antonio Santos has come to love the folklore which is so much part of the life in Munich. On this particular day, just before Christmas, he has travelled into the centre of the city on the underground in order to visit the Christkindl Markt. This is held every year in the days leading up to Christmas and is situated on the Marienplatz just in front of the town hall. One important aspect of the Christkindl Markt is the many stalls where you can drink Glühwein. Antonio has met Fritz Löb there and has got into conversation with him.

1   *Antonio*:   Prost!

    *Fritz*:   Prost!

    *Antonio*:   Der Glühwein ist schön warm, nicht wahr?

    *Fritz*:   Ja, schön warm.

5   *Antonio*:   Wohnen Sie hier in München?

    *Fritz*:   Ja, ich wohne in der Nietzschestraße.

    *Antonio*:   Wohnen Sie in einem Mietshaus?

    *Fritz*:   Ja, ich habe eine Einzimmerwohnung, in einem großen Mietshaus.

10  *Antonio*:   Haben Sie nur ein Zimmer?

    *Fritz*:   Na, ich habe ein Badezimmer und eine Küche.

    *Antonio*:   Und sonst?

    *Fritz*:   Sonst habe ich ein Wohn- und Schlafzimmer.

    *Antonio*:   Ist die Wohnung schön?

15  *Fritz*:   Ja, sie ist klein, aber ganz schön.

    Ich habe viele Bilder dort.

    *Antonio*:   Bilder?

*Christkindlmarkt, München*

Photograph: *Bavaria-Verlag/GEWE-Foto*

    *Fritz*:  Ja.
       Ich sammle Bilder.
20  *Antonio*:  Hmm. Interessant.


**Dialogue 2**
    Antonio and Fritz continue talking together.
1  *Antonio*:  Mein Onkel hat auch viele Bilder.

*Fritz*:   Wo wohnt er?
*Antonio*:   In Napoli.
*Fritz*:   Ach, in Neapel.
5   *Antonio*:   Er hat ein Einzelhaus.
*Fritz*:   Das ist schön.
*Antonio*:   Er hat sechs Schlafzimmer und zwei Gästezimmer.
*Fritz*:   Du liebe Zeit!
*Antonio*:   Stellen Sie sich mal vor!
10   Sechs Schlafzimmer!
*Fritz*:   Hat er auch einen Garten?
*Antonio*:   Und ob!
Er hat Bäume und Sträucher überall.
*Fritz*:   Sehr schön.
15   *Antonio*:   Aber ich . . .
Ich habe eine Sozialwohnung in der Kaufmannsstraße.
*Fritz*:   Wieviele Zimmer haben Sie?
*Antonio*:   Ich habe ein Eßzimmer und ein Schlafzimmer.
*Fritz*:   Haben Sie ein Badezimmer und eine Küche?
20   *Antonio*:   Selbstverständlich!
Und ich habe einen Balkon.
Das ist schön.

## 14.2 INFORMATION

### (a) Notes on Dialogue 1

Christkindl Markt

The Christkindl Markt in Munich consists of rows of brightly lit stalls where you can buy sweets, Christmas tree decorations and small items to give as presents. The air is full of the smell of frying sausages and sweetmeats which are being prepared on the spot. Many people take refuge from the very cold air by drinking Glühwein, a sort of punch made of hot red wine containing spices.

5. Wohnen Sie?

Notice that in English we form many questions by using the words 'do' or 'does'. For example:

Do you live in Munich?
Does he live in Stuttgart?
Do they live in London?

In German the question form is
made by inverting the order of
the subject and the verb. For
example:

Er wohnt in München
Wohnt er in München?
Wohnen Sie in Stuttgart?
Wohnt sie in Hamburg?

8. Ich habe ...

Notice that in English we often
use the verb 'have got'. For
example, we say 'I've got a flat
in King Street' or 'How many
rooms have you got?' German
does not have the word 'got'.
Consequently, there is no
equivalent for this word in a
sentence such as Ich habe eine
Einzimmerwohnung.

12. sonst

The expression Und sonst? is a
very useful one because it has
the function of inviting
somebody to enlarge on what he
or she has been saying.

13. Sonst habe ich ...

Note that when sonst is brought
to the beginning of the sentence
in order to give it emphasis,
then the subject comes after the
verb.

**(b) Notes on Dialogue 2**
1. auch

Note the position of the word
auch which means 'too' or
'also'.

4. Neapel

The names of certain towns
have a special German
equivalent. The German

equivalent of the Italian word
'Napoli' is Neapel.

8. Du liebe Zeit

This is a very useful expression
which can be used in many
situations in order to express
mild astonishment. It can be
used equally by men and women
in any sort of society, without
giving offence.

9. Stellen Sie sich mal vor

This expression is a bit of a
tongue-twister and may need
some practice before you can
get your tongue round it
adequately. It is, however, a
very useful expression which can
be used on many occasions in
order to express surprise tinged
with mild disbelief.

12. Und ob!

Like the above two expressions,
this has a very wide currency
and can be used very frequently
in order to give emphasis to
something which has been said
just previously.

**(c) Word list**

| | |
|---|---|
| Prost! | Cheers! |
| der **Glüh**wein | hot punch |
| die **Ein**zimmerwohnung (-en) | one-room flat |
| warm | warm |
| **woh**nen | to live |
| das **Miets**haus (¨er) | house divided up into flats |
| groß | big |
| nur | only |
| das **Zim**mer (-) | room |
| schön | beautiful |
| klein | small |
| aber | but |
| ganz | quite |
| viel- | many |
| das Bild (-er) | picture |

| | |
|---|---|
| **sam**meln | to collect |
| inter**essant** | interesting |
| der **On**kel (-) | uncle |
| über**all** | everywhere |
| selbstver**ständ**lich | of course |
| das **Haus** (¨er) | house |
| das **Ein**zelhaus (¨er) | detached house |
| das **Ein**familienhaus (¨er) | one-family house |
| die **Woh**nung (-en) | flat |
| die **Sozial**wohnung (-en) | council flat |
| die **Eigentums**wohnung (-en) | owner-occupied flat |
| die **Kü**che (-n) | kitchen |
| das **Ba**dezimmer (-) | bathroom |
| das **Wohn**zimmer (-) | living room |
| das **Eß**zimmer (-) | dining room |
| das **Schlaf**zimmer (-) | bedroom |
| das **WC** | toilet |
| das **Gäs**tezimmer (-) | guest room |
| der **Bal**kon (-e) | balcony |
| der **Gar**ten (¨) | garden |
| die **Gara**ge (-n) | garage |
| das **Schwimm**bad (¨er) | swimming pool |
| der **Ten**nisplatz (¨e) | tennis court |
| die **Terra**sse (-n) | terrace |
| der **Baum** (¨e) | tree |
| die **Blu**me (-n) | flower |
| der **Strauch** (¨er) | bush |
| der **En**kel (-) | grandson |
| der **Flü**gel (-) | wing |
| der **Schlüs**sel (-) | key |
| der **Ku**chen (-) | cake |
| der **Rei**fen (-) | tyre |
| der **Kof**fer (-) | suitcase |
| der **Kell**ner (-) | waiter |
| die **Hand** (¨e) | hand |
| die **Wand** (¨e) | wall |
| die **Stadt** (¨e) | town |
| das **Boot** (-e) | boat |
| das **Ding** (-e) | thing |
| der **Arm** (-e) | arm |
| der **Ort** (-e) | place |
| der **Schuh** (-e) | shoe |

| der **Ap**fel (⸚) | apple |
| der **Ha**fen (⸚) | harbour |
| der **Vo**gel (⸚) | bird |
| die Saat (-en) | seed |
| die Uhr (-en) | clock |
| die Tür (-en) | door |
| die Zahl (-en) | number |
| der Mann (⸚er) | man |
| der Wald (⸚er) | wood |
| das Dorf (⸚er) | village |

| der Flur (-e) | entrance hall, vestibule |
| die **Die**le (-n) | entrance hall, vestibule |

## 14.3 STRUCTURAL EXPLANATIONS

### (a) Structures to learn

#### (i) How to ask where someone lives

| Wo wohnen Sie? | Where do you live? |
| Wo wohnt er? | Where does he live? |
| Wohnen Sie hier in München? | Do you live here in Munich? |

#### (ii) How to ask in what sort of a house somebody lives

Wohnen Sie in einem { Haus / Einfamilienhaus / Mietshaus } ?

Do you live in a { house / one-family house / house divided up into flats } ?

### Other types of accommodation

| ein Zweifamilienhaus | a two-family house |
| eine Wohnung | a flat |
| eine Sozialwohnung | a council flat |
| ein Einzelhaus | a detached house |
| ein Reihenhaus | a terraced house |
| eine Mietwohnung | a rented flat |
| eine Eigentumswohnung | an owner-occupied flat |

N.B. Approximately half the population in Germany lives in rented accommodation. In the cities there are large numbers of blocks of flats while in the country districts it's more likely that rented flats are in large houses where the owner also lives.

## (iii) How to describe where one lives

| Wieviele Zimmer haben Sie? | How many rooms have you got? |
|---|---|
| Ich habe | I've got a |
| eine Küche | kitchen |
| ein Badezimmer | bathroom |
| ein Wohnzimmer | living room |
| ein Eßzimmer | dining room |
| ein Schlafzimmer | bedroom |
| ein WC | toilet |
| ein Gästezimmer | guest room |
| eine Einzimmerwohnung | one-room flat |
| eine Zweizimmerwohnung | two-room flat |

## (iv) How to ask about other amenities

| Haben Sie | Have you got a |
|---|---|
| einen Balkon | balcony |
| einen Garten ? | garden ? |
| eine Garage | garage |
| ein Schwimmbad | a swimming pool |

| Ich habe | I've got |
|---|---|
| einen Garten | a garden |
| einen Balkon | a balcony |
| einen Tennisplatz | a tennis court |
| eine Garage | a garage |
| eine Terrasse | a terrace |
| viele Bäume | many trees |
| viele Blumen | many flowers |
| viele Sträucher | many bushes |

## (b) Grammar

(i) The verb HABEN takes a *direct object* (see Chapter 5). The direct object of a sentence is said in German to be in the *accusative case*. The accusative case is 'marked' or 'signalled' by the indefinite article ein, thus:

Ich habe ein*en* Garten (der Garten)

Ich habe eine Garage (die Garage)
Ich habe ein Einzelhaus (das Einzelhaus)

N.B. Only the masculine singular article carries this marker.

(ii) Plurals of nouns
In English, we usually indicate that there are *more than one* of a thing
by adding the letters 's' or 'es' to a word.

| boy | – | boys | window | – | windows |
|-----|---|------|--------|---|---------|
| girl | – | girls | door | – | doors |

The plural of German nouns may be formed in any one of a number
of different ways. There is no foolproof way of predicting how a
German noun will make its plural and therefore the best thing to do is
to learn the plural form of each noun as it occurs. Below are given
some of the most frequently occurring plural formations with a
number of nouns in common use in each category.

No change in the plural
indicated thus (-)

| der Onkel (-) | uncle |
|---------------|-------|
| der Enkel (-) | grandson |
| der Flügel (-) | wing |
| der Schlüssel (-) | key |
| der Kuchen (-) | cake |
| der Reifen (-) | tyre |
| der Koffer (-) | case |
| der Kellner (-) | waiter |

Some nouns make their plurals
by adding an e. This is shown
like this (e)

| das Boot (-e) | boat |
|---------------|------|
| das Ding (-e) | thing |
| der Arm (-e) | arm |
| der Ort (-e) | place |
| der Schuh (-e) | shoe |

Other plurals are made by
adding an Umlaut over the
vowel and an e. This is
shown thus (¨e)

| die Hand (¨e) | hand |
|---------------|------|
| die Wand (¨e) | wall |
| die Stadt (¨e) | town |

Some nouns make their plural
by just adding an Umlaut. This
is shown thus (¨)

| der Apfel (¨) | apple |
|---------------|-------|
| der Garten (¨) | garden |
| der Hafen (¨) | harbour |
| der Vogel (¨) | bird |

Many nouns make their
plural by adding en. This is
indicated thus (-en)

| die Saat (-en) | seed |
|----------------|------|
| die Uhr (-en) | clock |
| die Tür (-en) | door |
| die Zahl (-en) | number |

Some nouns make their plural
by adding an Umlaut and er. It
is indicated like this (¨er)

| der Mann (¨er) | man |
|----------------|-----|
| der Wald (¨er) | wood |
| das Dorf (¨er) | village |
| das Buch (¨er) | book |
| das Haus (¨er) | house |

If you don't know a plural, here is a rule-of-thumb which will be correct some of the time.

1. Masculine nouns ending in -el, -en and -er don't change in the plural.
2. Many feminine nouns make their plural by adding -(e)n.
3. Many neuter nouns make their plural by adding -er, and an Umlaut if feasible, i.e. on a, o, u.
4. Many masculine nouns make their plural by adding -e. Many of these add an Umlaut if possible.

## 14.4 EXERCISES

**Section A**

**Exercise 1**

Imagine that this house belongs to you. Here is a conversation you might have with an acquaintance:

*Acquaintance*:   Haben Sie ein Wohnzimmer?

*You*:   Ja, ich habe ein Wohnzimmer.

Answer the following questions in the same way:
1. Haben Sie ein Wohnzimmer?
2. Haben Sie ein Eßzimmer?
3. Haben Sie eine Küche?
4. Haben Sie ein Badezimmer?
5. Haben Sie ein Schlafzimmer?
6. Haben Sie eine Toilette?

**Exercise 2**

Imagine that this house belongs to you. Here is a conversation which you might have with a friend:

*Friend*:   Haben Sie ein Wohnzimmer?
*You*:   Ja, ich habe ein Wohnzimmer.
*Friend*:   Haben Sie eine Garage?
*You*:   Nein, eine Garage habe ich nicht.

Answer the following questions in the same way:
1. Haben Sie ein Wohnzimmer?
2. Haben Sie eine Garage?
3. Haben Sie ein Eßzimmer?
4. Haben Sie eine Terrasse?
5. Haben Sie eine Küche?
6. Haben Sie einen Balkon?
7. Haben Sie ein Badezimmer?
8. Haben Sie einen Garten?

**Exercise 3**

The temptation to keep up with the Joneses sometimes simply cannot be resisted. The case of Helmut Schwarz is a case in point. He thought that he had built the most splendid house in the village but when a retired dentist from the city came and built an even larger house just beside his, he found that he had to keep up with the Winklers. Here is the beginning of a conversation between the two of them. You continue by playing the part of Helmut.

Example:

*Winkler*: Ich habe einen Garten.
*Helmut*: Ich habe auch einen Garten.

*Winkler*: Ich habe ein Schwimmbad
Ich habe einen Balkon
Ich habe einen Tennisplatz
Ich habe eine Terrasse
Ich habe viele Bäume
Ich habe viele Sträucher

**Section B**

**Exercise 4**

Listen to the recorded dialogues again or read the script in the book. Then answer the following questions.
1. Wohnt Fritz in München?
2. Hat er eine Zweizimmerwohnung?
3. Hat er ein Badezimmer?
4. Hat er eine Küche?
5. Hat er viele Bilder?
6. Wo wohnt Antonios Onkel?
7. Hat er eine Sozialwohnung?
8. Wieviele Schlafzimmer hat er?
9. Wieviele Gästezimmer hat er?

10. Hat Antonio ein Einzelhaus?
11. Hat er ein Eßzimmer?
12. Hat er ein Badezimmer?
13. Hat er eine Küche?
14. Hat er einen Garten?

# CHAPTER 15

# HOBBIES AND INTERESTS

## 15.1 DIALOGUES 📼

**Dialogue 1**
Fritz has taken the plunge and invited Elke to come home to his
flat after work to have some coffee and cakes.

1  *Fritz*:  Kommen Sie bitte herein.
  *Elke*:  Danke.
  *Fritz*:  Das ist meine Einzimmerwohnung.
  *Elke*:  Sie ist sehr schön.
5  *Fritz*:  Sie ist leider etwas zu klein.
  *Elke*:  Sie haben viele Bilder.
     Aber sie sind alle von Kirchen.
  *Fritz*:  Ja, ich interessiere mich für Kirchen.
  *Elke*:  Ja, das sehe ich.
10  *Fritz*:  Wissen Sie . . .
     Ich fotografiere sehr gern.
     Ich fotografiere gern Kirchen.
  *Elke*:  (meaningfully)
     Ja, das sehe ich.
  *Fritz*:  Möchten Sie eine Tasse Kaffee?
15  *Elke*:  O ja, bitte schön.
  *Fritz*:  Schauen Sie . . .
     die Kirche hier ist schön, nicht wahr?
  *Elke*:  (without enthusiasm)
     Hmm.
  *Fritz*:  Sie ist romanisch.
20  *Elke*:  Tatsächlich?
  *Fritz*:  Ja. Ich interessiere mich sehr für romanische Kirchen.
     Ich fotografiere sie sehr gern.

*Ich interessiere mich für Kirchen*

Photograph: Bavaria-Verlag/Dr Wilfred Bahnmüller

*Elke*: (yawning)
   Ja, das sehe ich.
*Fritz*: O, entschuldigen Sie.
25   Ihr Kaffee.
   Nehmen Sie Zucker?
*Elke*: Nein, danke.

**Dialogue 2**
Antonio is talking to a fellow student at the Meisterschule für
Mode.
1 *Student*:  Du! Antonio!
  *Antonio*:  Was ist los?
  *Student*:  Gar nichts.
    Ich wollte dir nur etwas sagen.
5 *Antonio*:  Na und ... ?
  *Student*:  Du weißt ... .
    Ich interessiere mich für italienisch.
  *Antonio*:  Ja, das weiß ich.
  *Student*:  Und ich esse sehr gern italienisches Essen.
10 *Antonio*:  Ja, das weiß ich auch.
  *Student*:  Also ... .
    Gestern war ich in einem italienischen Restaurant.
  *Antonio*:  Wo denn?
  *Student*:  In der St Markus Straße.
15    Restaurant Giovanni heißt es.
  *Antonio*:  Das kenne ich nicht.
    Ist es gut?
  *Student*:  Na, ich esse sehr gern Pizza.
    Und die Pizza war wirklich gut.
20 *Antonio*:  Warst du allein?
  *Student*:  Nein, die Birgit war dabei.
    Sie ißt lieber Canneloni.
  *Antonio*:  Hm. Waren die Cannelloni auch gut?
  *Student*:  Nicht schlecht.
25 *Antonio*:  Da muß ich auch hin.
    Ich esse furchtbar gern Pizza.

## 15.2 INFORMATION

**(a) Notes on Dialogue 1**
1. Kommen Sie

Note that the English translation gives the typically English rather tentative form where the German tends to be more direct.

8. für

Notice that where in English we say 'I'm interested *in* something', German uses the word für.

10. Wissen Sie

This is a very useful expression for indicating that you want to say something. It has the effect of telling other people 'Stop talking for a minute and listen to what I'm going to say'.

**(b) Notes on Dialogue 2**

5. Na und ... ?

This is another very useful phrase but you should take care to use it only with people you are on fairly good terms with. It can be slightly challenging and provocative. It has a touch of 'So what?' about it.

11. Also

One of the most useful words in German because it has the function of allowing you to say something, while you are still making up your mind what you want to say.

21. die Birgit

The word die is not necessary but it is very colloquial to say die Birgit or der Peter. It tends to be rather more frequently used in the south of Germany than in the north. It will make you sound very competent to use it occasionally but don't feel obliged to use it every time you say somebody's name.

**(c) Word list**

| | |
|---|---|
| **kom**men | to come |
| **et**was | somewhat |
| die **Ein**zimmer**wohnu**ng (-en) | one-roomed flat |
| sehr | very |
| schön | beautiful |
| **lei**der | unfortunately |
| klein | small |
| das Bild (-er) | picture |

| | |
|---|---|
| alle | all |
| die **Kir**che (-en) | church |
| sich interes**sier**en für | to be interested in |
| **seh**en | to see |
| **wiss**en | to know |
| fotogra**fier**en | to photograph |
| die **Tas**se (-n) | cup |
| der **Kaff**ee (-) | coffee |
| tat**säch**lich | indeed |
| **neh**men | to take |
| der **Zuck**er (-) | sugar |
| nur | only |
| **sa**gen | to say |
| **ess**en | to eat |
| das **Ess**en (-) | food |
| **ges**tern | yesterday |
| **heiß**en | to be called |
| **kenn**en | to know (a person or a place) |
| **wirk**lich | really |
| all**ein** | alone |
| dab**ei** | there |
| schlecht | bad |
| **furch**tbar | terribly |
| der **Fuß**ball (¨e) | football |
| die **Leich**tathletik (-) | athletics |
| das Land (¨er) | country |
| die **Brief**marke (-n) | stamp |
| die **Münz**e (-n) | coin |
| **tan**zen | to dance |
| **wan**dern | to go walking |
| **mal**en | to paint |
| **les**en | to read |
| **bast**eln | to make things as a hobby |
| **sing**en | to sing |
| **ko**chen | to cook |
| **spiel**en | to play |
| **fah**ren | to go |

**(d) Some phrases**

| | |
|---|---|
| **Kom**men Sie **bit**te her**ein** | Please come in |
| Das **sehe** ich | I can see that |
| Was ist los? | What's the matter? |
| Gar nichts | Nothing at all |
| Das weiß ich | I know |

## 15.3 STRUCTURAL EXPLANATIONS

### (a) Structures to learn

#### (i) How to ask about somebody's interests

Interessieren Sie sich für { Musik · Bilder · Bücher } ?

Musik – music
Bilder – pictures
Bücher – books

#### (ii) How to say what you are interested in

Ich interessiere mich für
Fotografie
Fußball
Leichtathletik
andere Länder

Fotografie – photography
Fußball – football
Leichtathletik – athletics
andere Länder – other countries

#### (iii) How to say that you collect things

Ich sammle { Briefmarken · Münzen · Kupferstiche · alte Bücher }

Briefmarken – stamps
Münzen – coins
Kupferstiche – etchings
alte Bücher – old books

#### (iv) How to say what you enjoy doing

Ich { tanze · wandere · male · lese · bastele · singe · koche } gern

tanzen – to dance
wandern – to go hiking or walking
malen – to paint
lesen – to read
basteln – to make things as a hobby
singen – to sing
kochen – to cook

#### (v)

Ich { spiele gern { Karten · Bridge · Klarinette · Klavier } · fahre gern { Ski · mit dem Rad } · koche gern { Spaghetti · Pizza } }

Karten spielen – to play cards
Klavier spielen – to play the piano
Ski fahren – to go skiing
mit dem Rad fahren – to go cycling

## (vi) Intensifiers

| | |
|---|---|
| gern | nicht gern |
| sehr gern | gar nicht gern |
| wirklich sehr gern | überhaupt nicht gern |
| außerordentlich gern | |
| furchtbar gern | |

These expressions allow you to convey your liking with increasing enthusiasm.

These expressions allow you to express your dislike with increasing strength.

Ich koche
- gern — I like cooking
- sehr gern — I like cooking very much
- wirklich sehr gern — I really like cooking a lot
- außerordentlich gern — I like cooking tremendously
- furchtbar gern — I adore cooking

Ich koche
- nicht gern — I don't like cooking
- gar nicht gern — I don't like cooking at all
- überhaupt nicht gern — I can't stand cooking

## (b) Grammar

(i) In German, you use the word **gern** in order to express the idea of *liking to do something*. Observe the position of the word gern in the sentence, when there is a simple verb.

| (1) | (2) | (3) | |
|-----|-----|------|---|
| Ich | lese | gern | I like reading |
| | reite | | I like riding |
| | male | | I like painting |

↑
Gern comes
after the verb

(ii) Observe the following sentences, and see where the word **gern** occurs.

| (1) | (2) | (3) | (4) | |
|-----|------|------|-----------|---|
| Ich | höre | gern | Musik | I like listening to music |
| | gehe | | schwimmen | I like going swimming |
| | fahre | | Auto | I like driving a car |

↑
Here you see
that the word
gern 'belongs
to' the verb

(iii) If you compare two activities, both of which you enjoy doing, it is possible that you prefer one to the other. The idea of preference is expressed in German as follows:

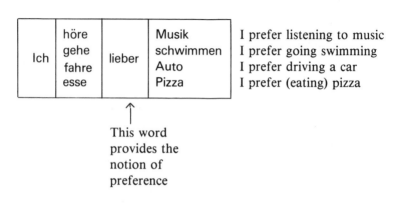

| Ich | höre<br>gehe<br>fahre<br>esse | lieber | Musik<br>schwimmen<br>Auto<br>Pizza | I prefer listening to music<br>I prefer going swimming<br>I prefer driving a car<br>I prefer (eating) pizza |

↑
This word
provides the
notion of
preference

(iv) If it is things, rather than activities, that you wish to compare, then you will need to know the *comparative form of adjectives*. Then you will be able to say that things are *bigger* and *better*.

Let us look first at some simple adjectives, and see how they make their comparative form.

| schön | — | schöner (more beautiful) |
| tief | — | tiefer (deeper) |
| leicht | — | leichter (easier) |
| angenehm | — | angenehmer (more pleasant) |

Note how there is only one way of expressing this comparison in German although we have two ways in English.

Let us put these comparative adjectives into sentences:

| Elke ist schöner als Petra | Elke is more beautiful than Petra |
| Der Atlantik ist tiefer als die Nordsee | The Atlantic is deeper than the North Sea |
| Deutsch ist leichter als französisch | German is easier than French |
| Schlafen ist angenehmer als Arbeit | Sleeping is more pleasant than work |

We can summarise the rule about making the comparative form of the adjective thus:

Add -er

(v) Perhaps you will want to say that something is *biggest* or *best*. Then you will need to know the *superlative form of adjectives.* Here is how the same adjectives make their superlative form

| schön | — | der, die, das schönste |
|---|---|---|
| tief | — | der, die, das tiefste |
| leicht | — | der, die, das leichteste |
| angenehm | — | der, die, das angenehmste |

Let us put these superlative adjectives into sentences.

| Elke ist die schönste Frau | Elke is the most beautiful woman |
|---|---|
| Der Stille Ozean ist das tiefste Meer | The Pacific is the deepest sea |
| Deutsch ist die leichteste Sprache | German is the easiest language |
| Schlafen ist die angenehmste Tätigkeit | Sleeping is the most pleasant activity |

We can summarise the rule about making the superlative form of the adjective thus:

Add -(e)st

(vi) Unfortunately, there are a number of irregular ways of forming comparative and superlative adjectives. You will find the rules set out in the appendix.

## 15.4 EXERCISES

### Section A

### Exercise 1
Here are five questions about what you like. Express your liking for each one of them with an increasing degree of enthusiasm.

1. Tanzen Sie gern?
2. Wandern Sie gern?
3. Malen Sie gern?
4. Lesen Sie gern?
5. Singen Sie gern?

**Exercise 2**

Here are three questions about your likes and dislikes. Answer each of them with an increasing degree of distaste.

1. Kochen Sie gern?
2. Basteln Sie gern?
3. Tanzen Sie gern?

**Exercise 3**

Imagine that you are one of those people who only likes doing those things which can be done comfortably at home, sitting down in the warmth. Answer the following questions appropriately.

1. Tanzen Sie gern?
2. Wandern Sie gern?
3. Malen Sie gern?
4. Spielen Sie gern Karten?
5. Fahren Sie gern Ski?
6. Lesen Sie gern?
7. Singen Sie gern?
8. Reiten Sie gern?

**Section B**

**Exercise 4**

There are two footballers playing in Germany at the moment. One is the veteran Beckenbauer and the other is the younger man Rumenigge. Here are some statements about Beckenbauer. See if you can trump them by making comparative statements about Rumenigge.

1. Beckenbauer ist groß.
2. Er ist schnell.
3. Er ist gesund.
4. Er ist stark.
5. Er ist jung.
6. Er ist klug.
7. Er spielt hart.
8. Er spielt gut.

(*See Grammatical Summary, Section D.*)

# CHAPTER 16

# 'WANT' AND 'MUST'

## 16.1 DIALOGUES

**Dialogue 1**

Elke is passionately fond of opera. She has succeeded in obtaining tickets to go to the Richard Wagner festival in Bayreuth.

1   *Elke*:   Fritz! Wissen Sie was?

    *Fritz*:   Nein.

    *Elke*:   Herr Zilling hat Karten für Parsifal, und er kann nicht gehen.

5   *Fritz*:   Das ist Pech.

    *Elke*:   Für ihn, aber nicht für uns.

    *Fritz*:   Wieso?

    *Elke*:   Wollen wir die Karten nehmen?

    *Fritz*:   Was kosten sie?

10  *Elke*:   Die Karte sechzig Mark.

    *Fritz*:   Das ist aber teuer.

    *Elke*:   Es ist doch Bayreuth, wissen Sie?

    *Fritz*:   Ja.

    Muß ich meinen Smoking anziehen?

15  *Elke*:   Das ist ja normal.

    Ich will mein neues Kleid anziehen.

    *Fritz*:   Schön!

    *Elke*:   Ich will auch meinen Nerzmantel tragen.

    *Fritz*:   Ha!

20  *Elke*:   Und natürlich meine Perlenkette.

    *Fritz*:   Wann müssen wir uns entscheiden?

    *Elke*:   O, sofort.

    Wir wollen doch gehen, oder?

    *Fritz*:   (hastily) O ja, selbstverständlich.

25     Wann müssen wir die Karten abholen?

*Bayreuth*

*Photograph: Bavaria-Verlag/Siegfried Lauterwasser-Bavaria*

## Dialogue 2

Frau Meyer has gone to see her doctor because she has been feeling a bit giddy recently.

1 *Doktor Storm*:   Nun, Frau Meyer, was fehlt Ihnen denn?
*Frau Meyer*:   Es ist mein Kopf, Herr Doktor.
Mir ist immer wieder schwindlig.

*Doktor Storm*:  Wie alt sind Sie, Frau Meyer?
5 *Frau Meyer*:  Ich bin fünfundsiebzig Jahre alt.
*Doktor Storm*:  Und wo wohnen Sie?
*Frau Meyer*:  In der Nietzschestraße.
*Doktor Storm*:  Wo ist Ihre Wohnung?
Im Parterre?
10 *Frau Meyer*:  Nein, Herr Doktor.
Im dritten Stock.
*Doktor Storm*:  Und Sie gehen jeden Tag einkaufen?
*Frau Meyer*:  Ja, und ich hole die kleine Sandra von der
Schule.
15 *Doktor Storm*:  Ja, ja. nun, Frau Meyer, Sie müssen etwas
weniger herumlaufen.
Wann stehen Sie morgens auf?
*Frau Meyer*:  Um sechs Uhr.
*Doktor Storm*:  Sie müssen etwas länger im Bett bleiben, und
20 Sie müssen sich jeden Nachmittag eine Stunde hinlegen.
*Frau Meyer*:  Muß ich daheim bleiben, Herr Doktor?
*Doktor Storm*:  Nein, Sie brauchen nicht daheim bleiben, aber
Sie müssen diese Tabletten nehmen.
*Frau Meyer*:  Muß ich sie abends nehmen?
25 Ich werde nicht einschlafen.
*Doktor Storm*:  Nein, Sie brauchen sie nicht abends nehmen.
*Frau Meyer*:  Gott sei Dank!


## 16.2 INFORMATION

### (a) Notes on Dialogue 1

| | |
|---|---|
| Bayreuth | Bayreuth is a town in the north of Bavaria where Richard Wagner established a theatre for the performance of his operas. Each summer there is a festival of his operas there. |
| 3. Parsifal | Parsifal is the name of one of Richard Wagner's operas. |
| 8. Wollen wir | Although the verb wollen means literally 'to want to', when it is used in this way wollen wir . . . ? it has the function of making a suggestion. It is |

consequently best translated in this case as 'Shall we ... ?'

10. Die Karte

In order to show the cost of each individual item, German places the name of the item first thus: Die Karte sechzig Mark – Each ticket sixty marks; das Glas eine Mark zwanzig – DM 1.20 per glass.

14. Smoking

Smoking is the term for a dinner jacket and matching trousers. It is here translated as evening dress.

23. doch

The word doch in this sentence is rendered in the English by 'do', which changes the straightforward statement into a request for confirmation: 'We *do* want to go, (don't we?)'.

23. oder?

The word oder? has the same function as nicht wahr?. It can be rendered in English as: 'don't we?' 'haven't I?' 'shan't we?' etc.

**(b) Notes on Dialogue 2**

2. Herr Doktor

When people speak to a doctor and refer to him by his title, the word Herr is used as well as the title.

3. immer wieder

This phrase indicates that something happens over and over again and can therefore be translated as 'always' or 'again and again'.

11. im

Note that German uses the word in where English uses the word 'on'. Im dritten Stock – 'on the third floor'.

17. morgens           This is a general term and has the force of 'every morning', or 'regularly every morning'.

## (c) Word list

| | |
|---|---|
| wissen | to know |
| die Karte (-n) | ticket |
| gehen | to go |
| wieso? | how? or why? |
| nehmen | to take |
| kosten | to cost |
| teuer | expensive |
| anziehen | to put on |
| das Kleid (-er) | dress |
| normal | usual |
| der Nerzmantel (¨) | mink coat |
| neu | new |
| tragen | to wear |
| natürlich | naturally |
| die Perlenkette (-n) | pearl necklace |
| wann? | when? |
| sich entscheiden | to decide |
| sofort | at once |
| selbstverständlich | of course |
| abholen | to fetch; pick up |
| der Kopf (¨e) | head |
| schwindlig | giddy |
| alt | old |
| das Jahr (-e) | year |
| die Wohnung (-en) | flat |
| der Stock (Stockwerke) | floor (of a building) |
| jed- | every |
| der Tag (-e) | day |
| einkaufen | to go shopping |
| holen | to fetch |
| die Schule (-n) | school |
| herumlaufen | to run about |
| aufstehen | to get up |
| lang | long, a long time |
| das Bett (-en) | bed |
| bleiben | to remain, stay |
| der Nachmittag (-e) | afternoon |
| die Stunde (-n) | hour |

| sich **hin**legen | to lie down |
| da**heim** | at home |
| die **Tab**lette (-n) | tablet; pill |
| a**bends** | in the evening |
| **ein**schlafen | to go to sleep |
| **ko**chen | to cook |
| **rau**chen | to smoke |
| **le**sen | to read |
| die **Zahn**bürste (-n) | toothbrush |
| die **Bad**ehose | swimming trunks |
| der **Reisepaß** (⁻e) | passport |
| die **Ein**trittskarte (-n) | (entry) ticket |
| das Geld | money |
| die **Land**karte (-n) | map |
| der **Ten**nisschläger (-) | tennis racket |
| der **Stie**fel (-) | boot |
| der **Re**genschirm (-e) | umbrella |

**(d)) Some phrases**

| Das ist Pech | That's bad luck |
| Was fehlt **Ih**nen? | What's the matter (with you)? |
| Im Par**terre** | On the groundfloor |
| Gott sei Dank! | Thank heavens! |

## 16.3 STRUCTURAL EXPLANATIONS

**(a) Structures to learn**

**(i) How to say what you want to do**

Ich will / Wir wollen { kochen / rauchen / gehen / lesen }

I want to / We want to { cook / smoke / go / read }

In order to express what you want to do, you use part of the verb WOLLEN, and the infinitive of some other verb.

(ii) Look at some of the sentences from the dialogues:

Ich will { mein neues Kleid / meinen Nerzmantel } anziehen

Wir wollen die Karten nehmen

I want to { put on my new dress / put on my mink coat }

We want to take the tickets

If you look at these sentences carefully, you will see that the infinitive is placed at the end of the sentence.

(iii) **How to express what you have to do**

$$
\left. \begin{array}{l} \text{Ich muß} \\ \text{Wir müssen} \end{array} \right\} \left\{ \begin{array}{l} \text{kochen} \\ \text{rauchen} \\ \text{gehen} \\ \text{lesen} \end{array} \right. \qquad \left. \begin{array}{l} \text{I must} \\ \text{We must} \end{array} \right\} \left\{ \begin{array}{l} \text{cook} \\ \text{smoke} \\ \text{go} \\ \text{read} \end{array} \right.
$$

(iv) When there are other elements in the sentence besides the modal verb, müssen or wollen, and an infinitive, then the infinitive is placed at the end of the sentence. Here are some sentences from the dialogue:

$$
\text{Sie müssen} \left\{ \begin{array}{l} \text{etwas weniger} \\ \text{etwas länger im Bett} \\ \text{sich} \\ \text{diese Tabletten} \end{array} \right\} \left\{ \begin{array}{l} \text{herumlaufen} \\ \text{bleiben} \\ \text{hinlegen} \\ \text{nehmen} \end{array} \right.
$$

(v) Exactly the same applies if you want to ask a question using a modal verb and an infinitive. Have a look at these sentences taken from the dialogue:

$$
\text{Wann müssen wir} \left\{ \begin{array}{l} \text{uns} \\ \text{die Karten} \end{array} \right\} \left\{ \begin{array}{l} \text{entscheiden?} \\ \text{abholen?} \end{array} \right.
$$

Or have a look at these sentences:

$$
\text{Muß ich} \left\{ \begin{array}{l} \text{sie abends} \\ \text{daheim} \\ \text{meinen Smoking} \end{array} \right\} \left\{ \begin{array}{l} \text{nehmen?} \\ \text{bleiben?} \\ \text{anziehen?} \end{array} \right.
$$

(vi) **How to say that you don't have to do something**
In these sentences, taken from the dialogue, the verb which expresses absence of obligation is the verb BRAUCHEN used in the negative.

$$
\text{Sie brauchen} \left\{ \begin{array}{l} \text{nicht daheim} \\ \text{sie nicht abends} \end{array} \right\} \left\{ \begin{array}{l} \text{bleiben} \\ \text{nehmen} \end{array} \right.
$$

You don't need to stay at home
You don't need to take them in the evening

**(b) Grammar**
(i) The three verbs you have been using in this chapter are:

WOLLEN – to want to
MÜSSEN – to 'must'/to have to
BRAUCHEN NICHT – to 'not have to'/not need to

In order to see how these verbs can be used in sentences, see Chapter 12.

(ii) Further notes on the modal verbs WOLLEN, MÜSSEN, BRAUCHEN
1. The verb wollen indicates a wish, willingness or intention.

| | |
|---|---|
| Wollen Sie Brot? | Do you want some bread? |
| Wollen Sie mit (kommen)? | Do you want to come (with me)? |
| Ich will ihn nicht stören | I don't want to disturb him |
| Ich will das nicht tun | I don't want to do it |

2. The verb müssen denotes some kind of compulsion.

| | |
|---|---|
| Ich muß nach Hause (gehen) | I must go home |
| Ich muß lachen | I must laugh, I can't help laughing |
| Ich muß einen Brief schreiben | I must/have to write a letter |

3. The verb brauchen is not normally considered to be amongst the set of modal verbs. Absence of obligation can be expressed by using the verb müssen in the negative form. However, it is probably easier to learn how to express this function of language by using a separate verb. That is why the verb brauchen has been introduced here. Here are some further examples of sentences showing its use.

| | |
|---|---|
| Sie brauchen keinen Brief schreiben | You don't have to write a letter |
| Sie brauchen jetzt nicht gehen | You don't have to go now |
| Sie brauchen nicht zu mir kommen | You don't have to come to me |

## 16.4 EXERCISES

### Section A

### Exercise 1
Which of the things in the list would you have to take with you (mitnehmen) under the following circumstances? For instance, if it was raining, you would need to take your raincoat and you would say Ich muß meinen Regenmantel mitnehmen.

1. What would you need to take if you were going shopping?
   die Zahnbürste
2. Suppose you wanted to play football. die Badehose
3. You want to play tennis. der Reisepaß
4. How about a drive in the country? die Eintrittskarten
5. You're just off to the theatre. das Geld
6. You want to go swimming. die Landkarte
7. You're going abroad for your holiday. der Tennisschläger
8. A weekend away? der Stiefel
9. It's raining der Regenschirm

**Exercise 2**
Below you will find a page from Fritz's diary. What does he have to
do on each day? The first one is done for you.
*Question*: Was muß Fritz am Sonntag machen?
*Answer*: Er muß Elke besuchen.

| So | Elke besuchen | Was muß Fritz am Sonntag machen? |
|----|---------------|----------------------------------|
| Mo | die Karten abholen | Was muß Fritz am Montag machen? |
| Di | nach Nürnberg fahren | Was muß Fritz am Dienstag machen? |
| Mi | eine Kette für Elke kaufen | Was muß Fritz am Mittwoch machen? |
| Do | einen Tennisschläger kaufen | Was muß Fritz am Donnerstag machen? |
| Fr | nach Stuttgart fahren | Was muß Fritz am Freitag machen? |
| Sa | im Bett bleiben (müde!) | Was muß Fritz am Samstag machen? |

**Exercise 3**
You have arranged to go on holiday with a friend. This friend is
notoriously careless at getting things ready and so you have collected
everything that he might need and put it in your car. When he rings
up, therefore, to find out if he should bring certain things with him,
you are able to say that you have already got everything organised.
The first answer is done for you to show you how to do it.
*Question*: Muß ich meinen Tennisschläger mitnehmen?
*Answer*: Nein, Sie brauchen Ihren Tennisschläger nicht mitnehmen.

Here are the questions.
1. Muß ich meine Stiefel mitnehmen?
2. Muß ich meine Landkarte mitnehmen?
3. Muß ich meine Badehose mitnehmen?
4. Muß ich meine Zahnbürste mitnehmen?
5. Muß ich meine Schuhe mitnehmen?
6. Muß ich meinen Smoking mitnehmen?
7. Muß ich meinen Mantel mitnehmen?
8. Muß ich meine Tabletten mitnehmen?
9. Muß ich mein Buch mitnehmen?
10. Muß ich meinen Tennisschläger mitnehmen?

# CHAPTER 17

# SUGGESTIONS AND PROPOSALS

## 17.1 DIALOGUES 🔲

**Dialogue 1**

The irrepressible Antonio Santos has spotted a rather nice-looking girl sitting outside a Gasthaus on the Leopoldstraße. Sensing the possibility of an upturn in his love-life, he sits down at the same table.

1 *Antonio*: Ist dieser Platz frei?
  *Mädchen*: Ja.
  *Antonio*: Schönes Wetter, nicht wahr?
  *Mädchen*: Ja. Sehr schön.
5 *Antonio*: Ich heiße Antonio.
  *Mädchen*: Hmm.
  *Antonio*: Antonio Santos.
  . . .
  *Antonio*: Wie heißen Sie?
  Wenn ich fragen darf?
10 *Mädchen*: Claudia.
  *Antonio*: Claudia. Ein schöner Name.
  *Mädchen*: Danke.

  . . .
  *Antonio*: Sagen Sie, Claudia?
  Können Sie Tennis spielen?
15 *Mädchen*: Ja.
  *Antonio*: Schön! Wollen wir Tennis spielen?
  *Mädchen*: Wann?
  *Antonio*: Morgen, vielleicht?
  *Mädchen*: Ja, gern.
20 *Antonio*: Spielen Sie oft?
  *Mädchen*: Ziemlich oft.

*Schönes Wetter, nicht wahr?*

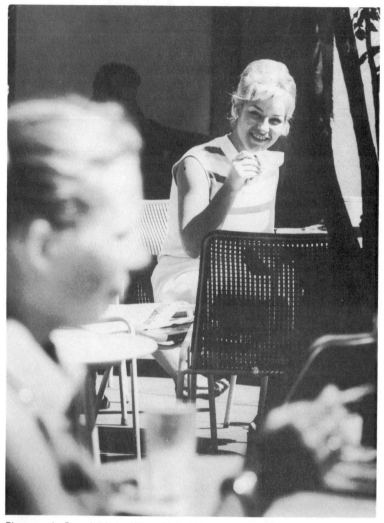

Photograph: Bavaria-Verlag/Klaus Meier-Ude

     Vier oder fünf mal in der Woche.
    *Antonio*:  Wo spielen Sie?
    *Mädchen*:  Im Carlton Club.
25  *Antonio*:  Ach?
     Spielen Sie gut?
    *Mädchen*:  Ach, ganz gut.
     Und Sie?
    *Antonio*:  Nicht sehr gut.
     (To himself) Das gibt's doch nicht!!

**Dialogue 2**

Fritz has decided that his relationship with Elke ought to take a more positive turn, so he goes to visit her at her flat. He is encouraged when she uses the familiar du form.

1 *Fritz*: Hallo, Elke!
  *Elke*: Du, Fritz!
    Komm doch herein!
  *Fritz*: Danke.
5   Wie geht's dir?
  *Elke*: Prima!
  *Fritz*: Du, Elke . . . .
    Wollen wir am Wochenende wegfahren?
  *Elke*: O, ja! Wohin?
10 *Fritz*: Ich kenne eine sehr hübsche Kirche.
    In der Nähe von Rosenheim.
  *Elke*: O nein, Fritz!
    Schon wieder eine Kirche!!!
  *Fritz*: Was ist denn los?
15 *Elke*: Jedes Mal eine Kirche!
  *Fritz*: Kirchen interessieren mich.
    Das weißt du.
  *Elke*: Aber du hast jede Woche eine andere Kirche.
    Das ist mir zu viel.

*Auf dem Idiotenhügel*

*Photograph: J. Allan Cash Ltd*

20 *Fritz*:  Es tut mir leid.
   *Elke*:  Wollen wir nach Kufstein fahren?
   Dort können wir Ski fahren.
   *Fritz*:  Aber ich kann nicht Ski fahren.
   *Elke*:  Aber ich kann sehr gut Ski fahren.
25 *Fritz*:  Na gut.
   Fahren wir nach Kufstein.
   *Elke*:  Ja, du kannst es lernen.
   (to herself) (Auf dem Idiotenhügel!)

## 17.2 INFORMATION

### (a) Notes on Dialogue 1

9. Wenn

Despite appearances to the contrary, this word very often means 'if'. Here it means 'if I may ask', or as we would say 'if you don't mind my asking'. Students wishing to inform themselves about the structure of 'subordinate' clauses introduced by wenn should consult the grammar books listed in the bibliography.

13. Sagen Sie

This phrase is excellent for indicating that you want to say something, or for breaking into a conversation, or simply for establishing that it is now your turn to speak. In English we would say, 'Tell me . . . ' or 'I say . . . '.

14. spielen

Note that this word comes at the end of the sentence. See Section 16.2.

17. Wann

Note this word carefully because it is very similar to the word in line 9. This word, however, is always used in a question: 'When?'

| 19. | gern | This short word is a very economic way of expressing the idea 'I'd like to'. |
|---|---|---|
| 26. | gut | This word can serve both as an adjective or an adverb. We would here have to translate it as 'well'. |

**(b) Notes on Dialogue 2**

| 7. | Du | This is a fairly emphatic, but very typical way of addressing somebody, in the familiar form. |
|---|---|---|
| 8. | wegfahren | Note the position of this word in the sentence. See Section 16.2. |
| 9. | Wohin | Germans are very punctilious about indicating the distinction between locality and direction. In English we would simply say 'Where?' In German, however, it is essential to indicate the meaning which we still have in our archaic form 'Whither?' It is probably best to think of the meaning of the word wohin? as 'where to?' |
| 11. | In der Nähe von | This rather long phrase is the German for 'near'. |
| 16. | interessieren mich | Note how German says: (things, e.g. churches) interest me. |
| 22. | Dort | This word is placed at the beginning of the sentence for emphasis. |
| 28. | Idiotenhügel | Although we would say 'nursery slope' in English, the term in German for the slopes where many people can learn to ski is very condescending. It is best translated as 'idiots' slope'. |

**(c) Word list**

| | |
|---|---|
| dies- | this |
| der Platz (¨e) | place; seat |
| frei | free; vacant |
| schön | nice, beautiful |
| das Wetter | weather |
| heißen | to be called |
| der Name (-n) | name |
| sagen | to say |
| können | to be able |
| spielen | to play |
| wollen | to wish; want to |
| wann? | when? |
| morgen | tomorrow |
| vielleicht | perhaps |
| oft | often |
| ziemlich | fairly |
| die Woche (-n) | week |
| gut | well (as an adverb) |
| ganz | quite |
| Prima! | splendid! |
| das Wochenende (-n) | weekend |
| wegfahren | to go away |
| wohin? | where to? |
| kennen | to know (a person or a place) |
| hübsch | pretty |
| die Kirche (-n) | church |
| interessieren | to interest |
| wissen | to know (a fact) |
| ander- | other |
| Ski fahren | to go ski-ing |
| lernen | to learn |
| der Fußball (¨e) | football |
| die Karte (-n) | card(s) |
| schwimmen | to swim |
| tanzen | to dance |
| essen | to eat |
| der Spaziergang (¨e) | walk |
| machen | to make, to do |
| reiten | to ride |
| malen | to paint |
| singen | to sing |
| ausgezeichnet | very well indeed |

**(d) Some phrases**

| | |
|---|---|
| Nicht wahr? | Isn't it, etc. |
| Wie **heiß**en Sie? | What is your name? |
| Komm doch her**ein** | Come in, won't you? (familiar form) |
| Wie geht's dir? | How are you? (familiar form) |
| Was ist denn los? | What's the matter? |
| Schon **wie**der! | Again! |
| **Je**des Mal | Every time |
| Das ist mir zu viel | That's too much (for me) |
| Es tut mir leid | I'm sorry |
| Sehr gut | Very well |
| **Ziem**lich gut | Fairly well |
| Nicht sehr gut | Not very well |
| Nur **et**was | Only a little bit |
| Im **groß**en und **ganz**en | On the whole |

## 17.3 STRUCTURAL EXPLANATIONS

### (a) Structures to learn

#### (i) How to make a suggestion or proposal

## (ii) How to ask what you can do

## (iii) How to say what you can do

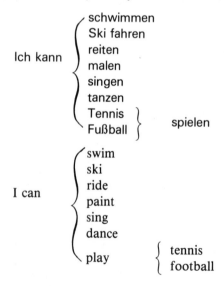

## (iv) How to ask how well someone can do something

Schwimmen Sie gut?
Reiten Sie gut?

Singen Sie gut?
Tanzen Sie gut?
BUT:
Fahren Sie gut Ski?
Spielen Sie gut Tennis?
Spielen Sie gut Fußball?

(v) **Here are some replies you can give**

| ausgezeichnet | – | very well indeed |
| sehr gut | – | very well |
| ziemlich gut | – | fairly well |
| nicht sehr gut | – | not very well |
| nur etwas | – | only a little bit |

**(b) Grammar**

(i) Here are the most frequently used parts of the two verbs we have been looking at in this chapter.

The verb WOLLEN – to want to

| ich will | I want to |
| er will | he wants to |
| sie will | she wants to |
| wir wollen | we want to |
| Sie wollen | you want to |

The verb KÖNNEN – to be able to

| ich kann | I can |
| er kann | he can |
| sie kann | she can |
| wir können | we can |
| Sie können | you can |

Both these verbs are *irregular* in that their stems change, and their endings do not conform to the standard pattern. However, they are amongst the most important verbs in the whole language and there is no alternative to learning them.

(ii) The most frequent sentence patterns in which these verbs operate is as follows:

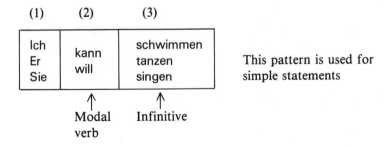

(1)  (2)  (3)

| Ich Er Sie | kann will | schwimmen tanzen singen |

↑ Modal verb   ↑ Infinitive

This pattern is used for simple statements

192

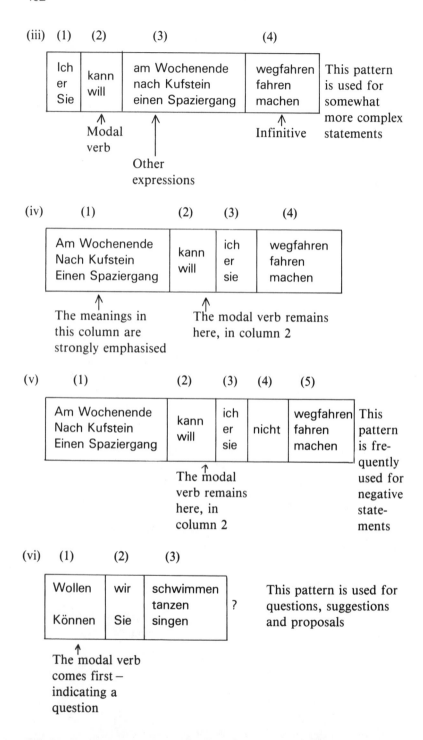

(iii)

| (1) | (2) | (3) | (4) |
|---|---|---|---|
| Ich<br>er<br>Sie | kann<br>will | am Wochenende<br>nach Kufstein<br>einen Spaziergang | wegfahren<br>fahren<br>machen |

↑ Modal verb  ↑ Other expressions  ↑ Infinitive

This pattern is used for somewhat more complex statements

(iv)

| (1) | (2) | (3) | (4) |
|---|---|---|---|
| Am Wochenende<br>Nach Kufstein<br>Einen Spaziergang | kann<br>will | ich<br>er<br>sie | wegfahren<br>fahren<br>machen |

↑ The meanings in this column are strongly emphasised

↑ The modal verb remains here, in column 2

(v)

| (1) | (2) | (3) | (4) | (5) |
|---|---|---|---|---|
| Am Wochenende<br>Nach Kufstein<br>Einen Spaziergang | kann<br>will | ich<br>er<br>sie | nicht | wegfahren<br>fahren<br>machen |

↑ The modal verb remains here, in column 2

This pattern is frequently used for negative statements

(vi)

| (1) | (2) | (3) |
|---|---|---|
| Wollen | wir | schwimmen<br>tanzen |
| Können | Sie | singen |

?

↑ The modal verb comes first — indicating a question

This pattern is used for questions, suggestions and proposals

(vii) You will find the verbs wollen and können in the appendix.

(viii) We now come to one of the trickiest problems in German; it concerns the two concepts of *position* and *direction*.

POSITION:         this concept enables you to *express where you are*, or *where something is*.

MOVEMENT TOWARDS:   this concept enables you to express movement towards a thing, a person, or a place.

Consider the following sentences:

1. a) Ich bin in dem (im) Garten    I am *in* the garden
   b) Ich gehe in den Garten        I go *into* the garden
2. a) Ich bin in dem (im) Haus     I am *in* the house
   b) Ich gehe in das (ins) Haus    I go *into* the house
3. a) Ich bin in dem (im) Park     I am *in* the park
   b) Ich gehe in den Park         I go *into* the park
4. a) Ich bin in der Kirche         I am *in* the church
   b) Ich gehe in die Kirche        I go *into* the church

Notice that in all the above pairs of sentences, the a) sentence expresses POSITION and has its definite article in the *dative case*. All the b) sentences express MOVEMENT TOWARDS something, and have their definite article in the *accusative case*.

This concept can be illustrated visually:

Jochen läuft in den Wald    Jochen runs into (i.e. towards) the wood

Jochen läuft in dem (im) Wald    Jochen is running in (i.e. within/inside) the wood

The above pictures show how important this concept is in German. The only difference between the two sentences is the definite article, once in the *accusative* indicating MOVEMENT TOWARDS the wood, and once in the *dative* indicating Jochen's POSITION inside the wood. Consequently, the only way German speakers have of understanding correctly what is meant is by correct use of the two cases.

Certain verbs, such as wohnen (to live), sein (to be) and sitzen (to be sitting) always indicate POSITION.

Other verbs, such as fahren (to go, to drive), and gehen (to go, to walk) always indicate MOVEMENT.

When you use one of these verbs, therefore, it is especially important to use the correct case.

The following three prepositions are the most frequently used for indicating either MOVEMENT TOWARDS or POSITION:

> an  — to, by
> auf — on, onto
> in  — in, into

The rule can be summarised thus:

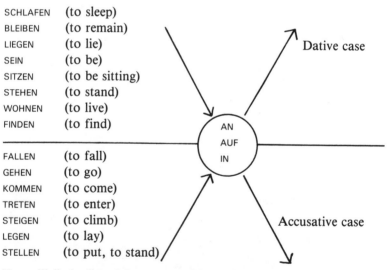

| | |
|---|---|
| SCHLAFEN | (to sleep) |
| BLEIBEN | (to remain) |
| LIEGEN | (to lie) |
| SEIN | (to be) |
| SITZEN | (to be sitting) |
| STEHEN | (to stand) |
| WOHNEN | (to live) |
| FINDEN | (to find) |

Dative case

AN
AUF
IN

| | |
|---|---|
| FALLEN | (to fall) |
| GEHEN | (to go) |
| KOMMEN | (to come) |
| TRETEN | (to enter) |
| STEIGEN | (to climb) |
| LEGEN | (to lay) |
| STELLEN | (to put, to stand) |

Accusative case

You will find a list of those prepositions which can be used with either the *accusative* or the *dative* case in the appendix.

Do not forget, however, that there are also prepositions which can *only* be used with the *accusative*, just as there are those which can *only* be used with the *dative*. You will find these in the appendix. They were dealt with in Chapters 5 and 9.

## 17.4 EXERCISES

**Section A**

**Exercise 1**

This is Karlheinz. He enjoys playing football and cards. He likes ski-ing and going for walks.

This is Gertraute. She likes dancing, swimming and riding and playing tennis.

Make some proposals to Karlheinz and Gertraute. Here are some sample conversations:

*You*: Karlheinz! Wollen wir Fußball spielen?
*Karlheinz*: Ja, gern.

*You*: Gertraute! Wollen wir Karten spielen?
*Gertraute*: Nein, ich kann nicht Karten spielen.

Suggest to Karlheinz that you
 1. play football,
 2. go riding,
 3. play cards,
 4. play tennis,
 5. go swimming.

Then propose to Gertraute that you
 6. go dancing,
 7. go ski-ing,
 8. go for a walk,
 9. play football,
10. play cards.

**Exercise 2**

You are one of those people who are either extremely good at a thing, or absolutely awful. As it happens your strengths lie in swimming, riding, tennis and cards, and your weaknesses in ski-ing, dancing, football, singing and painting. Answer the following questions:

1. Können Sie gut Tennis spielen?
2. Können Sie gut malen?
3. Können Sie gut reiten?
4. Können Sie gut Ski fahren?
5. Können Sie gut tanzen?
6. Können Sie gut schwimmen?
7. Können Sie gut singen?
8. Können Sie gut Fußball spielen?
9. Können Sie gut Karten spielen?

**Section B**

**Exercise 3**

Complete the following sentences:

1. Der Junge geht in d — Schule.
2. Der Lehrer arbeitet in d — Schule.
3. Die Klasse kommt in d — Klassenzimmer.
4. Die Mädchen warten in d — Klassenzimmer.
5. Das Radio steht auf d — Tisch.
6. Ich stelle die Milch in d — Kühlschrank.
7. Das Bild hängt an d — Wand.
8. Ich halte meine Zeitung unter d — Arm.
9. Ich gehe an d — Tür.
10. Ich stelle die Tasse auf d — Tisch.

# CHAPTER 18

# DREAMS AND WISHES

## 18.1 DIALOGUES 📼

### Dialogue 1

Elke and Fritz have been enjoying the ski-ing at Kufstein (she possibly somewhat more than he). Now they are lying side by side on camp beds in the sun at the top of the ski slope. Elke is looking through some travel brochures.

1  *Elke*:  Fritz?
   *Fritz*:  Ja?
   *Elke*:  Es ist schön hier, nicht?
   *Fritz*:  Ja. Sehr schön.
5  *Elke*:  Du bist wirklich lieb, weißt du?
   *Fritz*:  Ja?
   . . .
   *Elke*:  Fritz?
   *Fritz*:  Ja?
   *Elke*:  Weißt du was?
10  *Fritz*:  Nein?
   *Elke*:  Ich möchte nach Amerika fahren.
   *Fritz*:  Tatsächlich?
   *Elke*:  Ja. Ich möchte Hollywood sehen.
   *Fritz*:  Hollywood?
15  *Elke*:  Ja. Und ich möchte New York besuchen.
   *Fritz*:  Ach, New York ist doch nicht schön.
   *Elke*:  Doch, doch!
   Und ich möchte mit einer Straßenbahn in San Francisco fahren.
20  *Fritz*:  Warum möchtest du mit einer Straßenbahn fahren?
   Das kannst du in München tun.

*... ist das so romantisch*

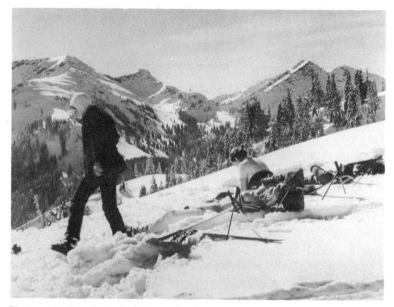

*Photograph: Bavaria-Verlag/Werner Stuhler*

*Elke*: Ach, du verstehst nicht.
In San Francisco ist das so romantisch.
*Fritz*: Aber teuer.
25 *Elke*: Das ist typisch ‚Mann'!!
Du denkst nur ans Geld.
Ich möchte reisen.
Ich möchte die Welt sehen.

## Dialogue 2

Frau Meyer is telephoning her best friend in order to impart the great news.

1 *Frau Meyer*: Leni? Weißt du was?
Die Inge kriegt ein Kind!
*Leni*: Nein. Das ist ja wunderbar!
Wo ist sie denn?
5 *Frau Meyer*: In Liverpool.
*Leni*: Ach ja, richtig.
In England.
*Frau Meyer*: Ich fahre natürlich nach Liverpool.
*Leni*: Ja, natürlich.

10 *Frau Meyer*: Ich muß meinen Pelzmantel reinigen lassen.
    *Leni*: Ja, selbstverständlich.
    *Frau Meyer*: Und ich muß mir ein neues Kleid machen lassen.
    *Leni*: Ja, freilich.
    *Frau Meyer*: Dann brauche ich einen Fotoapparat.
15 Ich muß meinen alten Fotoapparat reparieren lassen.
    *Leni*: Sicher.
    *Frau Meyer*: Dann muß ich auch etwas Geld wechseln.
    *Leni*: Ja, klar.
    *Frau Meyer*: Was für Geld haben sie dort in England?
20 Dollar, nicht?
    *Leni*: Nein. Sie haben Pfund und 'Pence'.
    *Frau Meyer*: Ach so. Ja.
    Dann muß ich mir die Haare waschen lassen.
    *Leni*: Moment, Irmgard.
25 Wann erwartet Inge ihr Kind?
    *Frau Meyer*: Nächstes Jahr.
    Im März.
    *Leni*: Hör' mal, Irmgard!
    Du hast doch noch viel Zeit.

## 18.2 INFORMATION

### (a) Notes on Dialogue 1

| | |
|---|---|
| 11. fahren | Note the difference in the word order between German and English. In German the infinitive comes at the end of the sentence. See also lines 13, 15, 19, 20 and 28. |
| 17. Doch, doch! | The word doch means 'yes' after someone has made a negative statement in the previous sentence. See line 16. |
| 26. ans Geld | The meaning of an in this sentence is 'of'. Denken an – 'to think of'. |

### (b) Notes on Dialogue 2

| | |
|---|---|
| 2. kriegt | There are two verbs in German which mean 'to get' or 'to |

receive'. They are kriegen and bekommen. Of the two, kriegen is slightly more colloquial. In this particular sentence the word kriegen is probably best rendered by 'to have', since in English we say 'to have a child'.

The present tense of the verb can be used to indicate something that is going to happen in the future. As the story makes clear, Inge's confinement lies in the future and the verb kriegt is consequently translated as 'is going to have'.

6. richtig

In German there are several expressions with which you can agree with what somebody else has just said. Leni uses a number of them.

> richtig (line 6)
> natürlich (line 9)
> selbstverständlich (line 11)
> freilich (line 13)
> sicher (line 16)
> klar (line 18)

14. brauche

As with the comment on line 2, this verb is formally in the present tense, though its meaning is to convey the future. Therefore it is translated as 'am going to need'.

17. etwas

This word when used together with a noun means 'some'. Etwas Geld – 'some money', etwas Milch – 'some milk', etwas Butter – 'some butter'.

19. Was für ... ?

This useful phrase means 'What sort of ... ?'

**(c) Word list**

| | |
|---|---|
| **wirk**lich | really |
| lieb | sweet, nice |
| tat**säch**lich | really; indeed |
| **seh**en | to see |
| be**su**chen | to visit |
| schön | beautiful |
| die **Straß**enbahn (-en) | tram |
| war**um**? | why? |
| ver**steh**en | to understand |
| ro**man**tisch | romantic |
| **teu**er | dear; expensive |
| **ty**pisch | typical |
| **den**ken | to think |
| nur | only |
| das Geld | money |
| **rei**sen | to travel |
| die Welt | world |
| **wis**sen | to know |
| **krie**gen | to get |
| das Kind (-er) | child |
| **wun**derbar | wonderful |
| **rich**tig | right; correct |
| na**tür**lich | naturally |
| der **Pelz**mantel (⸚) | fur coat |
| **rei**nigen | to clean |
| selbstver**ständ**lich | of course |
| neu | new |
| das Kleid (-er) | dress |
| **frei**lich | of course |
| **brau**chen | to need |
| der **Fo**toapparat (-e) | camera |
| alt | old |
| repa**rie**ren | to repair |
| **si**cher | certainly |
| **wech**seln | to change |
| klar | obviously |
| die **Haar**e (used in plural) | hair |
| **wa**schen | to wash |
| er**war**ten | to expect |
| das Jahr (-e) | year |
| die Zeit | time |

| | |
|---|---|
| **spre**chen | to speak |
| **zah**len | to pay |
| telefo**nier**en | to make a telephone call |
| **schla**fen | to sleep |
| **schmutz**ig | dirty |
| die **Arm**banduhr (-en) | wristwatch |
| ka**putt** | broken |
| **dre**ckig | dirty |
| das Hemd (-en) | shirt |
| die **Brille** | glasses, spectacles |

## 18.3 STRUCTURAL EXPLANATIONS

**(a) Structures to learn**

(i) **How to say you would like to do something and how to ask somebody what they would like to do**

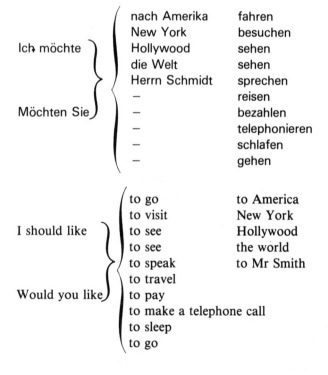

| Ich möchte | nach Amerika | fahren |
| | New York | besuchen |
| | Hollywood | sehen |
| | die Welt | sehen |
| | Herrn Schmidt | sprechen |
| | − | reisen |
| Möchten Sie | − | bezahlen |
| | − | telephonieren |
| | − | schlafen |
| | − | gehen |

| I should like | to go | to America |
| | to visit | New York |
| | to see | Hollywood |
| | to see | the world |
| | to speak | to Mr Smith |
| | to travel | |
| Would you like | to pay | |
| | to make a telephone call | |
| | to sleep | |
| | to go | |

## (ii) How to say that you would like to have something done

| Ich muß / Ich möchte | meinen Pelzmantel / meinen Fotoapparat / ein neues Kleid / mir die Haare | reinigen / reparieren / machen / waschen | lassen |

| I must / I should like to | have | my fur coat / my camera / a new dress / my hair | cleaned / repaired / made / washed |

(iii) When you have things done for you, you often want to ask when the services requested will be complete. Here are some ways of asking when things will be done:

| Wann ist | der Pelzmantel / der Fotoapparat / das Kleid | fertig? |

| When will | the fur coat / the camera / the dress | be ready? |

## (iv) How to ask when you can collect things

| Wann kann ich | den Pelzmantel / den Fotoapparat / das Kleid | abholen? |

| When can I collect | the fur coat / the camera / the dress | ? |

## 18.4 EXERCISES

### Section A

### Exercise 1
You had an accident on the way home and fell off your bicycle. All your clothes are dirty and all your breakables are broken. You have to set about restoring the damage. You go to the various shops. What do you say?

1. Dieser Mantel ist schmutzig.  Ich möchte . . . . . .
2. Diese Armbanduhr ist kaputt.  Ich möchte . . . . . .
3. Mein Hut ist dreckig.  Ich möchte . . . . . .
4. Mein Fotoapparat ist kaputt.  Ich möchte . . . . . .
5. Dieses Hemd ist schmutzig.  Ich möchte . . . . . .
6. Diese Hose ist dreckig.  Ich möchte . . . . . .
7. Meine Brille ist kaputt.  Ich möchte . . . . . .

**Exercise 2**
What would you say?
1. You're dreaming of far-off shores.
2. You want to leave the restaurant.
3. You want to speak to a friend on the phone.
4. You want to go to bed at last.
5. You want to leave.
6. You want to visit Peter.
7. You want to have a word with Miss Braun.
8. You want to see Munich.
9. You want to travel to Bonn.
10. You want to change your money.

**Section B**

**Exercise 3**
Unscramble the following sentences:

| | |
|---|---|
| 1. Ich möchte mir die Haare | a) Hamburg fahren. |
| 2. Er will seinen | b) wechseln. |
| 3. Elke will New York | c) Kleid machen lassen. |
| 4. Ich möchte die | d) Herrn Schmidt sprechen. |
| 5. Er möchte nach | e) reinigen lassen. |
| 6. Wir müssen das Geld | f) waschen lassen. |
| 7. Wir möchten | g) bezahlen. |
| 8. Sie muß sich ein neues | h) Apparat reparieren lassen. |
| 9. Kann ich bitte | i) Welt sehen. |
| 10. Sie will ihren Pelzmantel | j) besuchen. |

# CHAPTER 19

# TALKING ABOUT THE PAST

## 19.1 DIALOGUES 📼

**Dialogue 1**
Fritz is furious that Elke has kept him waiting – yet again.

1  *Fritz*: Mensch!
      Wo warst du denn?
    *Elke*: Was ist denn los?
      Mein Bus hatte Verspätung.
5  *Fritz*: Er hatte gestern Verspätung.
      Und heute hat er schon wieder Verspätung.
    *Elke*: Gestern hatte mein Bus nicht Verspätung.
    *Fritz*: Doch, doch!
      Er hatte dreißig Minuten Verspätung.
10  *Elke*: Das stimmt nicht.
    *Fritz*: Doch! Das stimmt.
      Ich war um sieben Uhr vor dem Kino.
      Und du warst erst um sieben Uhr dreißig da.
    *Elke*: Ich war pünktlich da.
15    Du warst einfach zu früh am Kino.
    *Fritz*: Und warum warst du vorgestern nicht pünktlich?
    *Elke*: Ich war im Geschäft.
    Fritz: Was? Bis acht Uhr?
      Das glaube ich nicht!
20  *Elke*: Ich hatte sehr viel zu tun.
    *Fritz*: Und der Chef war auch da, nicht wahr?
    *Elke*: Natürlich.
      Er hatte auch viel zu tun.
    *Fritz*: Ah hah. Jetzt verstehe ich . . .

**Dialogue 2**

Antonio is walking along the street when he sees Frau Meyer apparently searching for something.

1 *Antonio*: Kann ich Ihnen helfen?
  *Frau Meyer*: Ach, ich habe meine Armbanduhr verloren.
  *Antonio*: Hier, auf der Straße?
  *Frau Meyer*: Ja, das glaube ich.
5 Ich bin in die Stadt gefahren.
  Und ich habe dort Kaffee getrunken.
  *Antonio*: Haben Sie die Uhr vielleicht in der Stadt verloren?
  *Frau Meyer*: Nein.
  Ich habe sie in der Straßenbahn noch gesehen.
10 *Antonio*: Haben Sie an der Haltestelle gesucht?
  *Frau Meyer*: Ja, natürlich.
  Dort habe ich Frau Moezer getroffen.
  Ich bin mit ihr zur Post gegangen.
  *Antonio*: Haben Sie die Uhr vielleicht in der Post verloren?
15 *Frau Meyer*: Nein, das glaube ich nicht.
  *Antonio*: Sind Sie direkt von der Post hierher gekommen?
  *Frau Meyer*: Nein. Ich habe zuerst Äpfel gekauft.
  Bei Schötz.
  *Antonio*: Ach so. Bei Schötz.
20 Wie lange sind Sie bei Schötz geblieben?
  *Frau Meyer*: Ach, nicht lange.
  Fünf Minuten vielleicht.
  *Antonio*: Haben Sie in Ihrer Tasche gesucht?
  *Frau Meyer*: Was?
25 *Antonio*: Haben Sie in Ihrer Tasche gesucht?
  *Frau Meyer*: Um Gottes Willen!
  Da ist sie!

## 19.2 INFORMATION

### (a) Notes on Dialogue 1

1. Mensch!      This is a much-used expression in German, which you will hear very frequently if you go there. It conveys a certain feeling of indignation on the part of the speaker, and you should be wary of using it unless you feel you know the person you are speaking to well enough.

| 4. | Verspätung | Note that where in English we say something or someone *is* late, in German one says something has *lateness*. |
|---|---|---|
| 7. | Gestern | The word gestern is put at the beginning of the sentence for emphasis, and this means that the subject comes after the verb. |
| 10. | Das stimmt nicht | This phrase should be treated as an idiom, and not translated. |
| 12. | um sieben Uhr | In German, expressions of time always come before expressions of place. |
| 13. | erst | In expressions of time, this word means 'not until'. |

**(b) Notes on Dialogue 2**

| 2. | verloren | Note that the past participle comes at the end of the sentence. |
|---|---|---|
| 4. | das glaube ich | Get used to the order of the words in this expression, and use it as an idiom when you want to say 'I think so'. |
| 6. | getrunken | English very often uses the verb 'to have' with food or drink. German, however, always specifies whether one is eating or drinking. |
| 7. | vielleicht | This word means 'perhaps'. |
| 10. | Haben Sie ... ? | Remember that English very often forms its questions with the word 'Do' or 'Did'. In German the subject and the verb are inverted in order to make the question form. |

**(c) Word list**

| der Bus (¨se) | bus |
|---|---|
| **ges**tern | yesterday |

| | |
|---|---|
| heute | today |
| schon wieder | again |
| die Minute (-n) | minute |
| vor | in front of |
| das Kino (-s) | cinema |
| pünktlich | on time |
| einfach | simply |
| früh | early |
| vorgestern | the day before yesterday |
| das Geschäft (-e) | shop; business |
| bis | until |
| glauben | to believe |
| sehr viel | very much |
| tun | to do |
| der Chef | boss |
| verstehen | to understand |
| helfen | to help |
| die Armbanduhr (-en) | wristwatch |
| verlieren | to lose |
| die Straße (-n) | street |
| die Stadt (¨e) | town |
| die Straßenbahn | tram |
| der Kaffee | coffee |
| trinken | to drink |
| die Haltestelle | bus or tram stop |
| sehen | to see |
| suchen | to seek, look for |
| natürlich | of course, naturally |
| treffen | to meet |
| die Post | post office |
| direkt | straight directly |
| zuerst | first of all |
| der Apfel (¨) | apple |
| kaufen | to buy |
| wie lange? | how long? |
| bleiben | to stay; remain |
| nicht lange | not long |
| vielleicht | perhaps |
| die Tasche (-n) | pocket; bag |

**(d) Some phrases**

| | |
|---|---|
| Was ist denn los? | What's the matter? |
| Das stimmt nicht | That's not true, correct |

| | |
|---|---|
| Das **glau**be ich nicht | I don't believe it |
| Um **Got**tes **Wil**len! | Good Lord! |

## 19.3 STRUCTURAL EXPLANATIONS

**Grammar**

(i) When referring to the past, two tenses are used in German. The first past tense is known as the *Imperfect* or *Simple Past*, and the other is known as the *Perfect* tense or *Compound Past*.

(ii) **The Simple Past (also known as the Imperfect tense)**
When talking German and wishing to refer to the past, this tense is used mainly with the verbs haben and sein, and with a number of other verbs of speaking, i.e. sagen – 'to say'.
Here are some examples, taken from Dialogue 1:

Wo warst du denn?
Ich war um sieben Uhr vor dem Kino
Du warst erst um sieben Uhr dreißig da
Ich war pünktlich da
Ich war im Geschäft

Mein Bus hatte Verspätung
Er hatte gestern Verspätung
Ich hatte sehr viel zu tun
Er hatte auch viel zu tun

(iii) Here are the forms of the Simple Past tense of SEIN – to be.

| | |
|---|---|
| ich war | I was |
| du warst | you were (familiar) |
| er war | he was |
| sie war | she was |
| es war | it was |
| wir waren | we were |
| ihr ward | you were (familiar) |
| Sie waren | you were (formal or polite) |
| sie waren | they were |

(iv) Here are the forms of the Simple Past tense of HABEN – to have.

| | |
|---|---|
| ich hatte | I had |
| du hattest | you had (familiar) |
| er hatte | he had |

| sie hatte | she had |
| es hatte | it had |
| wir hatten | we had |
| ihr hattet | you had (familiar) |
| Sie hatten | you had (formal or polite) |
| sie hatten | they had |

(v) Remember when you want to say: 'I was', or 'we were', or 'I had', or 'they had', these are the forms to use.

You should use the same tense if you want to say 'I said'. The Simple Past tense of the verb 'to say' is given in the appendix.

### (vi) The Compound Past (also known as the Perfect tense)

In this course, you are going to learn the Compound Past of verbs *other than* haben, sein and sagen. As the word *compound* indicates, this tense is made by using parts of two verbs.

Consider the following sentences, taken from Dialogue 2 and try to discover how this tense is constructed.

| Ich *habe* meine Armbanduhr *verloren* | (verlieren – to lose) |
| Ich *habe* dort Kaffee *getrunken* | (trinken – to drink) |
| Ich *habe* sie in der Straßenbahn *gesehen* | (sehen – to see) |
| Ich *habe* zuerst Äpfel *gekauft* | (kaufen – to buy) |

Here is an analysis of these sentences.

|  (1)  |  (2)  |  (3)  |  (4)  |
|---|---|---|---|
| Ich | Part of the verb HABEN | meine Armbanduhr | verloren |
| Ich | | Kaffee | getrunken |
| Ich | | sie | gesehen |
| Ich | | Äpfel | gekauft |

In column 2 comes part of the present tense of the verb HABEN. This is called the *auxiliary* verb

In column 4, at the *end* of the sentence, comes part of the verb which carries the meaning. This part of the verb is called the *past participle*

(vii) Here are some more sentences from Dialogue 2. Look and see how they are constructed.

*Haben* Sie die Uhr in der Stadt *verloren?*
*Haben* Sie an der Haltestelle *gesucht?*
*Haben* Sie die Uhr in der Post *verloren?*
*Haben* Sie in Ihrer Tasche *gesucht?*

Here is an analysis of these sentences.

(1)        (2)        (3)                        (4)

| Part of the verb HABEN | Sie | die Uhr in der Stadt | verloren |
| | Sie | an der Haltestelle | gesucht |
| | Sie | die Uhr in der Post | verloren |
| | Sie | in Ihrer Tasche | gesucht |

The *auxiliary* verb is at the beginning of the sentence in column 1. This indicates that the sentences are questions

The *past participle* comes in column 4, at the end of the sentence

(viii) All the verbs we have looked at so far make their *Compound Past* tense by using the verb HABEN. Unfortunately, this is not always the case. A small group of very important verbs make the *Compound Past* by using the verb SEIN.

(ix) Consider the following sentences taken from Dialogue 2.

Ich bin in die Stadt gefahren.     (fahren – to go/drive)
Ich bin mit ihr zur Post gegangen.   (gehen – to go)

Here is an analysis of the sentences.

(1)   (2)        (3)              (4)

| Ich | Part of the verb SEIN | in die Stadt | gefahren |
| Ich | | zur Post | gegangen |

Part of the present tense of the verb SEIN

At the *end* of the sentence comes the *past participle*

(x) Here are some more sentences from Dialogue 2. Look and see how they are constructed.

> Sind Sie direkt von der Post hierher gekommen?
> (kommen – to come)
> Wie lange sind Sie bei Schötz geblieben?
> (bleiben – to stay/remain)

Here is an analysis of these sentences.

| (1) | (2) | (3) | (4) | (5) |
|-----|-----|-----|-----|-----|
| –<br>Wie lange | Part of<br>the verb<br>SEIN | Sie<br>Sie | von der Post<br>bei Schötz | gekommen?<br>geblieben? |

The *auxiliary*        The *past participle*
verb: SEIN          is at the *end* of
is here             the sentence

(xi) We can summarise the rule about making the Compound Past tense thus:

1. The *Compound Past* is made with part of the present tense of the verb HABEN or SEIN. This is called the *auxiliary verb*.
2. The other part of this tense is called the *past participle*.
3. The *past participle* comes at the end of the sentence, whether it is a question or a statement.

(xii) Two vital questions remain:
1. How does each individual verb make its past participle?
2. Which verbs make their Compound Past tense with HABEN, and which with SEIN?

These questions may be answered by consulting the list of verbs in the appendix.

## 19.4 EXERCISES

### Section A

### Exercise 1
Imagine that this is your diary. Say what you did on each day of the week. Here is an example:

Montag – Ich bin nach Solingen gefahren.

| Mo | *nach Solingen fahren.* |
|----|--------------------------|
| Di | *Armbanduhr kaufen.* |
| Mi | *Kette für Inge suchen.* |
| Do | *mit Elke ins Kino gehen.* |
| Fr | *Wein mit Peter trinken.* |
| Sa | *Bayern-München gegen Hamburg sehen.* |
| So | *in die Kirche gehen.* |

**Exercise 2**
Here is a page from your diary, which shows your movements throughout the day. Imagine that you are being questioned by a policeman, who says: 'Wo waren Sie um 9 Uhr?' You can answer: 'Ich war im Büro'. Now answer the following questions.

1. Wo waren Sie um 9 Uhr?
2. Wo waren Sie um 10 Uhr?
3. Wo waren Sie um 11 Uhr?
4. Wo waren Sie um 12 Uhr?
5. Wo waren Sie um 13 Uhr?
6. Wo waren Sie um 14 Uhr?
7. Wo waren Sie um 15 Uhr?

# Dienstag 2 Mai

| | |
|---|---|
| 09·00 | im Büro |
| 10·00 | in der Post |
| 11·00 | am Marktplatz |
| 12·00 | im Gasthaus Bauer |
| 13·00 | bei Müller |
| 14·00 | im Café |
| 15·00 | im Zug |
| 16·00 | |
| 17·00 | |
| 18·00 | |
| | |
| | |

**Section B**

**Exercise 3**
Put the following sentences into the Perfect tense.
1. Ich trinke Bier.
2. Ich gehe in die Stadt.
3. Er fährt nach Bremen.
4. Wir kommen um 8 Uhr.
5. Sie bleiben zu lange.
6. Sie kauft ein Hemd.
7. Wir suchen eine Wohnung.
8. Sie verliert ihre Armbanduhr.
9. Ich sehe einen guten Film.
10. Sie treffen Herrn Schüth.

# CHAPTER 20

# REVISION TESTS

In this chapter you will have an opportunity to consolidate the language you have learned in the previous nine chapters. Each test indicates whereabouts in the later part of the book you ought to search if you have forgotten a particular point.

**Test 1 – Ordering a Meal (Ch. 11)**
You're taking a friend out to dinner to celebrate his/her birthday.
*Waiter*: Guten Abend!
*You*: Greet him.
　Ask for a table for two.
*Waiter*: Kommen Sie, bitte.
*You*: Call for the waiter.
*Waiter*: Bitte schön?
*You*: Ask for the menu.
*Waiter*: Die Speisekarte, bitte schön.
*You*: Ask your friend if he/she would like an hors d'oeuvre.
*Friend*: Ja, bitte.
*You*: Ask your friend if he/she would like oysters.
*Friend*: Austern, O ja!
*You*: Order the oysters for both of you.
*Waiter*: Zweimal Austern.
*You*: Ask your friend if he/she would like a Zigeuner Steak.
*Friend*: Nein, danke, ich möchte ein Jägerschnitzel.
*You*: Order one Jägerschnitzel and a Wienerschnitzel.
*Waiter*: Jawohl.
*You*: Ask your friend if he/she would like something to drink.
*Friend*: O ja. Ich möchte einen Rotwein. Und Sie?
*You*: Say you'd like red wine too.
　Order two red wines.
*Waiter*: Jawohl, mein Herr.
If you are learning with a friend, take it in turns to play the parts.

**Test 2 – Finding a table in a restaurant (Ch. 11)**
Sort out these phrases spoken by a head waiter and a customer at his restaurant in order to make an intelligible conversation. If you are working with a partner, take a part each. The customer begins.

| *Customer* | *Head waiter* |
|---|---|
| Für zwei | Für wieviele Personen? |
| Ich möchte einen Tisch | Guten Abend |
| Guten Abend | Kommen Sie, bitte |

**Test 3 – Reserving a table by phone (Ch. 11)**
Now try to sort this one out. The customer begins.

| *Customer* | *Head waiter* |
|---|---|
| Um acht Uhr | Auf welchen Namen |
| Für zwei | Für wann? |
| Guten Tag! | Ist in Ordnung |
| Ich möchte einen Tisch | Für wieviele Personen? |
| Auf Wiederhören! | Um wieviel Uhr? |
| Schmidt | Guten Tag! |
| Für heute Abend | |

**Test 4 – Ordering food in a restaurant (Ch. 11)**
Order the following dishes:

| | |
|---|---|
| One apple pie | Three herring fillets |
| Two roast chickens | Two fruit cocktails |
| One boiled egg | One pepper steak |
| Two portions of duck | Two grape juices |
| Three portions of liver | One portion of pickled cabbage |
| One meat loaf | Three portions of pork |

**Test 5 – Asking to borrow things (Ch. 12)**
What would you say if you had very accommodating neighbours?
1. You want to borrow a table for a party.
2. Could you have a friend's dress, just for the evening?
3. There's one extra for dinner; you need another chair.
4. Your pullover has a stain.
5. You didn't have time to wash your shirt.
6. You ought really to have a blouse to go with that skirt.
7. There's a button off your jacket.
8. You have just torn your trousers.
9. It's raining and you have left your raincoat at the office.
10. The children need another nightdress for dressing up in.

**Test 6 – A Riddle (Ch. 13)**
How can you mention all the days of the working week, without saying Monday, Tuesday, Wednesday, etc.?

**Test 7 – Using the dative to express liking (Ch. 13)**
Answer the following questions. The ticks and crosses will give you a clue as to the answer you should give.
1. Gefällt Ihnen das Wetter? ✓
2. Gefällt Ihnen der Sonnenschein? ✓
3. Gefällt Ihnen der Regen? ✗
4. Gefällt Ihnen der Schnee? ✓
5. Gefällt Ihnen der Wind? ✗
6. Gefällt Ihnen die Landschaft? ✓
7. Gefällt Ihnen das Meer? ✓
8. Gefällt Ihnen der Nebel? (fog) ✗
9. Gefällt Ihnen der Strand? ✗
10. Gefallen Ihnen die Berge? ✓

**Test 8 – Types of accommodation (Ch. 14)**
 **(cf. also indefinite article, Ch. 5)**
Translate into German
1. I live in a house.
2. I live in an owner-occupied flat.
3. I live in a one-family house.
4. I live in a terraced house.
5. I live in a house divided up into flats.
6. I live in a detached house.
7. I live in a two-family house.
8. I live in a flat.
9. I live in a council flat.
10. I live in a rented flat.

**Test 9 – Saying what you like doing (Ch. 15)**
How would it be if you were the sort of person who only likes doing things which can be done in the open air and which involve being very energetic?
1. Reiten Sie gern?
2. Fahren Sie gern Ski?
3. Fahren Sie gern mit dem Rad?
4. Reisen Sie gern?
5. Spielen Sie gern Klavier?
6. Spielen Sie gern Karten?

**Test 10 – Describing hobbies and interests (Ch. 15)**
What would you say to somebody who said to you Haben Sie ein
Hobby?
1. Assuming that you were interested in music.
2. If you were interested in pictures.
3. If your passion was collecting books.
4. Assuming you were a keen photographer.
5. If you were a football fan.
6. If you liked watching athletics.

**Test 11 – Saying what you must/have to do (Ch. 16)**
Here is a page from Fritz's diary. Can you answer the questions
below?

| So | Elke besuchen |
|----|---------------|
| Mo | die Karten abholen |
| Di | nach Nürnberg fahren |
| Mi | eine Kette für Elke kaufen |
| Do | einen Tennisschläger kaufen |
| Fr | nach Stuttgart fahren |
| Sa | im Bett bleiben |

1. Was muß Fritz am Donnerstag machen?
2. Was muß er am Dienstag machen?
3. Was muß er am Sonntag machen?
4. Was muß er am Mittwoch machen?
5. Was muß er am Montag machen?
6. Was muß er am Freitag machen?
7. Was muß er am Samstag machen?

**Test 12 – Können and wollen (Ch. 17)**
Translate into German
1. Can you play tennis?
2. Shall we go for a walk?
3. Can you dance?
4. He can swim.

5. They want to play football.
6. We can play cards.
7. Shall we go to London?
8. Can she sing?
9. He doesn't want to drink.
10. You can't swim.

# II REFERENCE MATERIAL

# PRONUNCIATION KEY

The best way to get a good pronunciation is to practise with the sound recording. You should listen to each word as it is spoken on the tape, concentrating on the particular sound to be practised. This is indicated by underlining. You should pay particular attention to the vowel sounds because, in comparison with English pronunciation, a greater proportion of them in German are pure, that is to say they consist of one vowel sound only. There are, however, some diphthongs in German, and these are indicated separately. When a word, or part of a word, begins with a vowel, it is uttered with a slight explosion of breath at the back of the throat, similar to a very slight cough. This is called a 'glottal stop'. On the whole the consonants of German are the same as in English, and the learning problem here is to become used to the fact that certain letters of the alphabet indicate different sounds in German from English.

## VOWELS

/a/ is pronounced like /bunker/
Example: Danke – thank you

| | | |
|---|---|---|
| /a/ | – long is pronounced like /father/ | Example: Tag – day |
| /e/ | is pronounced like /pet/ | Example: welcher – which |
| /e/ | – long is pronounced like /fey/ | Example: Tee – tea |
| /i/ | is pronounced like /bit/ | Example: bitte – please |
| /ie/ | – long is pronounced like /here/ | Example: hier – here |
| /o/ | is pronounced like /coffer/ | Example: Koffer – suitcase |
| /o/ | – long is pronounced like /grown/ | Example: wohnen – to live |
| /u/ | is pronounced like /pull/ | Example: und – and |
| /u/ | – long is pronounced like /moot/ | Example: Guten Tag – Good Day |

## MODIFIED VOWELS

The vowel sounds shown above are changed slightly by the addition of an *Umlaut* (¨).

| | | |
|---|---|---|
| /ä/ | is pronounced like /peck/ | Example: Äpfel – apples |
| /ä/ | – long is pronounced like /late/ | Example: spät – late |
| /ö/ | – is pronounced like /cur/ | Example: Streichhölzer – matches |

/ö/    – long is pronounced like /turn/    Example: schön – beautiful

/ü/    This sound does not exist in English, and the way to make it is to purse your lips as if to whistle, and then without moving them say a short /i/   Example: hübsch – pretty

/ü/    – long   Purse the lips the same way, as if to whistle, and without moving them say /ee/   Example: Bücher – books

/ei/    is pronounced like /mine/    Example: nein – no

/au/    is pronounced like /howl/    Example: Frau – Mrs

/eu/    is pronounced like /coy/    Example: heute – today

/äu/    is pronounced like /coy/    Example: Fräulein – Miss

When a vowel comes before two consonants, it is usually 'short', e.g. Äpfel, bitte. When a vowel comes before a single consonant, or the letter 'h', it is usually 'long', e.g. wohnen, hier.

## CONSONANTS

These are the main differences from English:

/j/    is pronounced like /yacht/    Example: ja – yes

/r/    This sound is made at the back of the mouth when it comes at the beginning or the middle of a word. Example: Frau – Mrs

/v/    is pronounced like /fan/    Example: von – from

/w/    is pronounced like /vase/    Example: wieder – again

/z/    is pronounced like /cats/    Example: Zimmer – room
      Note that English has this sound, but does not put it at the beginning of a word as German does.

/ch/    when it follows the vowels a, o, u, or au is pronounced like /loch/ Example: Bach – stream

/ch/    when it comes anywhere else is pronounced like /huge/ Example: ich – I

/sch/    is pronounced like /ship/    Example: schön – beautiful

/sp/    is pronounced like /shp/    Example: spät – late

/st/    is pronounced like /sht/    Example: Stein – stone

/s/    when it comes before vowels has a buzzing sound like /zoo/ Example: Sie – you

/s/    in other positions is pronounced like /house/ Example: ist – is
                    Rathaus – town hall

/b/    when it occurs at the end of a word or a syllable is pronounced like /p/ Example: grob – vulgar

/d/    when it comes at the end of a word or a syllable is pronounced like /t/ Example: Hand – hand

/g/    when it comes after /i/ (-ig) is pronounced like /ch/ as in the Scottish 'loch'   Example: hungrig – hungry

Students are warned that the pronunciation key given here is only an approximation. Treat the key as a rough guide. If you are able to implement it, it will make you understandable amongst speakers of German, but to obtain a really good accent you should practise with the sound recording.

## STRESS

The best way to learn how the syllables of German words are stressed is to listen carefully to the recorded dialogues.

As an additional help, the *word lists* show the stressed syllables in bold type. The letters of the German alphabet are virtually the same as in English. There are four exceptions. These are asterisked.

| | |
|---|---|
| Aa | The two dots over the vowels /a/o/u/ |
| Ää * | are called an UMLAUT. |
| Bb | |
| Cc | The symbol between /s/ and /t/ is called sz |
| Dd | |
| Ee | |
| Ff | |
| Gg | |
| Hh | |
| Ii | |
| Jj | |
| Kk | |
| Ll | |
| Mm | |
| Nn | |
| Oo | |
| Öö * | |
| Pp | |
| Qq | |
| Rr | |
| Ss | |
| ß * | |
| Tt | |
| Uu | |
| Üü * | |
| Vv | |
| Ww | |
| Xx | |
| Yy | |
| Zz | |

# ANSWERS TO EXERCISES

## Chapter 1 Greetings and Introductions

### Answers to Exercise 1
1. Gute Nacht!
2. Viel Glück!
3. Prost/Zum Wohl!
4. Guten Morgen!
5. Gute Reise!
6. Gute Besserung!
7. Guten Abend!
8. Viel Spaß/Viel Vergnügen!
9. Guten Tag/Grüß Gott!

### Answers to Exercise 2
1. Guten Abend, Herr Doktor!
2. Darf ich meine Frau vorstellen?
3. Angenehm.
4. Kommen Sie herein.
5. Bitte, nehmen Sie Platz.
6. Danke schön für die Einladung.
7. Eine Tasse Kaffee?
8. Bitte sehr!
9. Nein, danke.
10. Entschuldigen Sie!

### Answers to Exercise 3
1. Guten Abend!
2. Danke/Danke schön.
3. Sehr gut, danke.
4. Angenehm.
5. Danke.
6. It depends, doesn't it? Either Bitte sehr or Nein, danke.

## Chapter 2 Getting about

**Answers to Exercise 1**
1. Wie komme ich zum Krankenhaus?
2. Wie komme ich zur Sparkasse?
3. Wie komme ich zum Bahnhof?
4. Wie komme ich zum Sportplatz?
5. Wie komme ich zum Hallenbad?
6. Wie komme ich zum Freibad?
7. Wie komme ich zur Grundschule?
8. Wie komme ich zum Altenheim?
9. Wie komme ich zur Kapuzinerkirche?
10. Wie komme ich zum Campingplatz?
11. Wie komme ich zum Kindergarten?
12. Wie komme ich zur Reithalle?
13. Wie komme ich zum Minigolfplatz?
14. Wie komme ich zum Waldrestaurant?
15. Wie komme ich zum Marktplatz?
16. Wie komme ich zur Post?
17. Wie komme ich zum Rathaus?
18. Wie komme ich zum Dom?
19. Wie komme ich zum Parkplatz?

**Answers to Exercise 2**
1. Wie komme ich zur Audi-Werkstatt?
2. Wie komme ich zur Volkswagen-Werkstatt?
3. Wie komme ich zur Opel-Werkstatt?
4. Wie komme ich zur Ford-Werkstatt?
5. Hard luck, you'd better go on to Munich.

**Answers to Exercise 3**
1. Wie komme ich nach Warburg?
2. Wie komme ich nach Brakel?
3. Wie komme ich nach Eissen?
4. Wie komme ich nach Manrode?
5. Wie komme ich nach Offendorf?
6. Wie kommen wir nach Paderborn?
7. Wie kommen wir nach Detmold?
8. Wie kommen wir nach Peckelsheim?
9. Wie kommen wir nach Steinheim?
10. Wie kommen wir nach Holzminden?

**Answers to Exercise 4**
1. *A*: Wie weit ist es nach Dessau?
   *B*: Einundzwanzig Kilometer ungefähr.
2. *A*: Wie weit ist es nach Halle?
   *B*: Zweiundfünfzig Kilometer ungefähr.
3. *A*: Wie weit ist es nach Jena?
   *B*: Hundertein Kilometer ungefähr.

4. *A*: Wie weit ist es nach Linz?
   *B*: Dreiundzwanzig Kilometer ungefähr.
5. *A*: Wie weit ist es nach Kitzbühel?
   *B*: Neununddreißig Kilometer ungefähr.
6. *A*: Wie weit ist es nach Kufstein?
   *B*: Neun Kilometer ungefähr.
7. *A*: Wie weit ist es nach Zürich?
   *B*: Sechsundfünfzig Kilometer ungefähr.
8. *A*: Wie weit ist es nach Tübingen?
   *B*: Einundsiebzig Kilometer ungefähr.
9. *A*: Wie weit ist es nach Ansbach?
   *B*: Sechsundfünfzig Kilometer ungefähr.
10. *A*: Wie weit ist es nach Fulda?
    *B*: Fünfundvierzig Kilometer ungefähr.

## Chapter 3 Staying in hotels

### Section A

### Answers to Exercise 1

1. *Guest*: Haben Sie ein Zimmer frei?
   *Hotel*: Jawohl. Was für ein Zimmer?
   *Guest*: Ein Einzelzimmer.
   *Hotel*: Für wie lange?
   *Guest*: Für eine Nacht.

2. *Guest*: Haben Sie ein Zimmer frei?
   *Hotel*: Jawohl. Was für ein Zimmer?
   *Guest*: Ein Einzelzimmer mit Dusche.
   *Hotel*: Für wie lange?
   *Guest*: Für eine Nacht.

3. *Guest*: Haben Sie ein Zimmer frei?
   *Hotel*: Jawohl. Was für ein Zimmer?
   *Guest*: Ein Doppelzimmer mit Bad.
   *Hotel*: Für wie lange?
   *Guest*: Für zwei Nächte.

4. *Guest*: Haben Sie ein Zimmer frei?
   *Hotel*: Jawohl. Was für ein Zimmer?
   *Guest*: Ein Einzelzimmer mit Dusche.
   *Hotel*: Für wie lange?
   *Guest*: Für eine Woche.

5. *Guest*: Haben Sie ein Zimmer frei?
   *Hotel*: Jawohl. Was für ein Zimmer?
   *Guest*: Ein Zweibettzimmer.
   *Hotel*: Für wie lange?
   *Guest*: Für zwei Nächte.

6. *Guest*: Haben Sie ein Zimmer frei?
   *Hotel*: Jawohl. Was für ein Zimmer?

*Guest*: Ein Doppelzimmer mit Dusche.
*Hotel*: Für wie lange?
*Guest*: Für eine Woche.

7. *Guest*: Haben Sie ein Zimmer frei?
*Hotel*: Jawohl. Was für ein Zimmer?
*Guest*: Ein Einzelzimmer mit Bad.
*Hotel*: Für wie lange?
*Guest*: Für drei Nächte.

8. *Guest*: Haben Sie ein Zimmer frei?
*Hotel*: Jawohl. Was für ein Zimmer?
*Guest*: Ein Doppelzimmer.
*Hotel*: Für wie lange?
*Guest*: Für vier Nächte.

9. *Guest*: Haben Sie ein Zimmer frei?
*Hotel*: Jawohl. Was für ein Zimmer?
*Guest*: Ein Einzelzimmer.
*Hotel*: Für wie lange?
*Guest*: Für drei Nächte.

10. *Guest*: Haben Sie ein Zimmer frei?
*Hotel*: Jawohl. Was für ein Zimmer?
*Guest*: Ein Einzelzimmer mit Dusche.
*Hotel*: Für wie lange?
*Guest*: Für zwei Nächte.

**Answers to Exercise 2**

*Schmidt*
1. Guten Tag!

3. Haben Sie ein Zimmer frei?

5. Haben Sie ein Einzelzimmer frei?

7. Für eine Nacht.

9. Ich nehme das Zimmer.

*Empfang*

2. Guten Tag, der Herr!

4. Ja, ein Zimmer habe ich.

6. Für wie lange, bitte?

8. Für eine Nacht.
Das geht in Ordnung.

10. Tragen Sie sich bitte ein!

**Answers to Exercise 3**

*Müller*
1. Guten Tag!

3. Haben Sie ein Zimmer frei?

5. Haben Sie ein Doppelzimmer
frei? – mit Bad?

*Rezeption*

2. Grüß Gott!

4. Ja, das ist möglich.

6. Ja, ein Doppelzimmer habe ich
noch. Für wieviele Nächte,
bitte?

7. Von heute bis Sonntag.

9. Ich nehme das Zimmer.

8. Ja, das geht.

10. Bitte, tragen Sie sich ein.

## Section B

### Answers to Exercise 4
1. Haben Sie ein Einzelzimmer?
2. Wie lange bleiben Sie?
3. Ich nehme das Zimmer.
4. Entschuldigen Sie, bitte.
5. Wie komme ich nach Stauting?
6. Fahren Sie hier geradeaus.
7. Er biegt hier nach links ab.
8. Nehmen Sie dann die erste Straße links.
9. Gehen Sie die Marktstraße hoch.
10. Haben Sie einen Tisch für zwei?
11. Ich habe einen Tisch um 8 Uhr.
12. Sie bleiben eine Nacht.
13. Sie kommen zur Adriastraße.

### Answers to Exercise 5
1. Der zweite Mai neunzehnhundertachtundsiebzig.
2. Der sechzehnte Juni neunzehnhundertzweiundachtzig.
3. Der einunddreißigste Dezember neunzehnhundertneunundsiebzig.
4. Der elfte August neunzehnhundertzweiundachtzig.
5. Der siebenundzwanzigste März neunzehnhundertdreiundachtzig.
6. Der siebzehnte Mai neunzehnhundertfünfundachtzig.

## Chapter 4 Travelling by train

## Section A

### Answers to Exercise 1
1. Um wieviel Uhr/Wann fährt der Zug nach Nürnberg?
2. Um wieviel Uhr/Wann fährt der Zug nach Würzburg?
3. Um wieviel Uhr/Wann fährt der Zug nach Innsbruck?
4. Um wieviel Uhr/Wann fährt der Zug nach Frankfurt?
5. Um wieviel Uhr/Wann fährt der Zug nach Treuchtlingen?
6. Um wieviel Uhr/Wann fährt der Zug nach Erlangen?
7. Um wieviel Uhr/Wann fährt der Zug nach Ansbach?
8. Um wieviel Uhr/Wann fährt der Zug nach Großhabersdorf?
9. Um wieviel Uhr/Wann fährt der Zug nach Forchheim?
10. Um wieviel Uhr/Wann fährt der Zug nach Schwabach?

### Answers to Exercise 2
1. *Reisender*: Zweimal zweiter Klasse nach Hamburg, bitte.
   *Angestellte*: Hin und zurück?
   *Reisender*: Nein, einfach.

2. *Reisender*:   Einmal zweiter Klasse nach Bremen, bitte.
   *Angestellte*:   Hin und zurück?
   *Reisender*:   Ja, hin und zurück, bitte.

3. *Reisender*:   Einmal erster Klasse nach Hamm, bitte.
   *Angestellte*:   Hin und zurück?
   *Reisender*:   Nein, einfach.

4. *Reisender*:   Einmal erster Klasse nach Münster, bitte.
   *Angestellte*:   Hin und zurück?
   *Reisender*:   Ja, hin und zurück, bitte.

5. *Reisender*:   Dreimal zweiter Klasse nach Dortmund, bitte.
   *Angestellte*:   Hin und zurück?
   *Reisender*:   Nein, einfach.

6. *Reisender*:   Zweimal zweiter Klasse nach Düsseldorf, bitte.
   *Angestellte*:   Hin und zurück?
   *Reisender*:   Nein, einfach.

7. *Reisender*:   Zweimal zweiter Klasse nach Bonn, bitte.
   *Angestellte*:   Hin und zurück?
   *Reisender*:   Ja, hin und zurück bitte.

8. *Reisender*:   Einmal erster Klasse nach Koblenz, bitte.
   *Angestellte*:   Hin und zurück?
   *Reisender*:   Ja, hin und zurück, bitte.

9. *Reisender*:   Zweimal zweiter Klasse nach Köln, bitte.
   *Angestellte*:   Hin und zurück?
   *Reisender*:   Nein, einfach.

10. *Reisender*:   Dreimal erster Klasse nach München, bitte.
   *Angestellte*:   Hin und zurück?
   *Reisender*:   Ja, hin und zurück, bitte.

**Section B**

**Answers to Exercise 3**
1. Oma ruft am Samstag an.
2. Ingrid geht am Dienstag aus.
3. Die Kinder räumen den Laden auf.
4. Mutter räumt die Spielsachen auf.
5. Peter wäscht die Teller ab.
6. Inge kauft Lebensmittel ein.
7. Helmut wäscht am Sonntag ab.
8. Der Chef gibt seine Arbeit auf.
9. Maria schließt den Laden ab.
10. Oma geht am Samstag aus.

**Answers to Exercise 4**
1. Wann fährt der Zug nach Bonn ab?
2. Wir schließen den Laden ab.
3. Oma geht am Dienstag aus.
4. Peter ruft am Mittwoch an.

5. Der Chef kauft Lebensmittel ein.
6. Mutter wäscht die Teller ab.
7. Die Kinder trocknen die Teller ab.
8. Er kauft Lebensmittel ein.
9. Der Chef gibt seine Arbeit auf.
10. Ich räume die Spielsachen auf.

## Chapter 5 Travelling by taxi, bus or tram

## Section A

### Answers to Exercise 1
Fährt dieser Bus nach Egersdorf?
Fährt dieser Bus nach Steinach?
Fährt dieser Bus zum Stadttheater?
Fährt dieser Bus zum Rathaus?
Fährt dieser Bus zum Flughafen?
Fährt dieser Bus zur Stadtmitte?
Fährt dieser Bus zur Goethestraße?

Fährt diese Straßenbahn nach Egersdorf?
Fährt diese Straßenbahn nach Steinach?
Fährt diese Straßenbahn zum Stadttheater?
Fährt diese Straßenbahn zum Rathaus?
Fährt diese Straßenbahn zum Flughafen?
Fährt diese Straßenbahn zur Stadtmitte?
Fährt diese Straßenbahn zur Goethestraße?

Fährt dieser Zug nach Egersdorf?
Fährt dieser Zug nach Steinach?
Fährt dieser Zug zum Stadttheater?
Fährt dieser Zug zum Rathaus?
Fährt dieser Zug zum Flughafen?
Fährt dieser Zug zur Stadtmitte?
Fährt dieser Zug zur Goethestraße?

Fährt die Nummer 15 nach Egersdorf?
Fährt die Nummer 15 nach Steinach?
Fährt die Nummer 15 zum Stadttheater?
Fährt die Nummer 15 zum Rathaus?
Fährt die Nummer 15 zum Flughafen?
Fährt die Nummer 15 zur Stadtmitte?
Fährt die Nummer 15 zur Goethestraße?

### Answers to Exercise 2
1. Fährt die (Nummer) 17 zum Rathaus?
2. Fährt die (Nummer) 17 zur Oper?
3. Fährt die (Nummer) 17 nach Perlach?
4. Fährt die (Nummer) 23 zur Stadtmitte?
5. Fährt die (Nummer) 31 zum Flughafen?
6. Fährt die (Nummer) 1 zum Freibad?

7. Welche Straßenbahn fährt zum Hauptbahnhof?
8. Welcher Bus fährt zur Heidenstraße?
9. Welcher Bus fährt nach Egersdorf?
10. Welcher Bus fährt nach Göttingen?

**Answers to Exercise 3**
1. Er hat kein Auto.
2. Sie möchte keinen Kaffee.
3. Er ist kein Professor.
4. Sie hat keine Einladung.
5. Wir haben keinen Hund.
6. Das ist nicht der Bahnhof.
7. Der Garten ist nicht groß.
8. Der Vater ist nicht alt.
9. Frau Meier ist nicht jung.
10. Santos ist nicht in Hamburg.

**Chapter 6 Illness**

**Section A**

**Answers to Exercise 1**
1. Ich habe Zahnschmerzen.
2. Ich habe Bauchschmerzen.
3. Ich habe Kopfschmerzen.
4. Ich habe Halsschmerzen.
5. Ich habe Ohrenschmerzen.
6. Ich habe Fieber.
7. Meine Füße tun weh.
8. Ich habe Durchfall.
9. Mein Knie tut weh.
10. Ich habe Fieber.

**Answers to Exercise 2**

| *Patient* | *Arzt* |
|---|---|
| 1. Guten Tag, Herr Doktor. | |
| | 2. Guten Tag. Was fehlt Ihnen? |
| 3. Ich habe Halsschmerzen. | |
| | 4. Seit wann haben Sie Halsschmerzen? |
| 5. Seit drei Tagen. | |
| | 6. Ich verschreibe Ihnen etwas für die Halsschmerzen. |

**Answers to Exercise 3**

| | |
|---|---|
| Mein Kopf tut weh. | Mein Arm tut weh. |
| Mein Bein tut weh. | Mein Bauch tut weh. |
| Mein Fuß tut weh. | Mein Ohr tut weh. |
| Meine Hand tut weh. | Mein Knie tut weh. |
| Mein Rücken tut weh. | Mein Zahn tut weh. |

**Section B**

**Answers to Exercise 4**
1. Nein, das ist kein gutes Buch.
2. Nein, das ist keine schöne Frau.
3. Nein, das ist keine ruhige Straße.
4. Nein, das ist kein ruhiges Zimmer.
5. Nein, das war kein schöner Abend.
6. Nein, das war keine gute Reise.
7. Nein, das war keine ruhige Nacht.
8. Nein, das war kein schöner Ausblick.

**Answers to Exercise 5**
1. Nein, ich habe keine ruhige Frau.
2. Nein, ich habe kein gutes Zimmer.
3. Nein, ich habe keinen schönen Ausblick.
4. Nein, ich habe kein neues Buch.
5. Nein, ich habe keinen neuen Fußball.
6. Nein, ich habe keinen guten Doktor.
7. Nein, ich habe keine nette Schwester.
8. Nein, ich habe keine ruhige Straße.

**Chapter 7 Shopping**

**Section A**

**Answers to Exercise 1**
1. *Verkäuferin*: Was darf es sein?
   *Kundin*: Ich möchte einen Rock.
   *Verkäuferin*: Welche Größe brauchen Sie?
   *Kundin*: Größe 40.
   *Verkäuferin*: An welches Material hatten Sie gedacht?
   *Kundin*: Popeline.
   *Verkäuferin*: Welche Farbe möchten Sie?
   *Kundin*: Ich möchte dunkelrot, bitte.
   *Verkäuferin*: Der ist sehr elegant.
   *Kundin*: Ja, er gefällt mir.
      Was kostet er?

2. *Verkäuferin*: Was darf es sein?
   *Kundin*: Ich möchte eine Bluse.
   *Verkäuferin*: Welche Größe brauchen Sie?
   *Kundin*: Größe 42.
   *Verkäuferin*: An welches Material hatten Sie gedacht?
   *Kundin*: Krepp.
   *Verkäuferin*: Welche Farbe möchten Sie?
   *Kundin*: Ich möchte rosa, bitte.
   *Verkäuferin*: Die ist sehr elegant.
   *Kundin*: Ja, sie gefällt mir.
      Was kostet sie?

3. *Verkäuferin*: Was darf es sein?
   *Kunde*: Ich möchte ein Hemd.
   *Verkäuferin*: Welche Größe brauchen Sie?
   *Kunde*: Größe 38.
   *Verkäuferin*: An welches Material hatten Sie gedacht?
   *Kunde*: Seide.
   *Verkäuferin*: Welche Farbe möchten Sie?
   *Kunde*: Ich möchte weiß, bitte.
   *Verkäuferin*: Das ist sehr elegant.
   *Kunde*: Ja, es gefällt mir.
   Was kostet es?

4. *Verkäuferin*: Was darf es sein?
   *Kunde*: Ich möchte eine Jacke.
   *Verkäuferin*: Welche Größe brauchen Sie?
   *Kunde*: Größe 46.
   *Verkäuferin*: An welches Material hatten Sie gedacht?
   *Kunde*: Leder.
   *Verkäuferin*: Welche Farbe möchten Sie?
   *Kunde*: Ich möchte dunkelbraun.
   *Verkäuferin*: Die ist sehr elegant.
   *Kunde*: Ja, sie gefällt mir.
   Was kostet sie?

**Answers to Exercise 2**
1. Ja, der gefällt mir. Was kostet er?
2. Ja, die gefällt mir. Was kostet sie?
3. Ja, das gefällt mir. Was kostet es?
4. Ja, die gefällt mir. Was kostet sie?
5. Ja, die gefällt mir. Was kostet sie?
6. Ja, der gefällt mir. Was kostet er?
7. Ja, der gefällt mir. Was kostet er?
8. Ja, die gefällt mir. Was kostet sie?
9. Ja, die gefällt mir. Was kostet sie?
10. Ja, das gefällt mir. Was kostet es?

**Section B**

**Answers to Exercise 3**
1. I'm only looking.
2. I'd like a pullover.
3. I don't know exactly.
4. Which material were you thinking of?
5. The blue pullover is certainly very nice.
6. I need a new pair of shoes.
7. I always wear size 40.
8. Can I try it on?
9. Have you any shoes with leather soles?
10. That's too expensive for me.

**Answers to Exercise 4**
1. Was kosten sie?

2. Die Schuhe gefallen mir gar nicht.
3. Sind die Sohlen aus Leder?
4. Haben Sie diese Art eine Größe kleiner?
5. Was kosten die braunen Schuhe im Schaufenster?
6. Ich möchte ein Nachthemd.
7. Ich schaue mich nur um.
8. Das Hemd ist aus Seide.
9. Was kosten die Schuhe?
10. Der Pullover ist mir zu teuer.

**Answers to Exercise 5**
1. Das weiße Hemd.
2. Die rote Hose.
3. Die schwarzen Schuhe.
4. Das lange Kleid.
5. Die braune Jacke.
6. Das hellblaue Hemd.
7. Der braune Anzug.
8. Der kurze Regenmantel.
9. Die grüne Bluse.
10. Das kleine schwarze Kleid.

## Chapter 8 Families and nationalities

**Section A**

**Answers to Exercise 1**
1. *Pfarrer*:   Sagen Sie, Herr Schmidt.
       Sind Sie verheiratet?
   *Herr Schmidt*:   Geschieden.
   *Pfarrer*:   Und haben Sie Kinder?
   *Herr Schmidt*:   Nein, ich habe keine Kinder.
   *Pfarrer*:   Es ist besser so.

2. *Pfarrer*:   Sagen Sie, Herr Schmidt.
       Sind Sie verheiratet?
   *Herr Schmidt*:   Nein, ich bin verwitwet.
   *Pfarrer*:   Und haben Sie Kinder?
   *Herr Schmidt*:   Ja, ich habe drei Kinder.
   *Pfarrer*:   Ach so!

3. *Pfarrer*:   Sagen Sie, Herr Schmidt.
       Sind Sie verheiratet?
   *Herr Schmidt*:   Ja, aber wir leben getrennt.
   *Pfarrer*:   Und haben Sie Kinder?
   *Herr Schmidt*:   Ja, ich habe ein Kind.
   *Pfarrer*:   Ach so!

4. *Pfarrer*:   Sagen Sie, Herr Schmidt.
       Sind Sie verheiratet?
   *Herr Schmidt*:   Nein, ich bin nicht verheiratet.

**Answers to Exercise 2**

1. *Question*: Sind Sie verheiratet?
   *Answer*: Ja.
   *Question*: Und haben Sie Kinder?
   *Answer*: Ja, wir haben ein Baby.

2. *Question*: Sind Sie verheiratet?
   *Answer*: Ja.
   *Question*: Und haben Sie Kinder?
   *Answer*: Ja, wir haben einen Sohn und eine Tochter.

3. *Question*: Sind Sie verheiratet?
   *Answer*: Ja.
   *Question*: Und haben Sie Kinder?
   *Answer*: Ja, wir haben zwei Töchter.

4. *Question*: Sind Sie verheiratet?
   *Answer*: Ja.
   *Question*: Und haben Sie Kinder?
   *Answer*: Ja, wir haben drei Söhne.

5. *Question*: Sind Sie verheiratet?
   *Answer*: Ja.
   *Question*: Und haben Sie Kinder?
   *Answer*: Ja, wir haben vier Söhne und eine Tochter.

**Section B**

**Answers to Exercise 3**

1. Ich bin Architekt.
2. Ich bin Lehrerin.
3. Ich bin Polizistin.
4. Ich bin Arzt.
5. Ich bin Studentin.
6. Ich bin Lehrer.
7. Ich bin Verkäufer.
8. Ich bin Verkäuferin.

**Chapter 9 Places and weather**

**Answers to Exercise 1**

1. Nicht weit von Bremen.
2. Nicht weit von Hannover.
3. Nicht weit von Bielefeld.
4. Nicht weit von Koblenz.
5. Nicht weit von Frankfurt.
6. Nicht weit von Mannheim.
7. Nicht weit von Nürnberg.
8. Nicht weit von München.
9. Nicht weit von Stuttgart.
10. Nicht weit von Salzburg.

**Answers to Exercise 2**
1. Kiel ist in Norddeutschland.
2. Passau ist in Süddeutschland.
3. Lübeck ist in Norddeutschland.
4. München ist in Süddeutschland.
5. Hamburg ist in Norddeutschland.
6. Augsburg ist in Süddeutschland.
7. Oldenburg ist in Norddeutschland.
8. Ulm ist in Süddeutschland.
9. Bremen ist in Norddeutschland.
10. Freiburg ist in Süddeutschland.

**Answers to Exercise 3**
1. Zu Weihnachten.
2. Bei meinen Eltern.
3. Aus diesem Grund.
4. Aus Versehen.
5. Bei diesem Wetter.
6. Mit dem Zug.
7. Zu Fuß.
8. Nach meiner Meinung/Meiner Meinung nach.
9. Bei der Arbeit.
10. Nach einer halben Stunde.

**Answers to Exercise 4**
1. Sie kommt mit einem eleganten Kleid.
2. Er hat einen süddeutschen Akzent.
3. Es gibt eine schöne Kirche dort.
4. Mein kleiner Bruder wohnt in Hamburg.
5. Bad Reichenhall ist nicht weit von einem hohen Berg.
6. Dort gibt es ein großes Kurhaus.
7. Bei Schaffhausen ist ein großer See.
8. Die Zugspitze ist ein hoher Berg.
9. Er hat ein weißes Hemd.
10. Sie trägt einen blauen Pullover.

**Chapter 10 Revision**

**Answers to Test 1**
Das ist meine Frau.
Das ist mein Vater.
Das ist meine Mutter.
Das ist mein Sohn.
Das ist meine Tochter.
Das ist mein Onkel.
Das ist meine Tante.

**Answers to Test 2**
Das ist unser Garten.
Das ist unsere Küche.

Das ist unser Schlafzimmer.
Das ist unsere Garage.
Das ist unser Hund.
Das ist unsere Katze.

## Answers to Test 3
1. Guten Morgen!
2. Prost/Zum Wohl!
3. Entschuldigen Sie bitte!
4. Viel Spaß/Viel Vergnügen!
5. Entschuldigen Sie vielmals!
6. Gute Besserung!
7. Gute Nacht!
8. Entschuldigung!/Entschuldigen Sie!
9. Entschuldigen Sie, bitte!
10. Guten Appetit!

## Answers to Test 4
Hiermit bestätige ich meine Reservierung für:
1. ein Doppelzimmer mit Bad
2. ein Einzelzimmer mit Dusche
3. ein Zweibettzimmer mit Dusche
4. ein Einzelzimmer
5. ein Doppelzimmer

für die Zeit vom:
1. 1. August bis zum 13. August einschließlich
2. 4. April bis zum 7. April einschließlich
3. 10. Juni bis zum 12. Juni einschließlich
4. 10. August bis zum 17. August einschließlich
5. 26. Februar bis zum 28. Februar einschließlich
Hochachtungsvoll.

## Answers to Test 5
*Empfang*:  Grüß Gott!
*You*:  Grüß Gott!
     Haben Sie ein Zimmer frei, bitte?
*Empfang*:  Möchten Sie ein Einzelzimmer oder ein Doppelzimmer?
*You*:  Ich möchte ein Doppelzimmer bitte.
*Empfang*:  Ja, das ist möglich.
     Fur wieviele Nächte, bitte?
*You*:  Für 3 Nächte bitte.
*Empfang*:  Möchten Sie das Zimmer mit Bad oder mit Dusche?
*You*:  Mit Dusche, bitte.
*Empfang*:  Ja, ein Doppelzimmer mit Dusche habe ich.
     Das geht in Ordnung.
*You*:  Was kostet das Zimmer?
*Empfang*:  Das Zimmer kostet 55 Mark pro Nacht.
*You*:  Ist das mit Frühstück?
*Empfang*:  Jawohl.
*You*:  Ist das mit Mehrwertsteuer?
*Empfang*:  Ja, selbstverständlich.

*You*: Ich nehme das Zimmer.
*Empfang*: Tragen Sie sich bitte ein.

## Answers to Test 6

1. *Reisender*: Wann fährt der Zug nach Freiburg ab?
   *Angestellte*: Er fährt um 9 Uhr 45 ab.
   *Reisender*: Wann kommt er in Freiburg an?
   *Angestellte*: Er kommt um 17.03 an.
   *Reisender*: Muß ich umsteigen?
   *Angestellte*: Nein, der Zug fährt direkt.

2. *Reisender*: Wann fährt der Zug nach Fulda ab?
   *Angestellte*: Er fährt um 11 Uhr 14 ab.
   *Reisender*: Wann kommt er in Fulda an?
   *Angestellte*: Er kommt um 13.36 an.
   *Reisender*: Muß ich umsteigen?
   *Angestellte*: Nein, der Zug fährt direkt.

3. *Reisender*: Wann fährt der Zug nach Basel ab?
   *Angestellte*: Er fährt um 12.10 ab.
   *Reisender*: Wann kommt er in Basel an?
   *Angestellte*: Er kommt um 17.46 an.
   *Reisender*: Muß ich umsteigen?
   *Angestellte*: Nein, der Zug fährt direkt.

4. *Reisender*: Wann fährt der Zug nach Freiburg ab?
   *Angestellte*: Er fährt um 15.34 ab.
   *Reisender*: Wann kommt er in Freiburg an?
   *Angestellte*: Er kommt um 17.03 an.
   *Reisender*: Muß ich umsteigen?
   *Angestellte*: Nein, der Zug fährt direkt.

5. *Reisender*: Wann fährt der Zug nach Karlsruhe ab?
   *Angestellte*: Er fährt um 13.37 ab.
   *Reisender*: Wann kommt er in Karlsruhe an?
   *Angestellte*: Er kommt um 16.02 an.
   *Reisender*: Muß ich umsteigen?
   *Angestellte*: Nein, der Zug fährt direkt.

6. *Reisender*: Wann fährt der Zug nach Basel ab?
   *Angestellte*: Er fährt um 17.04 ab.
   *Reisender*: Wann kommt er in Basel an?
   *Angestellte*: Er kommt um 17.46 an.
   *Reisender*: Muß ich umsteigen?
   *Angestellte*: Nein, der Zug fährt direkt.

7. *Reisender*: Wann fährt der Zug nach Freiburg ab?
   *Angestellte*: Er fährt um 14.42 ab.
   *Reisender*: Wann kommt er in Freiburg an?
   *Angestellte*: Er kommt um 17.03 an.
   *Reisender*: Muß ich umsteigen?
   *Angestellte*: Nein, der Zug fährt direkt.

8. *Reisender*: Wann fährt der Zug nach Frankfurt ab?
*Angestellte*: Er fährt um 10.00 ab.
*Reisender*: Wann kommt er in Frankfurt an?
*Angestellte*: Er kommt um 14.36 an.
*Reisender*: Muß ich umsteigen?
*Angestellte*: Nein, der Zug fährt direkt.

9. *Reisender*: Wann fährt der Zug nach Frankfurt ab?
*Angestellte*: Er fährt um 11 Uhr 14 ab.
*Reisender*: Wann kommt er in Frankfurt an?
*Angestellte*: Er kommt um 14.36 an.
*Reisender*: Muß ich umsteigen?
*Angestellte*: Nein, der Zug fährt direkt.

10. *Reisender*: Wann fährt der Zug nach Basel ab?
*Angestellte*: Er fährt um 16.03 ab.
*Reisender*: Wann kommt er in Basel an?
*Angestellte*: Er kommt um 17.46 an.
*Reisender*: Muß ich umsteigen?
*Angestellte*: Nein, der Zug fährt direkt.

**Answers to Test 7**
1. Oma ruft am Samstag an.
2. Ingrid geht am Dienstag aus.
3. Die Kinder räumen den Laden auf.
4. Mutter räumt die Spielzeuge auf.
5. Peter wäscht die Teller ab.
6. Inge kauft Lebensmittel ein.
7. Helmut wäscht am Sonntag auf.
8. Der Chef gibt seine Arbeit auf.
9. Maria schließt den Laden ab.
10. Oma geht am Samstag aus.

**Answers to Test 8**
**Dialogue A**
*Müller*: Entschuldigen Sie, bitte!
*Meier*: Ja, bitte?
*Müller*: Fährt dieser Bus nach Opladen?
*Meier*: Nach Opladen?
Nein, dieser Bus fährt nach Ludwigshafen.
*Müller*: Welcher Bus fährt nach Opladen?
*Meier*: Sie brauchen die Nummer 14.

**Dialogue B**
*Schmidt*: Entschuldigen Sie, bitte!
*Schüth*: Ja. Kann ich Ihnen helfen?
*Schmidt*: Fährt diese Straßenbahn zum Schauspielhaus?
*Schüth*: Nein, nicht zum Schauspielhaus.
Sie fährt zum Hofgarten.
*Schmidt*: Welche Straßenbahn fährt zum Schauspielhaus?
*Schüth*: Sie brauchen die Nummer 1.

Sie fährt zum Schauspielhaus.
*Schmidt*: Danke schön.

## Answers to Test 9
1. Der Professor heißt Doktor Schmidt.
2. Wo ist die Tasse?
3. Hier ist das Buch.
4. Der Kaffee ist heiß.
5. Hier ist die Frau.
6. Das Auto fährt schnell.
7. Der Mann heißt Herr Müller.
8. Die Einladung kommt heute.
9. Das Schlafzimmer ist groß.
10. Die Küche ist klein.

## Answers to Test 10

| *Arzt* | *Patient* |
|---|---|
| 1. Guten Tag. | |
| | 2. Guten Tag, Herr Doktor. |
| 3. Was fehlt Ihnen denn? | |
| | 4. Mein Bein tut weh. |
| 5. Ihr Bein? Ist es ein leichter Schmerz? | |
| | 6. Nein, es ist ein stichartiger Schmerz. |
| 7. Ach so, stichartig. Seit wann tut es weh? | |
| | 8. Seit drei Tagen. |
| 9. So, so. Drei Tage schon. Kein Fußball für Sie. | |
| | 10. O weh. |

## Answers to Test 11
Sepp: Ja, mein Kopf tut weh.
Ja, mein Bein tut weh.
Ja, mein Knie tut weh.
Ja, mein Rücken tut weh.
Ja, mein Hals tut weh.
Ja, mein Ellbogen tut weh.
Ja, mein Ohr tut weh.
Ja, meine Nase tut weh.
Ja, meine Schulter tut weh.
Ja, mein Finger tut weh.

## Answers to Test 12
1. Haben Sie dieses Material in blau?
2. Haben Sie diese Art eine Nummer kleiner?
3. Haben Sie diese Farbe in Wolle?
4. Haben Sie diese Farbe eine Nummer größer?
5. Haben Sie dieses Material in hellblau?
6. Haben Sie diese Art in Baumwolle?

7. Haben Sie diese Farbe in Polyester?
8. Haben Sie diese Art in schwarz?
9. Haben Sie diese Art in Velours?
10. Haben Sie diese Größe in weiß?

**Answers to Test 13**
1. Es ist sehr heiß im Sommer und es regnet im Winter.
2. Es ist sehr heiß im Sommer und es schneit im Winter.
3. Es regnet im Sommer und es regnet im Winter.
4. Es ist sehr heiß im Sommer und es ist sehr kalt im Winter.
5. Es ist sehr heiß im Sommer und es regnet im Winter.

## Chapter 11 Eating out

### Section A

**Answers to Exercise 1**
1. *A*:  Herr Ober! (Fräulein!)
    Ich möchte bestellen.
  *B*:  Ja, bitte schön?
  *A*:  Einmal Eisbein mit Sauerkraut.
  *B*:  Einmal Eisbein mit Sauerkraut.
    Möchten Sie etwas zu trinken?
  *A*:  Nein, danke.

2. *A*:  Herr Ober! (Fräulein!)
    Ich möchte bestellen.
  *B*:  Ja, bitte schön?
  *A*:  Zweimal Austern
  *B*:  Zweimal Austern
  *A*:  Zweimal Seezungenfilet.
  *B*:  Zweimal Seezungenfilet.
  *A*:  Zweimal Zigeunersteak.
  *B*:  Zweimal Zigeunersteak.
  *A*:  Zweimal Ananas.
  *B*:  Zweimal Ananas.
    Möchten Sie etwas zu trinken?
  *A*:  Eine Flasche Rheinwein, bitte.
  *B*:  Jawohl.

3. *A*:  Herr Ober! (Fräulein!)
    Ich möchte bestellen.
  *B*:  Ja, bitte schön?
  *A*:  Einmal Rührei mit Schinken.
  *B*:  Einmal Rührei.
  *A*:  Einmal Frankfurter.
  *B*:  Einmal Frankfurter.
  *A*:  Und einmal Forelle.
  *B*:  Einmal Forelle.
    Möchten Sie etwas zu trinken?
  *A*:  Dreimal Mineralwasser, bitte.
  *B*:  Jawohl.

244

## MENU

### HORS D'OEUVRES

Prawn cocktail
Jellied eel
Oysters

### SOUPS

Chicken soup with noodles
Goulash soup
Onion soup

### EGG DISHES

Scrambled egg
Fried eggs with ham
Omelette – various

### FISH DISHES

Rollmop herring
Poached trout with green salad and
 boiled potatoes
Fillet of Dover sole with French
 beans and boiled potatoes

### MEAT DISHES

Pickled knuckle of pork with
 sauerkraut
'Texas' steak with chips
 and mixed salad
Veal (or pork) escalope garnished
 with mushroom sauce and chips
Veal (or pork) escalope with
 breadcrumbs garnished with fried
 egg, salad and roast potatoes
Veal (or pork) escalope garnished
 with paprika sauce with onions,
 rice and green salad

### FOR CHILDREN

Scrambled egg with ham
Two Frankfurters with chips

### CHEESE

Emmenthal, butter, bread
Mixed cheese platter, butter, bread

### DESSERTS

Mixed cold stewed fruit
Grapefruit
Pancakes
Pineapple flambé with cherry
 brandy

### BEVERAGES

Beer   Pils
       Export
Quarter litre Moselle wine
              Rhine wine
Red wine

Sekt (German champagne)
Cognac
German brandy
Mineral water

Cup of coffee or tea
Pot (of coffee or tea)
**OUR PRICES INCLUDE SERVICE AND VAT**

4. *A*:   Herr Ober! (Fräulein!)
       Ich möchte bestellen.
   *B*:   Ja, bitte schön?
   *A*:   Einmal Rührei.
   *B*:   Einmal Rührei.
   *A*:   Einmal Spiegeleier mit Schinken.
   *B*:   Einmal Spiegeleier.
   *A*:   Einmal die Käseplatte.
   *B*:   Einmal die Käseplatte.
       Möchten Sie etwas zu trinken?
   *A*:   Zweimal Kaffee, bitte.
   *B*:   Jawohl.

245

**Answers to Exercise 2**
1. Haben Sie einen Tisch für drei?
2. Fräulein!
3. Ich möchte bestellen.
4. Zweimal Krabbencocktail und einmal Aal in Aspik.
5. Dreimal Texas Steak.
6. Zwei Viertel Rotwein und einen Pils.
7. Zahlen, bitte!

**Section B**

**Answers to Exercise 3**
1. Möchten Sie auch eine Vorspeise?
2. Möchten Sie auch ein Mineralwasser?
3. Möchten Sie auch einen Cognac?
4. Möchten Sie auch eine Gulaschsuppe?
5. Möchten Sie auch eine Forelle?
6. Möchten Sie auch Salzkartoffeln?
7. Möchten Sie auch Eisbein?
8. Möchten Sie auch ein Wiener Schnitzel?
9. Möchten Sie auch eine Käseplatte?
10. Möchten Sie auch ein gemischtes Kompott?

**Answers to Exercise 4**
1. Wieviel Uhr ist es?
   Es ist ein Uhr.
2. Wieviel Uhr ist es?
   Es ist Mittag.
3. Wieviel Uhr ist es?
   Es ist fünf (Minuten) nach neun.
4. Wieviel Uhr ist es?
   Es ist viertel nach sechs.
5. Wieviel Uhr ist es?
   Es ist fünfundzwanzig (Minuten) nach vier.
6. Wieviel Uhr ist es?
   Es ist halb zehn.
7. Wieviel Uhr ist es?
   Es ist zehn (Minuten) nach elf.
8. Wieviel Uhr ist es?
   Es ist zwanzig (Minuten) nach sechs.
9. Wieviel Uhr ist es?
   Es ist halb zehn.
10. Wieviel Uhr ist es?
    Es ist viertel vor drei.

**Chapter 12 Asking permission**

**Answers to Exercise 1**
Kann ich Ihr Auto borgen, bitte?
Kann ich Ihre Zahnbürste borgen, bitte?
Kann ich Ihre Zahnpasta borgen, bitte?

Kann ich Ihren Rasierapparat borgen, bitte?
Kann ich Ihre Zeitung borgen, bitte?

**Answers to Exercise 2**
1. Selbstverständlich
2. Auf keinen Fall
3. Aber natürlich
4. Nein, das ist unmöglich
5. Selbstverständlich
6. Nein, es tut mir leid
7. Auf keinen Fall
8. Auf keinen Fall
9. Aber natürlich
10. Selbstverständlich

**Answers to Exercise 3**
1. Darf ich hier parken?
2. Kann ich Ihr Fahrrad borgen, bitte?
3. Kann ich etwas Zucker borgen, bitte?
4. Kann ich das Auto nehmen, bitte?
5. Kann ich Ihre Zahnbürste borgen, bitte?

**Answers to Exercise 4**
1. Kann ich Ihre Zeitung sehen, bitte?
2. Kann ich Ihr Auto borgen, bitte?
3. Kann ich Ihre Lampe haben, bitte, Frau Fiebiger?
4. Kann ich Ihren Fernsehapparat nehmen, bitte?
5. Kann ich Ihr Radio borgen, bitte, Herr Fiebiger?
6. Kann ich bitte Ihren Regenmantel nehmen, Frau Fiebiger?
7. Kann ich bitte Ihren Rasierapparat haben, Herr Fiebiger?
8. Kann ich bitte Ihre Zahnpasta borgen?
9. Kann ich bitte Ihr Buch sehen, Frau Fiebiger?
10. Kann ich bitte Ihren Kamm haben, Herr Fiebiger?

**Chapter 13 Jobs and professions**

**Section A**

**Answers to Exercise 1**
1. Herr Moezer ist Bäcker.
2. Frau Hacker ist Friseuse.
3. Fräulein Siegling ist Studentin.
4. Herr Mader ist Taxifahrer.
5. Frau Meyer ist Hausfrau.
6. Fräulein Bauer ist Sekretärin.
7. Frau Augustin ist Kellnerin.
8. Herr Flohr ist Polizist.
9. Herr Kahle ist Techniker.
10. Herr Löb ist Lehrer (Hauptschullehrer).

**Answers to Exercise 2**

1. *A*: Was sind Sie von Beruf, Herr Löb?
   *B*: Ich bin Lehrer.
   *A*: Wann beginnen Sie mit der Arbeit?
   *B*: Um acht Uhr.
   *A*: Wann haben Sie Feierabend?
   *B*: Ich habe um vierzehn Uhr (zwei Uhr) Feierabend.

2. *A*: Was sind Sie von Beruf, Frau Hacker?
   *B*: Ich bin Friseuse.
   *A*: Wann beginnen Sie mit der Arbeit?
   *B*: Um neun Uhr.
   *A*: Wann haben Sie Feierabend?
   *B*: Ich habe um achtzehn Uhr (sechs Uhr) Feierabend.

3. *A*: Was sind Sie von Beruf, Frau Augustin?
   *B*: Ich bin Kellnerin.
   *A*: Wann beginnen Sie mit der Arbeit?
   *B*: Um vierzehn Uhr (zwei Uhr).
   *A*: Wann haben Sie Feierabend?
   *B*: Ich habe um zweiundzwanzig Uhr dreißig (halb elf) Feierabend.

4. *A*: Was sind Sie von Beruf, Herr Mader?
   *B*: Ich bin Taxifahrer.
   *A*: Wann beginnen Sie mit der Arbeit?
   *B*: Um fünf Uhr.
   *A*: Wann haben Sie Feierabend?
   *B*: Ich habe um dreizehn Uhr (ein Uhr) Feierabend.

5. *A*: Was sind Sie von Beruf, Herr Moezer?
   *B*: Ich bin Bäcker.
   *A*: Wann beginnen Sie mit der Arbeit?
   *B*: Um vier Uhr.
   *A*: Wann haben Sie Feierabend?
   *B*: Ich habe um elf Uhr Feierabend.

**Section B**

**Answers to Exercise 3**

1. Gefällt Ihnen die Farbe?
2. Gefällt Ihnen die Landschaft?
3. Gefällt Ihnen das Auto?
4. Gefallen Ihnen die Schuhe?
5. Gefällt Ihnen der Wind?
6. Gefällt Ihnen das Material?
7. Gefällt Ihnen das Wetter?
8. Gefällt Ihnen der Schnee?
9. Gefallen Ihnen die Geschäfte?
10. Gefällt Ihnen der Regen?

**Chapter 14 Accommodation**

**Section A**

**Answers to Exercise 1**
1. Ja, ich habe ein Wohnzimmer.
2. Ja, ich habe ein Eßzimmer.
3. Ja, ich habe eine Küche.
4. Ja, ich habe ein Badezimmer.
5. Ja, ich habe ein Schlafzimmer.
6. Ja, ich habe eine Toilette.

**Answers to Exercise 2**
1. Ja, ich habe ein Wohnzimmer.
2. Nein, eine Garage habe ich nicht.
3. Nein, ein Eßzimmer habe ich nicht.
4. Nein, eine Terrasse habe ich nicht.
5. Ja, ich habe eine Küche.
6. Nein, einen Balkon habe ich nicht.
7. Ja, ich habe ein Badezimmer.
8. Nein, einen Garten habe ich nicht.

**Answers to Exercise 3**
*Winkler*: Ich habe ein Schwimmbad.
*Helmut*: Ich habe auch ein Schwimmbad.
*Winkler*: Ich habe einen Balkon.
*Helmut*: Ich habe auch einen Balkon.
*Winkler*: Ich habe einen Tennisplatz.
*Helmut*: Ich habe auch einen Tennisplatz.
*Winkler*: Ich habe eine Terrasse.
*Helmut*: Ich habe auch eine Terrasse.
*Winkler*: Ich habe viele Bäume.
*Helmut*: Ich habe auch viele Bäume.
*Winkler*: Ich habe viele Sträuche.
*Helmut*: Ich habe auch viele Sträuche.

**Section B**

**Answers to Exercise 4**
1. Ja, er wohnt in München.
2. Nein, er hat eine Einzimmerwohnung.
3. Ja, er hat ein Badezimmer.
4. Ja, er hat eine Küche.
5. Ja, er hat viele Bilder.
6. Antonios Onkel wohnt in Neapel (Napoli).
7. Nein, er hat ein Einzelhaus.
8. Er hat sechs Schlafzimmer.
9. Er hat zwei Gästezimmer.
10. Nein, Antonio hat eine Sozialwohnung.
11. Ja, er hat ein Eßzimmer.
12. Ja, er hat ein Badezimmer.

13. Ja, er hat eine Küche.
14. Nein, er hat einen Balkon.

## Chapter 15 Hobbies and Interests

### Section A

**Answers to Exercise 1**
1. Ich tanze gern.
2. Ich wandere sehr gern.
3. Ich male wirklich sehr gern.
4. Ich lese außerordentlich gern.
5. Ich singe furchtbar gern.

**Answers to Exercise 2**
1. Ich koche nicht gern.
2. Ich bastele gar nicht gern.
3. Ich tanze überhaupt nicht gern.

**Answers to Exercise 3**
1. Nein, ich tanze nicht gern.
2. Nein, ich wandere nicht gern.
3. Ja, ich male gern.
4. Ja, ich spiele gern Karten.
5. Nein, ich fahre nicht gern Ski.
6. Ja, ich lese gern.
7. Nein, ich singe nicht gern.
8. Nein, ich reite nicht gern.

### Section B

**Answers to Exercise 4**
1. Ja, aber Rumenigge ist größer.
2. Ja, aber Rumenigge ist schneller.
3. Ja, aber Rumenigge ist gesünder.
4. Ja, aber Rumenigge ist stärker.
5. Ja, aber Rumenigge ist jünger.
6. Ja, aber Rumenigge ist klüger.
7. Ja, aber Rumenigge spielt härter.
8. Ja, aber Rumenigge spielt besser.

## Chapter 16 'Want' and 'Must'

**Answers to Exercise 1**
1. Ich muß mein Geld mitnehmen.
2. Ich muß meine Stiefel mitnehmen.
3. Ich muß meinen Tennisschläger mitnehmen.
4. Ich muß meine Landkarte mitnehmen.
5. Ich muß meine Eintrittskarten mitnehmen.

6. Ich muß meine Badehose mitnehmen.
7. Ich muß meinen Reisepaß mitnehmen.
8. Ich muß meine Zahnbürste mitnehmen.
9. Ich muß meinen Regenschirm mitnehmen.

**Answers to Exercise 2**
1. Er muß Elke besuchen.
2. Er muß die Karten abholen.
3. Er muß nach Nürnberg fahren.
4. Er muß eine Kette für Elke kaufen.
5. Er muß einen Tennisschläger kaufen.
6. Er muß nach Stuttgart fahren.
7. Er muß im Bett bleiben.

**Answers to Exercise 3**
1. Nein, Sie brauchen Ihre Stiefel nicht mitnehmen.
2. Nein, Sie brauchen Ihre Landkarte nicht mitnehmen.
3. Nein, Sie brauchen Ihre Badehose nicht mitnehmen.
4. Nein, Sie brauchen Ihre Zahnbürste nicht mitnehmen.
5. Nein, Sie brauchen Ihre Schuhe nicht mitnehmen.
6. Nein, Sie brauchen Ihren Smoking nicht mitnehmen.
7. Nein, Sie brauchen Ihren Mantel nicht mitnehmen.
8. Nein, Sie brauchen Ihre Tabletten nicht mitnehmen.
9. Nein, Sie brauchen Ihr Buch nicht mitnehmen.
10. Nein, Sie brauchen Ihren Tennisschläger nicht mitnehmen.

**Chapter 17 Suggestions and Proposals**

**Answers to Exercise 1**
1. a) Karlheinz! Wollen wir Fußball spielen?
   b) Ja, gern.
2. a) Karlheinz! Wollen wir reiten?
   b) Nein, ich kann nicht reiten.
3. a) Karlheinz! Wollen wir Karten spielen?
   b) Ja, gern.
4. a) Karlheinz! Wollen wir Tennis spielen?
   b) Nein, ich kann nicht Tennis spielen.
5. a) Karlheinz! Wollen wir schwimmen gehen?
   b) Nein, ich kann nicht schwimmen.
6. a) Gertraute! Wollen wir tanzen gehen.
   b) Ja, gern.
7. a) Gertraute! Wollen wir Ski fahren?
   b) Nein, ich kann nicht Ski fahren.
8. a) Gertraute! Wollen wir einen Spaziergang machen?
   b) Ja, gern.
9. a) Gertraute! Wollen wir Fußball spielen?
   b) Nein, ich kann nicht Fußball spielen.
10. a) Gertraute! Wollen wir Karten spielen?
    b) Nein, ich kann nicht Karten spielen.

**Answers to Exercise 2**
1. Ja, ausgezeichnet.
2. Nein, nicht sehr gut.
3. Ja, ausgezeichnet.
4. Nein, nicht sehr gut.
5. Nein, nicht sehr gut.
6. Ja, ausgezeichnet.
7. Nein, nicht sehr gut.
8. Nein, nicht sehr gut.
9. Ja, ausgezeichnet.

**Answers to Exercise 3**
1. Der Junge geht in die Schule.
2. Der Lehrer arbeitet in der Schule.
3. Die Klasse kommt in das Klassenzimmer.
4. Die Mädchen warten in dem Klassenzimmer.
5. Das Radio steht auf dem Tisch.
6. Ich stelle die Milch in den Kühlschrank.
7. Das Bild hängt an der Wand.
8. Ich halte meine Zeitung unter dem Arm.
9. Ich gehe an die Tür.
10. Ich stelle die Tasse auf den Tisch.

**Chapter 18 Dreams and Wishes**

**Answers to Exercise 1**
1. Ich möchte ihn reinigen lassen.
2. Ich möchte sie reparieren lassen.
3. Ich möchte ihn reinigen lassen.
4. Ich möchte ihn reparieren lassen.
5. Ich möchte es reinigen lassen.
6. Ich möchte sie reinigen lassen.
7. Ich möchte sie reparieren lassen.

**Answers to Exercise 2**
1. Ich möchte reisen (die Welt sehen).
2. Ich möchte bezahlen.
3. Ich möchte telefonieren.
4. Ich möchte schlafen.
5. Ich möchte gehen.
6. Ich möchte Peter besuchen.
7. Ich möchte Fräulein Braun sprechen.
8. Ich möchte München sehen.
9. Ich möchte nach Bonn fahren.
10. Ich möchte mein Geld wechseln.

**Answers to Exercise 3**
1. Ich möchte mir die Haare waschen lassen.
2. Er will seinen Apparat reparieren lassen.

3. Elke will New York besuchen.
4. Ich möchte die Welt sehen.
5. Er möchte nach Hamburg fahren.
6. Wir müssen das Geld wechseln.
7. Wir möchten bezahlen.
8. Sie muß sich ein neues Kleid machen lassen.
9. Kann ich bitte Herrn Schmidt sprechen.
10. Sie will ihren Pelzmantel reinigen lassen.

## Chapter 19 Talking about the past

**Answers to Exercise 1**
Montag – Ich bin nach Solingen gefahren.
Dienstag – Ich habe eine Armbanduhr gekauft.
Mittwoch – Ich habe eine Kette für Inge gesucht.
Donnerstag – Ich bin mit Elke ins Kino gegangen.
Freitag – Ich habe Wein mit Peter getrunken.
Samstag – Ich habe Bayern-München gegen Hamburg gesehen.
Sonntag – Ich bin in die Kirche gegangen.

**Answers to Exercise 2**
1. Ich war im Büro.
2. Ich war in der Post.
3. Ich war am Marktplatz.
4. Ich war im Gasthaus Bauer.
5. Ich war bei Müller.
6. Ich war im Café.
7. Ich war im Zug.

**Answers to Exercise 3**
1. Ich habe Bier getrunken.
2. Ich bin in die Stadt gegangen.
3. Er ist nach Bremen gefahren.
4. Wir sind um 8 Uhr gekommen.
5. Sie sind zu lange geblieben.
6. Sie hat ein Hemd gekauft.
7. Wir haben eine Wohnung gesucht.
8. Sie hat ihre Armbanduhr verloren.
9. Ich habe einen guten Film gesehen.
10. Sie haben Herrn Schüth getroffen.

## Chapter 20 Revision

**Answers to Test 1**
*Kellner*:   Guten Abend!
*Sie*:   Guten Abend!
   Haben Sie einen Tisch für zwei?
*Kellner*:   Kommen Sie, bitte.
*Sie*:   Herr Ober!
*Kellner*:   Bitte schön?

Sie: Die Speisekarte, bitte.
Kellner: Die Speisekarte, bitte schön.
Sie: Möchten Sie eine Vorspeise?
Freund(in): Ja, bitte.
Sie: Möchten Sie Austern?
Freund(in): Austern. O ja!
Sie: Zweimal Austern, bitte.
Kellner: Zweimal Austern.
Sie: Möchten Sie das Zigeuner Schnitzel?
Freund(in): Nein, danke. Ich möchte ein Jägerschnitzel.
Sie: Einmal Jägerschnitzel und einmal Wienerschnitzel.
Kellner: Jawohl.
Sie: Möchten Sie etwas zu trinken?
Freund(in): O ja. Ich möchte dein Jägerschnitzel.
Sie: Ich möchte auch einen Rotwein.
Zwei Viertel Rotwein, bitte.
Kellner: Jawohl, mein Herr.

**Answers to Test 2**

| Customer | Head waiter |
|---|---|
| Guten Abend! | Guten Abend! |
| Ich möchte einen Tisch | Fur wieviele Personen? |
| Für zwei | Kommen Sie, bitte. |

**Answers to Test 3**

| Customer | Head waiter |
|---|---|
| Guten Tag! | Guten Tag! |
| Ich möchte einen Tisch | Für wann? |
| Für heute abend. | Auf welchen Namen? |
| Schmidt | Für wieviele Personen? |
| Für zwei | Um wieviel Uhr? |
| Um acht Uhr | Ist in Ordnung |
| Auf Wiederhören! | |

**Answers to Test 4**

| | |
|---|---|
| Einmal Apfelkuchen | Dreimal Matjesfilet |
| Zweimal Brathähnchen | Zweimal Obstsalat |
| Ein gekochtes Ei | Einmal Pfeffersteak |
| Zweimal Ente | Zweimal Traubensaft |
| Dreimal Leber | Einmal Sauerkraut |
| Einmal Leberkäs | Dreimal Schweinefleisch |

**Answers to Test 5**
1. Kann ich einen Tisch borgen, bitte?
2. Kann ich ein Kleid borgen, bitte?
3. Kann ich einen Stuhl borgen, bitte?
4. Kann ich einen Pullover borgen, bitte?
5. Kann ich ein Hemd borgen, bitte?
6. Kann ich eine Bluse borgen, bitte?
7. Kann ich eine Jacke borgen, bitte?

8. Kann ich eine Hose borgen, bitte?
9. Kann ich einen Regenmantel borgen, bitte?
10. Kann ich ein Nachthemd borgen, bitte?

### Answer to Test 6
(Assume today is Wednesday):
Heute, gestern, vorgestern, morgen, übermorgen.

### Answers to Test 7
1. Ja, das Wetter gefällt mir.
2. Ja, der Sonnenschein gefällt mir.
3. Nein, der Regen gefällt mir nicht.
4. Ja, der Schnee gefällt mir.
5. Nein, der Wind gefällt mir nicht.
6. Ja, die Landschaft gefällt mir.
7. Ja, das Meer gefällt mir.
8. Nein, der Nebel gefällt mir nicht.
9. Nein, der Strand gefällt mir nicht.
10. Ja, die Berge gefallen mir.

### Answers to Test 8
1. Ich wohne in einem Haus.
2. Ich wohne in einer Eigentumswohnung.
3. Ich wohne in einem Einfamilienhaus.
4. Ich wohne in einem Reihenhaus.
5. Ich wohne in einem Mietshaus.
6. Ich wohne in einem Einzelhaus.
7. Ich wohne in einem Zweifamilienhaus.
8. Ich wohne in einer Wohnung.
9. Ich wohne in einer Sozialwohnung.
10. Ich wohne in einer Mietwohnung.

### Answers to Test 9
1. Ja, ich reite gern.
2. Ja, ich fahre gern Ski.
3. Ja, ich fahre gern mit dem Rad.
4. Ja, ich reise gern.
5. Nein, ich spiele nicht gern Klavier.
6. Nein, ich spiele nicht gern Karten.

### Answers to Test 10
1. Ich interessiere mich für Musik.
2. Ich interessiere mich für Bilder.
3. Ich interessiere mich für Bücher.
4. Ich interessiere mich für Fotografie.
5. Ich interessiere mich für Fußball.
6. Ich interessiere mich für Leichtathletik.

### Answers to Test 11
1. Am Donnerstag muß er einen Tennisschläger kaufen.
2. Am Dienstag muß er nach Nürnberg fahren.

3. Am Sonntag muß er Elke besuchen.
4. Am Mittwoch muß er eine Kette für Elke kaufen.
5. Am Montag muß er die Karten abholen.
6. Am Freitag muß er nach Stuttgart fahren.
7. Am Samstag muß er im Bett bleiben.

**Answers to Test 12**

1. Können Sie Tennis spielen?
2. Wollen wir spazieren gehen?
3. Können Sie tanzen?
4. Er kann schwimmen.
5. Sie wollen Fußball spielen.
6. Wir können Karten spielen.
7. Wollen wir nach London fahren?
8. Kann sie singen?
9. Er will nicht trinken.
10. Sie können nicht schwimmen.

# TRANSLATIONS
# OF DIALOGUES

The following translations give equivalents of the German dialogues.

**Chapter 1 Greetings and Introductions**

**Dialogue 1**
1   *Secretary*:   Ah Professor Hecht! Good Morning (Good Afternoon).
      *Professor Hecht*:   Good morning, Mrs Hausmann.
      Is Mr Kirchhof there?
      *Secretary*:   Yes, just a moment.
5      Mr Kirchhof ...
      Professor Hecht is here.
      . . .
      *Mr Kirchhof*:   Good morning, Professor Hecht.
      *Prof. Hecht*:   Good morning, Mr Kirchhof.
      *Mr Kirchhof*:   Please come in.
10   *Prof. Hecht*:   Thank you.
      How are you?
      *Mr Kirchhof*:   Very well, thank you.
      Please sit down.
      *Prof. Hecht*:   Thank you.
15   *Mr Kirchhof*:   Would you like a cup of coffee?
      *Prof. Hecht*:   Oh yes, please.
      *Mr Kirchhof*:   Mrs Hausmann, two cups of
      coffee, please.
      *Mrs Hausmann*:   Certainly.
20   *Mr Kirchhof*:   Now, how is your wife?
      *Prof. Hecht*:   Very well indeed.
      *Mr Kirchhof*:   And how are Andreas and Daniella?
      *Prof. Hecht*:   Very well, too.
      *Mr Kirchhof*:   And here is the catalogue.
25   *Prof. Hecht*:   Yes, the catalogue.

**Dialogue 2**
1   *Elke*:   Good evening!
      *Doctor Neumann*:   Elke, good evening!
      *Elke*:   How nice.
      Do come in.

5  *Dr Neumann*:  Thank you.
     Can I introduce my wife?
     *Elke*:  Good evening, Mrs Neumann.
     Welcome!
     *Mrs Neumann*:  Good evening
10  Thank you for the invitation.
     *Elke*:  Not at all.
     That's Fritz.
     *Fritz*:  Good evening!
     My name is Löb.
15  *Elke*:  Eckhard!
     *Eckhard*:  Elke!
     *Elke*:  You here!
     This is marvellous!
     *Eckhard*:  Elke, you are as beautiful as ever.
20  *Elke*:  Oh no.
     *Eckhard*:  Yes you are.
     *Elke*:  Oh yes.
     That's Fritz.
     *Eckhard*:  My name is Becker.
25  Pleased to meet you.
     *Fritz*:  My name is Löb.
     Pleased to meet you.
     *Elke*:  Excuse me!

     *Prof. Hecht*:  Goodbye.
30  Thank you very much.
     *Elke*:  Not at all.
     Goodbye.

## Chapter 2: Getting about

**Dialogue 1**
1  *Mrs Meyer*:  Excuse me!
     How do I get to the Amalienstraße,
     please?
     *Pedestrian*:  Sorry?
     *Mrs Meyer*:  The Amalienstraße.
5  How do I get to the Amalienstraße?
     *Pedestrian*:  Now let me see, the Amalienstraße.
     *Mrs Meyer*:  Terrible!
     quite terrible!
     *Pedestrian*:  Sorry?
10  *Mrs Meyer*:  Everything is new here.
     *Pedestrian*:  Yes, that's right.
     To the Adriastraße, wasn't it?
     *Mrs Meyer*:  No, not the Adriastraße,
     to the Amalienstraße.
     How do I get to the Amalienstraße?
15  *Pedestrian*:  Oh yes.
     go straight on,

then take the first street on the
left.
*Mrs Meyer*:  The first street on the left.
*Pedestrian*:  That's Market Street.
20  Go up Market Street,
   then you come to the Amalienstraße.
*Mrs Meyer*:  Thank you.
*Pedestrian*:  That's quite all right.

**Dialogue 2**
1  *Elke*:  Excuse me!
   How do we get to Mittenwald?
*Boy*:  Sorry?
*Elke*:  To Mittenwald.
5  *Boy*:  I don't know.
*Elke*:  Thank you.
   (Under her breath)
   Silly idiot!
   You, Fritz, ask that girl over there.
*Fritz*:  Excuse me!
10  How do we get to Mittenwald?
*Girl*:  To Mittenwald?
   Go straight on.
*Fritz*:  Straight on.
*Girl*:  To Garmisch.
15  Turn left when you get there.
   That is the B28.
*Fritz*:  Is it far?
*Girl*:  No.
   About twenty kilometres.
20  *Fritz*:  Thank you.
*Girl*:  Keep going towards Innsbruck.
*Fritz*:  Towards Innsbruck.
   Thank you.
*Girl*:  That's all right.

**Chapter 3 Staying in hotels**

**Dialogue 1**
1  *Antonio*:  Good evening!
*Receptionist*:  Good evening!
*Antonio*:  I want to reserve a room.
*Receptionist*:  Yes, how long for?
5  *Antonio*:  Five nights
   Monday to Saturday.
*Receptionist*:  A single room or a
   double room?
*Antonio*:  A double room.
*Receptionist*:  With bath or shower?
10  *Antonio*:  With a shower.
   A quiet room.

*Receptionist*:   Yes the room is nice and quiet.
*Antonio*:   Good.
*Receptionist*:   What is the name, please?
15   *Antonio*:   Santos. S-A-N-T-O-S.
*Receptionist*:   Thank you very much.
*Antonio*:   How much is the room?
*Receptionist*:   It costs 60 marks a night.
*Antonio*:   Is that with breakfast?
20   *Receptionist*:   Yes, that's with breakfast
and VAT.
*Antonio*:   Thank you.
*Receptionist*:   That's all right.


**Dialogue 2**

1   *Elke*:   Good afternoon!
*Receptionist*:   Good afternoon!
*Elke*:   Have you a room, please?
*Receptionist*:   Yes.
5      What sort of room?
*Elke*:   A single room.
With bathroom.
*Receptionist*:   For how many nights?
*Elke*:   I'm staying two nights.
10   *Receptionist*:   A single room with a bathroom.
Yes, I can do that.
*Elke*:   What does the room cost?
*Receptionist*:   It costs 95 marks a night
with breakfast.
*Elke*:   I'll take it.
15   *Receptionist*:   Would you please sign the register.
. . .
Your room is on the fifth floor.
*Elke*:   Has the room got a view?
*Receptionist*:   Yes, it's got a lovely view
over the Alster.
20   *Elke*:   How nice.
*Receptionist*:   Have you any luggage?
*Elke*:   Yes, my luggage is here.
*Receptionist*:   Porter!


**Dialogue 3**

1   *Receptionist*:   Hotel Bayerischer Hof.
*Fritz*:   Good afternoon!
Have you a room available for next
Saturday, please?
*Receptionist*:   For the 12th?
5   *Fritz*:   Yes, for Saturday the 12th.
*Receptionist*:   No, I'm sorry,
we're completely booked up.
*Fritz*:   Thank you.
*Receptionist*:   Not at all.

### Chapter 4: Travelling by train

**Dialogue 1**

1   *Mrs Meyer*:   Good morning!
    *Clerk*:   Good morning!
    *Mrs Meyer*:   Second class ticket to Augsburg,
    please.
    *Clerk*:   Single or return?
5   *Mrs Meyer*:   Return please.
    How much is that?
    *Clerk*:   Thirty-two marks.
    *Mrs Meyer*:   What? As much as that!
    *Clerk*:   Sorry!
10   *Mrs Meyer*:   That's terrible!
    *Clerk*:   There's nothing I can do about it.
    *Mrs Meyer*:   Forty marks.
    *Clerk*:   (counts) 33, 34, 35, 40, thank you.
    *Mrs Meyer*:   Thank you.
15   (still grumbling) Thirty two marks.
    That's terrible!

    *Mrs Meyer*:   Excuse me!
    *Information*:   Yes?
    *Mrs Meyer*:   What time is the train to Augsburg?
20   *Information*:   Augsburg ... Augsburg ....
    The train leaves at 9.27 a.m.,
    and arrives at 10.13.
    *Mrs Meyer*:   Thank you.
    Do I have to change?
25   *Information*:   No. It's a through train.
    *Mrs Meyer*:   Thank you.
    *Information*:   You're welcome.

**Dialogue 2**

1   *Antonio*:   Good morning!
    *Clerk*:   Good morning!
    *Antonio*:   Two second class tickets to Innsbruck.
    please.
    *Clerk*:   Single or return?
5   *Antonio*:   Single, please.
    *Clerk*:   Two singles to Innsbruck.
    Ninety-eight marks, please.
    *Antonio*:   Just a minute.
    A ticket to Innsbruck, too.
10   *Clerk*:   Single?
    *Antonio*:   No.
    Return.
    *Clerk*:   Two singles.
    One return.
15   Is that right?
    *Antonio*:   Yes, that's right.
    *Clerk*:   That's 196 marks, please.

*Antonio*:   What time does the train leave for
        Innsbruck?
*Information*:   At 9.31.
20   *Antonio*:   Thank you.
        Which platform?
*Information*:   Platform 3.
*Antonio*:   Thank you.
*Information*:   That's OK.


**Chapter 5: Travelling by taxi, bus or tram**

**Dialogue 1**
1   *Elke*:   I want a taxi,
        please.
*Clerk*:   What name?
*Elke*:   Kustmann.
5   *Clerk*:   What's your address?
*Elke*:   Fürstenstraße 15.
*Clerk*:   Where do you want to go to?
*Elke*:   To the Nietzschestraße.
*Clerk*:   The taxi will be there in 10 minutes.
10   *Elke*:   Thank you.

*Taxi Driver*:   Mrs Kustmann?
*Elke*:   Yes.
*Taxi Driver*:   Your taxi is here.
15   *Elke*:   Nietzschestraße,
        please.
        Number 30.
*Taxi Driver*:   All right.

        Here you are.
20   *Elke*:   How much is that?
*Taxi driver*:   6 marks 50.
*Elke*:   Thank you.
        That's all right.
25   *Taxi driver*:   Thank you.
        Goodbye.

**Dialogue 2**
1   *Mrs Meyer*:   Excuse me!
        Does the number 23 go to the town hall?
*Man*:   No, not the 23.
*Mrs Meyer*:   Good heavens!
5   Which tram does go to the
        town hall then?
*Man*:   You need number 18.
        The 18 goes to the town hall.
*Mrs Meyer*:   I see, thank you very much.
        The number 18.
10   *Man*:   Yes, that goes to the town hall.

*Mrs Meyer*: (to herself)
That's unheard of!!
It was always the 23!!

## Chapter 6: Illness

### Dialogue 1

1   *Receptionist*:  Doctor Storm's surgery.
   Good morning.
   *Mrs Meyer*:  Good morning.
   I'd like to see the doctor.
5   *Receptionist*:  Have you got an appointment?
   *Mrs Meyer*:  No.
   Is this morning possible?
   *Receptionist*:  No.
   I'm sorry.
10   There's no time available this morning.
   *Mrs Meyer*:  Oh heavens above!
   Isn't there any time available?
   *Receptionist*:  No.
   I'm sorry.
15   *Mrs Meyer*:  Is this afternoon possible?
   *Receptionist*:  Yes. Come at 4 o'clock.
   *Mrs Meyer*:  Thank goodness!
   At 4 o'clock.
   Yes, that's all right.
20   Thank you.
   *Receptionist*:  Goodbye.
   *Mrs Meyer*:  Goodbye.

### Dialogue 2

1   *Doctor Storm*:  Now, what's the matter?
   *Fritz*:  I've got a headache.
   *Doctor Storm*:  Is that all?
   *Fritz*:  No, doctor.
5   I've got a pain in my stomach and I've got diarrhoea.
   *Doctor Storm*:  How long have you had diarrhoea?
   *Fritz*:  Since yesterday.
   *Doctor Storm*:  I'll prescribe something
   for the diarrhoea.
   *Fritz*:  Thank you, doctor.

### Dialogue 3

1   *Doctor Storm*:  Now, where does it hurt?
   *Antonio*:  Here,
   It's my back.
   *Doctor Storm*:  Here?
5   *Antonio*:  Ow!! Yes!
   *Doctor Storm*:  Is it a sharp pain?
   *Antonio*:  Yes! It's a shooting pain.

*Doctor Storm*:   Is it always a shooting pain?
*Antonio*:   No.
10     In the night it was a dull pain.
*Doctor Storm*:   I see.
No more football for you.
*Antonio*:   Oh dear.


**Chapter 7: Shopping**

**Dialogue 1**
1    *Saleswoman*:   Can I help you?
*Fritz*:   (speaking by instinct)
I'm just looking round.
*Saleswoman*:   Yes, of course.
*Fritz*:   (clears his throat)
Miss!
5    *Saleswoman*:   Yes? Can I help you?
*Fritz*:   I want a pullover.
*Saleswoman*:   Yes. A gentleman's or a lady's pullover?
*Fritz*:   I'm looking for a lady's pullover.
*Saleswoman*:   Yes. What size does the lady take?
10   *Fritz*:   Oh I don't know exactly.
Medium size, I think.
*Saleswoman*:   Like me?
*Fritz*:   (embarrassed and trying not to look too closely)
Yes, about like that.
*Saleswoman*:   Yes, that's size 40.
15     What material were you thinking of?
*Fritz*:   Oh yes. The material? Of course.
*Saleswoman*:   Wool? Cotton? Nylon?
*Fritz*:   Wool! Yes, wool.
*Saleswoman*:   I've got a lovely red pullover here.
20     It's made of wool.
*Fritz*:   No. She's already got a red pullover.
Have you got this sort of thing in blue?
*Saleswoman*:   Has the lady got blue eyes?
*Fritz*:   Yes, (she has) actually.
25   *Saleswoman*:   I've got a blue pullover here.
*Fritz*:   Yes. The blue pullover is really very nice.
What does it cost?
*Saleswoman*:   65 Marks.
*Fritz*:   I'll take it.

**Dialogue 2**
1    *Salesman*:   Can I help you?
*Mrs Meyer*:   I need some new shoes.
*Salesman*:   Yes, of course.
(looking at Mrs Meyer's shoes)
You take size 4½, I think.
5    *Mrs Meyer*:   No. I always take size 4.

*Salesman*:   (sceptically)
    Really?
*Mrs Meyer*:   How much do the brown shoes cost in the window?
*Salesman*:   They are size 4½.
10  *Mrs Meyer*:   Have you got the brown shoes a size smaller?
*Salesman*:   Yes, I've got the same shoes here.
    But they're black.
*Mrs Meyer*:   Can I try them on?
15  *Salesman*:   Of course you can try them on.
*Mrs Meyer*:   (taking a few steps)
    Ow!!! That hurts!
    They're too small.
*Salesman*:   Would you like to try on the brown shoes?
*Mrs Meyer*:   Are the soles made of leather?
20  *Salesman*:   No. The brown shoes have got crepe soles.
*Mrs Meyer*:   Crepe soles! That's terrible!
    I don't like that at all.
    Haven't you got any shoes with leather soles?
25  *Salesman*:   Certainly.
    Look!
    These blue shoes are very elegant.
    They are made entirely of leather.
*Mrs Meyer*:   What size are they?
30  *Salesman*:   Size 4½.
*Mrs Meyer*:   How much do they cost?
*Salesman*:   They cost 145 marks.
*Mrs Meyer*:   What? That's too expensive!
    Goodbye!
35  *Salesman*:   Goodbye!
*Mrs Meyer*:   (grumbling to herself) Disgusting! It's
    disgusting! 145 marks!


## Chapter 8 Families and nationalities

**Dialogue 1**
1  *Antonio*:   Good day!
*Owner*:   Good day!
*Antonio*:   I've come about the job
    as a waiter.
*Owner*:   Oh yes.
5    Do you have any experience?
*Antonio*:   No, unfortunately.
*Owner*:   Hmm. Can you speak Italian?
*Antonio*:   Of course.
    I am Italian.
10  *Owner*:   Oh, you are Italian.
    Where do you come from?
*Antonio*:   I come from Naples.
*Owner*:   Naples! Naples!
    I come from Benevento.
15  *Antonio*:   That's wonderful!

My Aunt Concetta comes from
Benevento.
*Owner*: No!
*Antonio*: Yes, she does.
*Owner*: That's fantastic!
20    When can you begin?

**Dialogue 2**
1  *Parson*: The church is very old, Mr
Löb.
*Fritz*: Yes, one can see that.
*Parson*: Over three hundred years old.
*Fritz*: Really?
5  *Parson*: Yes
Look.
The altar is beautiful, isn't it?
*Fritz*: That's true.
It's very beautiful.
10  *Parson*: Riemenschneider.
*Fritz*: Really.
Tilman Riemenschneider.
*Parson*: Yes.
Tell me, Mr Löb.
15  What do you do (What are you by profession?)
if I may ask? (If you don't mind my asking?)
*Fritz*: I'm a teacher.
In Munich.
*Parson*: Really.
Are you married?
20  *Fritz*: Yes. That's to say, we're
separated.
*Parson*: I'm sorry.
*Fritz*: Thank you.
*Parson*: Have you got any children?
*Fritz*: No, I haven't got any children.
25  *Parson*: Perhaps it's better that way.
*Fritz*: Yes, it's better that way.
Young children need a father.
*Parson*: That's right.

**Chapter 9: Places and weather**

**Dialogue 1**
1  *Man*: I beg your pardon!
*Elke*: Yes?
*Man*: I just wanted to say ...
that's a very elegant dress.
5  *Elke*: Oh, thank you.
That's very nice of you.
*Man*: You have a north German accent.

266

*Elke*:  Yes. I come from Mölln.
*Man*:  Mölln? Where is Mölln?
10 *Elke*:  In North Germany.
   Not far from Hamburg.
*Man*:  Oh yes. Near Hamburg.
*Elke*:  Yes. Between Hamburg and Lübeck.
*Man*:  What is the countryside like there?
15 *Elke*:  There's a large lake there,
   and a very beautiful church.
*Man*:  Have you still got any family there?
*Elke*:  Yes. My brother lives in Mölln,
   with my parents.
*Man*:  Oh, you've got a brother.
20 *Elke*:  Yes. He's coming to Munich next week.
   He's an enthusiastic skier.
*Man*:  Isn't there any snow in Mölln then?
*Elke*:  No. It rains a lot in winter.
   But there's not much snow.
25 *Man*:  Oh, I see.


**Dialogue 2**
1 *Antonio*:  Cheers!
*Girl*:  Cheers!
*Antonio*:  Are you from Munich
*Girl*:  No. I come from Bad Reichenhall.
5 *Antonio*:  Where is Bad Reichenhall?
*Girl*:  Not far from Salzburg.
   And you?
*Antonio*:  I come from Naples.
   But I'm a 'Münchener' now.
10 *Girl*:  Oh, I see.
*Antonio*:  What is there to see there,
   in Bad Reichenhall?
*Girl*:  There is a fine pump room,
   and nice shops.
*Antonio*:  And the countryside?
   What is the countryside like there?
15 *Girl*:  Oh the countryside is wonderful!
   There are high mountains.
*Antonio*:  That's nice.
*Girl*:  Yes. The Predigtstuhl for example.
   That is a very high mountain.
20 *Antonio*:  What's the weather like?
*Girl*:  It's usually nice.
   There is a lot of snow in winter.
*Antonio*:  And in summer?
*Girl*:  It rains sometimes in summer.
25   Unfortunately.

**Chapter 11: Eating out**

**Dialogue 1**
1   *Owner*:   Blue House Restaurant.
     Good morning (or good afternoon).
     *Fritz*:   Good morning!
     I should like a table for this evening.
5   *Owner*:   For how many people?
     *Fritz*:   For two.
     *Owner*:   At what time?
     *Fritz*:   At 8 o'clock.
     *Owner*:   Yes, at 8 o'clock.
10    I have a table for 8 o'clock.
     *Fritz*:   Good.
     *Owner*:   What name please?
     *Fritz*:   Löb (spells his name) L – Ö – B.
     *Owner*:   Mr Löb.
15    That's all right, Mr Löb.
     *Fritz*:   Goodbye.
     *Owner*:   Goodbye.

     *Fritz*:   Good evening!
     *Reception*:   Good evening!
20   *Fritz*:   I have reserved a table.
     *Reception*:   For how many people?
     *Fritz*:   For two people.
     *Reception*:   What name, please?
     *Fritz*:   Löb.
25   *Reception*:   Oh, yes.
     Mr Löb
     This way, please.

**Dialogue 2**
1   *Fritz*:   Would you like a starter?
     *Elke*:   I'd like some soup –
     some onion soup.
     *Fritz*:   And then?
     *Elke*:   A Texas steak.
5    And you?
     What would you like?
     *Fritz*:   I think I'd like some soup, too –
     some goulash soup.
     And then ... Texas steak as well.
10   *Waiter*:   Have you chosen?
     *Fritz*:   One onion soup.
     One goulash soup.
     *Waiter*:   One onion soup.
     One goulash soup.
15   *Fritz*:   And then – two Texas steaks.

*Elke*: Without chips, please.
*Waiter*: Two Texas steaks.
One with chips.
One without.
20    Very good.
*Fritz*: Would you like something to drink?
*Elke*: Yes, I'd like a quarter of red wine, please.
*Fritz*: Two quarters of red wine, please.
*Waiter*: Two quarters of red wine.
25    Thank you.


## Chapter 12: Asking permission

### Dialogue 1

1   *Antonio*: Excuse me!
(louder) Excuse me!
*Policeman*: Yes?
*Antonio*: Can I park here?
5  *Policeman*: No. Sorry.
You're not allowed to park here.
*Antonio*: (pointing) What about over there?
Can I park over there?
*Policeman*: No.
10  You're not allowed to park there either.
*Antonio*: Damn!
Where can I park then?
*Policeman*: In the multi-storey car park.
Drive to the multi-storey car park.
15  *Antonio*: To the car park! To the car park!
OK, to the car park.

### Dialogue 2

1   *Mrs Meyer*: Yes?
Oh, it's you, Mr Löb.
*Fritz*: Good morning, Mrs Meyer!
Excuse me for disturbing you.
5  *Mrs Meyer*: What can I do for you?
*Fritz*: Mrs Meyer, my car won't start.
The battery has run out, I think.
*Mrs Meyer*: I'm sorry.
*Fritz*: Can I borrow your bicycle?
10  *Mrs Meyer*: My bicycle?
Yes, of course you can.
It's downstairs in the cellar.
*Fritz*: Thank you very much.
Oh, can I borrow the pump as well?
15  *Mrs Meyer*: Of course you can.
You can borrow the pump too.
*Fritz*: Thank you very much.
*Mrs Meyer*: That's quite all right.

Mind how you go.
20 *Fritz*:  Yes, of course.


## Chapter 13: Jobs and professions

### Dialogue 1
1 *Mrs Meyer*:  Yes?
   Oh, it's you. Mr Löb.
   *Fritz*:  Good morning, Mrs Meyer.
   Excuse me for disturbing you.
5   Here is your bicycle.
   *Mrs Meyer*:  Thank you very much.
   Was everything all right?
   *Fritz*:  Yes, everything was all right.
   Thank you very much.
10 *Mrs Meyer*:  You are a teacher, aren't you?
   *Fritz*:  Yes, that's right.
   *Mrs Meyer*:  Do you like your work?
   *Fritz*:  Oh yes, very much.
   *Mrs Meyer*:  When do you begin in the morning?
15 *Fritz*:  We begin at eight o'clock.
   *Mrs Meyer*:  Oh, I see.
   And when do you normally come home?
   *Fritz*:  I usually come home about two o'clock.
   *Mrs Meyer*:  How many days do you work a week?
20 *Fritz*:  Only five.
   Thank heavens!
   *Mrs Meyer*:  When I was a schoolgirl,
   we had school on Saturdays too.
   *Fritz*:  Yes, we are better off.
25   Now, thank you very much again for the bicycle.
   *Mrs Meyer*:  That's quite all right, Mr Löb.
   Goodbye.


### Dialogue 2
1 *Man*:  What do you do (for a living),
   if you don't mind my asking?
   *Elke*:  I'm a sales assistant.
   *Man*:  Here in Munich?
   *Elke*:  Yes, at Zilling Fashions.
5   In the Leopoldstraße.
   *Man*:  Do you like the work?
   *Elke*:  Oh, yes and no.
   The pay is very good.
   *Man*:  When do you begin work?
10 *Elke*:  At eight o'clock.
   *Man*:  And do you have a midday break?
   *Elke*:  Yes. From twelve to one.
   *Man*:  I have a midday break from twelve to one too.
   *Elke*:  (ironically) Well now!

15 *Man*:  When do you come home in the evening?
     *Elke*:  I'm free at five o'clock.
     *Man*:  Me too.
       Could I pick you up at your shop?
       I have a car.
20     Perhaps we could drive out into the country.
     *Elke*:  Thank you very much.
       But I have my own car.
     *Man*:  Oh, I see.
     *Elke*:  And today my boyfriend is coming at five o'clock.
25     We want to go shopping in the Viktualien Market.
     *Man*:  Oh, that's a pity.
       Some other time perhaps.
     *Elke*:  Perhaps.

## Chapter 14: Accommodation

### Dialogue 1

1 *Antonio*:  Cheers!
  *Fritz*:  Cheers!
  *Antonio*:  The punch is nice and warm, isn't it?
  *Fritz*:  Yes, nice and warm.
5 *Antonio*:  Do you live here in Munich?
  *Fritz*:  Yes, I live in the Nietzschestraße.
  *Antonio*:  Do you live in a block of flats?
  *Fritz*:  Yes, I have a one-room flat,
    in a large house divided up into flats.
10 *Antonio*:  Have you only got one room?
  *Fritz*:  Well, I have a bathroom,
    and a kitchen.
  *Antonio*:  Anything else?
  *Fritz*:  Apart from that I have a bed-sitting room.
  *Antonio*:  Is the flat nice?
15 *Fritz*:  Yes, it's small but quite nice.
    I have a lot of pictures there.
  *Antonio*:  Pictures?
  *Fritz*:  Yes.
    I collect pictures.
20 *Antonio*:  Hmm, interesting.

### Dialogue 2

1 *Antonio*:  My uncle has got lots of pictures too.
  *Fritz*:  Where does he live?
  *Antonio*:  In Naples.
  *Fritz*:  Ah, in Naples.
5 *Antonio*:  He's got a detached house.
  *Fritz*:  That's nice.
  *Antonio*:  He's got six bedrooms
    and two guest-rooms.
  *Fritz*:  Good heavens!

*Antonio*: Just imagine that!
10     Six bedrooms!
*Fritz*: Has he got a garden too?
*Antonio*: I should say so!
    He's got trees
    and bushes everywhere.
*Fritz*: Very nice.
15   *Antonio*: As for me ...
    I've got a council flat,
    in the Kaufmannstraße.
*Fritz*: How many rooms have you got?
*Antonio*: I've got a dining-room,
    and a bedroom.
*Fritz*: You've got a bathroom
    and a kitchen?
20   *Antonio*: Of course!
    And I've got a balcony.
    That's nice.


**Chapter 15: Hobbies and Interests**


**Dialogue 1**
1   *Fritz*: Won't you come in?
*Elke*: Thank you.
*Fritz*: This is my one-room flat.
*Elke*: It's very nice.
5   *Fritz*: It's unfortunately a bit too small.
*Elke*: You've got a lot of pictures,
    but they are all of churches.
*Fritz*: Yes, I'm interested in churches.
*Elke*: Yes, so I see.
10   *Fritz*: You know,
    I like photography.
    I like taking pictures of churches.
*Elke*: Yes, so I see.
*Fritz*: Would you like a cup of coffee?
15   *Elke*: Oh yes, please.
*Fritz*: Look ...
    this church is beautiful, isn't it?
*Elke*: Hmm.
*Fritz*: It's Romanesque.
20   *Elke*: Really?
*Fritz*: Yes. I'm very interested in Romanesque churches.
    I like taking photographs of them.
*Elke*: Yes, so I see.
*Fritz*: Oh, excuse me.
25   Your coffee.
    Do you take sugar?
*Elke*: No, thank you.

**Dialogue 2**

 1  *Student*:  Antonio!
    *Antonio*:  What's the matter?
    *Student*:  Nothing.
       I just wanted to tell you something.
 5  *Antonio*:  Well then?
    *Student*:  As you know,
       I'm interested in Italian.
    *Antonio*:  Yes, I know.
    *Student*:  And I like Italian food very much.
10  *Antonio*:  Yes, I know that as well.
    *Student*:  Well,
       yesterday I was in an Italian restaurant.
    *Antonio*:  Whereabouts?
    *Student*:  In St Mark's Street.
15     It's called the Trattoria Giovanni.
    *Antonio*:  I don't know it.
       Is it good?
    *Student*:  Well, I like pizza very much
       and the pizza was really good.
20  *Antonio*:  Were you alone?
    *Student*:  No, Birgit was there.
       She prefers cannelloni.
    *Antonio*:  Hmm. Was the cannelloni good as well?
    *Student*:  Not bad, I believe.
25  *Antonio*:  I must go there too.
       I love pizza.


**Chapter 16: 'Want' and 'Must'**

**Dialogue 1**

 1  *Elke*:  Fritz! Do you know what?
    *Fritz*:  No.
    *Elke*:  Herr Zilling has got tickets for Parsifal
       and he can't go.
 5  *Fritz*:  That's bad luck
    *Elke*:  For him
       but not for us.
    *Fritz*:  How's that?
    *Elke*:  Shall we take the tickets?
    *Fritz*:  What do they cost?
10  *Elke*:  Sixty marks each.
    *Fritz*:  That's expensive.
    *Elke*:  It is Bayreuth, you know.
    *Fritz*:  Yes.
       Must I put on my evening dress (i.e. dinner jacket)?
15  *Elke*:  Well, that is normal.
       I want to put on my new dress.
    *Fritz*:  Nice!
    *Elke*:  I want to wear my mink coat, too.

*Fritz*:   Aha!
20 *Elke*:   And of course my pearl necklace.
*Fritz*:   When must we decide?
*Elke*:   Oh, immediately.
    We do want to go, don't we?
*Fritz*:   Oh yes, of course we do.
25     When must we pick up the tickets?


## Dialogue 2

1 *Doctor Bauer*:   Now, Mrs Meyer,
    what's the matter with you?
*Mrs Meyer*:   It's my head, doctor.
    I keep on getting giddy.
*Doctor Bauer*:   How old are you, Mrs Meyer?
5 *Mrs Meyer*:   I'm 75 years old.
*Doctor Bauer*:   And where do you live?
*Mrs Meyer*:   In the Nietzschestraße.
*Doctor Bauer*:   Where is your flat?
    On the ground floor?
10 *Mrs Meyer*:   No, doctor.
    On the third floor.
*Doctor Bauer*:   And you go shopping every day?
*Mrs Meyer*:   Yes, and I fetch little Sandra from school.
15 *Doctor Bauer*:   Yes, yes. Now Mrs Meyer,
    You must run about a little bit less.
    When do you get up in the morning?
*Mrs Meyer*:   At six o'clock.
*Doctor Bauer*:   You must stay in bed a bit longer,
20     and you must lie down for an hour every afternoon.
*Mrs Meyer*:   Must I stay at home, doctor?
*Doctor Bauer*:   No, you don't need to stay at home,
    but you must take these tablets.
*Mrs Meyer*:   Must I take them in the evening?
25     I shan't go to sleep.
*Doctor Bauer*:   No, you don't need to take them in the evening.
*Mrs Meyer*:   Thank heavens!


## Chapter 17: Suggestions and Proposals

## Dialogue 1

1 *Antonio*:   Is this seat free?
*Girl*:   Yes.
*Antonio*:   Nice weather, isn't it?
*Girl*:   Yes. Very nice.
5 *Antonio*:   My name is Antonio.
*Girl*:   Hmm.
*Antonio*:   Antonio Santos.
   ...
*Antonio*:   What's your name?
    If you don't mind my asking?

10  *Girl*:  Claudia.
    *Antonio*:  Claudia. A nice name.
    *Girl*:  Thank you.
    . . .
    *Antonio*:  Tell me, Claudia.
    Can you play tennis?
15  *Girl*:  Yes.
    *Antonio*:  Good. Shall we play tennis?
    *Girl*:  When?
    *Antonio*:  Tomorrow, perhaps?
    *Girl*:  Yes, I'd like to.
20  *Antonio*:  Do you play often?
    *Girl*:  Fairly often.
    Four or five times a week.
    *Antonio*:  Where do you play?
    *Girl*:  In the Carlton Club.
25  *Antonio*:  Oh?
    Do you play well?
    *Girl*:  Hmm, quite well.
    And you?
    *Antonio*:  No, not very well.
    That's marvellous!!! (spoken ironically)

**Dialogue 2**
1  *Fritz*:  Hello, Elke!
    *Elke*:  It's you, Fritz!
    Come in!
    *Fritz*:  Thank you.
5  How are you?
    *Elke*:  Fine!
    *Fritz*:  Elke . . . .
    Shall we go away at the weekend?
    *Elke*:  Oh yes! Where to?
10  *Fritz*:  I know a very pretty church
    near Rosenheim.
    *Elke*:  Oh no, Fritz!
    Another church!
    *Fritz*:  What's the matter?
15  *Elke*:  Every time a church!
    *Fritz*:  I'm interested in churches.
    You know that.
    *Elke*:  But you have a different church every week.
    That's just too much.
20  *Fritz*:  I'm sorry.
    *Elke*:  Shall we go to Kufstein?
    We can go ski-ing there.
    *Fritz*:  But I can't ski.
    *Elke*:  But I can ski very well.
25  *Fritz*:  All right.
    Let's go to Kufstein.
    *Elke*:  Yes, you can learn
    (on the nursery slopes).

## Chapter 18: Dreams and Wishes

### Dialogue 1
1   *Elke*:  Fritz?
      *Fritz*:  Yes?
      *Elke*:  It's nice here, isn't it?
      *Fritz*:  Yes. Lovely.
5   *Elke*:  You are really nice, you know.
      *Fritz*:  Yes?
      . . .
      *Elke*:  Fritz?
      *Fritz*:  Yes?
      *Elke*:  Do you know what?
10  *Fritz*:  No.
      *Elke*:  I should like to go to America.
      *Fritz*:  Really?
      *Elke*:  Yes. I should like to see Hollywood.
      *Fritz*:  Hollywood?
15  *Elke*:  Yes. And I should like to visit New York.
      *Fritz*:  Oh, New York isn't nice.
      *Elke*:  Yes, it is!
          And I should like to go on a tramcar in San Francisco.
20  *Fritz*:  Why do you want to go on a tramcar?
          You can do that in Munich.
      *Elke*:  Oh, you don't understand.
          It's so romantic in San Francisco.
      *Fritz*:  But expensive.
25  *Elke*:  That's typically male!!
          You only think about money.
          I want to travel.
          I want to see the world.

### Dialogue 2
1   *Mrs Meyer*:  Leni?  Do you know what?
               Inge is going to have a baby!
      *Leni*:  No. That's wonderful!
          Where is she?
5  *Mrs Meyer*:  In Liverpool.
      *Leni*:  Oh yes, that's right.
          In England.
      *Mrs Meyer*:  Of course I shall go to Liverpool.
      *Leni*:  Yes, of course.
10  *Mrs Meyer*:  I must have my fur coat cleaned.
      *Leni*:  Yes, of course.
      *Mrs Meyer*:  And I must have a new dress made.
      *Leni*:  Yes, of course.
      *Mrs Meyer*:  And then I shall need a camera.
15         I must have my old camera repaired.
      *Leni*:  Of course.
      *Mrs Meyer*:  Then I must get some money changed too.
      *Leni*:  Yes, of course.
      *Mrs Meyer*:  What sort of money do they have in England?

20    Dollars, isn't it?
     *Leni*:  No. They have pounds and pennies.
     *Mrs Meyer*:  Oh yes. Of course.
     Then I must have my hair washed.
     *Leni*:  Wait a minute, Irmgard.
25    When is Inge expecting her child?
     *Mrs Meyer*:  Next year.
     In March.
     *Leni*:  Look, Irmgard.
     You have got a lot of time.

## Chapter 19: Talking about the past

### Dialogue 1

1  *Fritz*:  Good heavens!
     Where have you been?
     *Elke*:  What's the matter?
     My bus was late.
5  *Fritz*:  It was late yesterday.
     And today it was late again.
     *Elke*:  My bus wasn't late yesterday.
     *Fritz*:  Yes, it was!
     It was thirty minutes late.
10  *Elke*:  That's not true.
     *Fritz*:  Yes, it is true.
     I was at the cinema at seven o'clock.
     And you weren't there until seven thirty.
     *Elke*:  I was there on time.
15  You were simply at the cinema too early.
     *Fritz*:  And why weren't you on time the day before yesterday?
     *Elke*:  I was in the shop.
     *Fritz*:  What? Until eight o'clock?
     I don't believe it!
20  *Elke*:  I had a lot to do.
     *Fritz*:  And the boss was there too, wasn't he?
     *Elke*:  Of course.
     He had a lot to do, too.
     *Fritz*:  Ah hah. Now I understand ... !

### Dialogue 2

1  *Antonio*:  Can I help you?
     *Mrs Meyer*:  Oh, I have lost my wristwatch.
     *Antonio*:  Here on the street?
     *Mrs Meyer*:  Yes, I think so,
5  I went into town.
     And I had some coffee there.
     *Antonio*:  Do you think you have lost your watch in town?
     *Mrs Meyer*:  No.
     I saw it in the tram.
10  *Antonio*:  Have you looked at the tram stop?
     *Mrs Meyer*:  Yes, of course.

I met Mrs Moezer there.

I went to the Post Office with her.

*Antonio*:  Do you think you have lost the watch in the post office?

15  *Mrs Meyer*:  No, I don't think so.

*Antonio*:  Have you come here straight from the post office?

*Mrs Meyer*:  No. I bought some apples first.

At Schötz's.

*Antonio*:  I see. At Schötz's.

20  How long did you stay at Schötz's?

*Mrs Meyer*:  Oh, not long.

Five minutes perhaps.

*Antonio*:  Have you looked in your bag?

*Mrs Meyer*:  What?

25  *Antonio*:  Have you looked in your bag?

*Mrs Meyer*:  Good Lord!

There it is!

# GRAMMATICAL SUMMARY

## SECTION A – WORD FAMILIES

### 1. Cardinal numbers

The cardinal numbers are as follows:

| | | | | | |
|---|---|---|---|---|---|
| 1 | ein(s) | 14 | vierzehn | 70 | siebzig |
| 2 | zwei | 15 | fünfzehn | 80 | achtzig |
| 3 | drei | 16 | sechzehn | 90 | neunzig |
| 4 | vier | 17 | siebzehn | 100 | hundert |
| 5 | fünf | 18 | achtzehn | 120 | hundert(und) zwanzig |
| 6 | sechs | 19 | neunzehn | 221 | zweihundert- einundzwanzig |
| 7 | sieben | 20 | zwanzig | 1,000 | tausend |
| 8 | acht | 21 | einundzwanzig | 1,101 | eintausendein hundertundeins |
| 9 | neun | 22 | zweiundzwanzig | 1,000,000 | eine Million |
| 10 | zehn | 30 | dreißig | 2,000,000 | zwei Millionen |
| 11 | elf | 40 | vierzig | | |
| 12 | zwölf | 50 | fünfzig | | |
| 13 | dreizehn | 60 | sechzig | | |

Tausend is not generally used in dates: das Jahr neunzehnhundertzweiund-achtzig, 'the year 1982'.

Slight irregularities are to be noticed in the numbers 16, 17, 30, 60 and 70.

Compound numbers of hundreds, tens and units (e.g. zweihunderteinund-zwanzig) are usually written as one word.

### 2. Ordinal numbers

The ordinal numbers below 20 (except those meaning first, third and eighth) are formed by adding -t to the corresponding cardinal number; from 20 onwards they are formed by adding -st. When the number is a compound one, only the last part of the cardinal is changed into an ordinal:

| | | | |
|---|---|---|---|
| 1st | der erste | 8th | der achte |
| 2nd | der zweite | 9th | der neunte |
| 3rd | der dritte | 10th | der zehnte |

| | | | |
|---|---|---|---|
| 4th | der vierte | 20th | der zwanzigste |
| 5th | der fünfte | 100th | der hundertste |
| 6th | der sechste | 101st | der hundert(und)erste |
| 7th | der siebente/siebte | 120th | der hundert(und)zwanzigste |
| | | 221st | der zweihunderteinund-zwanzigste |

Der siebente is better than der siebte, which is sometimes used.

## 3. Days of the week

| | |
|---|---|
| Sonntag | Sunday |
| Montag | Monday |
| Dienstag | Tuesday |
| Mittwoch | Wednesday |
| Donnerstag | Thursday |
| Freitag | Friday |
| Samstag/Sonnabend | Saturday |

## 4. Parts of the body (Plural forms are given where relevant)

| | | | |
|---|---|---|---|
| der Arm (-e) | arm | das Knie (-n) | knee |
| der Fuß (⸚e) | foot | das Auge (-n) | eye |
| die Lippe (-n) | lip | das Bein (-e) | leg |
| die Hand (⸚e) | hand | das Ohr (-en) | ear |
| der Zahn (⸚e) | tooth | der Finger (-) | finger |
| der Kopf (⸚e) | head | der Zeh (-en) | toe |
| die Schulter (-n) | shoulder | der Ellbogen (-) | elbow |

| | |
|---|---|
| der Mund | mouth |
| die Nase | nose |
| der Bauch | stomach |
| der Hals | neck |

## 5. Nouns of nationality

Nouns of nationality make their feminine form in two ways:

(i) Nouns of nationality which end in e make their feminine form by changing the e into in. Here are some examples:

| | |
|---|---|
| der Franzose | die Französin |
| der Däne | die Dänin |
| der Ire | die Irin |
| der Finne | die Finnin |
| der Grieche | die Griechin |
| der Nordire | die Nordirin |
| der Rumäne | die Rumänin |
| der Schotte | die Schottin |
| der Russe | die Russin |
| der Brite | die Britin |
| der Schwede | die Schwedin |

(ii) Other nouns which end in er make their feminine form by adding in. Here are some examples:

| | |
|---|---|
| der Engländer | die Engländerin |
| der Österreicher | die Österreicherin |
| der Belgier | die Belgierin |
| der Amerikaner | die Amerikanerin |
| der Holländer | die Holländerin |
| der Italiener | die Italienerin |
| der Norweger | die Norwegerin |
| der Spanier | die Spanierin |
| der Schweizer | die Schweizerin |
| der Waliser | die Waliserin |

(iii) German nationality is the only exception:

| | | |
|---|---|---|
| der Deutsche | die Deutsche | Plural: die Deutschen |
| but: | | |
| ein Deutscher | eine Deutsche | Plural: Deutsche |

## 6. Sprechen Sie Deutsch?

The German for the most common European languages is as follows:

Bulgarisch
Dänisch
Deutsch
Englisch
Finnisch
Französisch
Griechisch
Holländisch
Italienisch
Norwegisch
Portugiesisch
Russisch
Schwedisch
Spanisch

## 7. The seasons

der Frühling/im Frühling
der Sommer/im Sommer
der Herbst/im Herbst
der Winter/im Winter

## 8. The months

| | |
|---|---|
| Januar | Juli |
| Februar | August |
| März | September |
| April | Oktober |
| Mai | November |
| Juni | Dezember |

## SECTION B – VERBS

Important points to remember:

(i) All the infinitives end in -en or -n.

(ii) German does not distinguish between simple forms (I go), and continuous forms (I am going).

(iii) The questioning, or interrogative, form is made by putting the verb first and the subject second. There is no 'do' or 'does' in German.

### 9. Some important regular verbs used in *Mastering German*

These verbs are given in the present tense.

The verb KOMMEN – to come

| | |
|---|---|
| ich komme | I come |
| du kommst | you come (familiar) |
| er kommt | he comes |
| sie kommt | she comes |
| wir kommen | we come |
| ihr kommt | you come (familiar plural) |
| Sie kommen | you come (formal or polite) |
| sie kommen | they come |

The verb GEHEN – to go

| | |
|---|---|
| ich gehe | I go |
| du gehst | you go (familiar) |
| er geht | he goes |
| sie geht | she goes |
| wir gehen | we go |
| ihr geht | you go (familiar plural) |
| Sie gehen | you go (formal or polite) |
| sie gehen | they go |

The verb BLEIBEN – to stay/remain

| | |
|---|---|
| ich bleibe | I stay/remain |
| du bleibst | you stay/remain (familiar) |
| er bleibt | he stays/remains |
| sie bleibt | she stays/remains |
| wir bleiben | we stay/remain |
| ihr bleibt | you stay/remain (familiar plural) |
| Sie bleiben | you stay/remain (formal or polite) |
| sie bleiben | they stay/remain |

The verb SUCHEN – to seek/look for

| | |
|---|---|
| ich suche | I'm looking for |
| du suchst | you're looking for (familiar) |
| er sucht | he's looking for |
| sie sucht | she's looking for |
| wir suchen | we're looking for |
| ihr sucht | you're looking for (familiar plural) |
| Sie suchen | you're looking for (formal or polite) |
| sie suchen | they're looking for |

The verb GLAUBEN – to believe/think

| | |
|---|---|
| ich glaube | I believe/think |
| du glaubst | you believe (familiar) |
| er glaubt | he believes |
| sie glaubt | she believes |
| wir glauben | we believe |
| ihr glaubt | you believe (familiar plural) |
| Sie glauben | you believe (formal or polite) |
| sie glauben | they believe |

The verb BRAUCHEN – to need

| | |
|---|---|
| ich brauche | I need |
| du brauchst | you need (familiar) |
| er braucht | he needs |
| sie braucht | she needs |
| wir brauchen | we need |
| ihr braucht | you need (familiar plural) |
| Sie brauchen | you need (formal or polite) |
| sie brauchen | they need |

## 10. Some important irregular verbs used in *Mastering German*

The verb FAHREN – to go (by vehicle)

| | |
|---|---|
| ich fahre | I go |
| du fährst | you go (familiar) |
| er fährt | he goes |
| sie fährt | she goes |
| wir fahren | we go |
| ihr fahrt | you go (familiar plural) |
| Sie fahren | you go (formal or polite) |
| sie fahren | they go |

The verb NEHMEN – to take

| | |
|---|---|
| ich nehme | I take |
| du nimmst | you take (familiar) |
| er nimmt | he takes |
| sie nimmt | she takes |
| wir nehmen | we take |
| ihr nehmt | you take (familiar plural) |
| Sie nehmen | you take (formal or polite) |
| sie nehmen | they take |

The verb HABEN – to have

| | |
|---|---|
| ich habe | I have |
| du hast | you have (familiar) |
| er hat | he has |
| sie hat | she has |
| wir haben | we have |
| ihr habt | you have (familiar plural) |
| Sie haben | you have (formal or polite) |
| sie haben | they have |

The verb TRAGEN – to wear

| | |
|---|---|
| ich trage | I wear |
| du trägst | you wear (familiar) |
| er trägt | he wears |
| sie trägt | she wears |
| wir tragen | we wear |
| ihr tragt | you wear (familiar plural) |
| Sie tragen | you wear (formal or polite) |
| sie tragen | they wear |

## 11. The *modal* verbs

The verb KÖNNEN – to 'can'/to be able to

| | |
|---|---|
| ich kann | I can |
| du kannst | you can (familiar) |
| er kann | he can |
| sie kann | she can |
| wir können | we can |
| ihr könnt | you can (familiar plural) |
| Sie können | you can (formal or polite) |
| sie können | they can |

The verb DÜRFEN – to 'may'/be allowed to

| | |
|---|---|
| ich darf | I may |
| du darfst | you may (familiar) |
| er darf | he may |
| sie darf | she may |
| wir dürfen | we may |
| ihr dürft | you may (familiar plural) |
| Sie dürfen | you may (formal or polite) |
| sie dürfen | they may |

The verb WOLLEN – to want to

| | |
|---|---|
| ich will | I want to |
| du willst | you want to (familiar) |
| er will | he wants to |
| sie will | she wants to |
| wir wollen | we want to |
| ihr wollt | you want to (familiar plural) |
| Sie wollen | you want to (formal or polite) |
| sie wollen | they want to |

The verb MÜSSEN – to 'must'/have to

| | |
|---|---|
| ich muß | I must/have to |
| du mußt | you must/have to (familiar) |
| er muß | he must/has to |
| sie muß | she must/has to |
| wir müssen | we must/have to |
| ihr müßt | you must/have to (familiar plural) |
| Sie müssen | you must/have to (formal or polite) |
| sie müssen | they must/have to |

The verb BRAUCHEN NICHT – to don't have to/don't need to

| | |
|---|---|
| ich brauche nicht | I don't have to/need to |
| du brauchst nicht | you don't have to/need to (familiar) |
| er braucht nicht | he doesn't have to/need to |
| sie braucht nicht | she doesn't have to/need to |
| wir brauchen nicht | we don't have to/need to |
| ihr braucht nicht | you don't have to/need to (familiar plural) |
| Sie brauchen nicht | you don't have to/need to (formal or polite) |
| sie brauchen nicht | they don't have to/need to |

A very important part of the verb MÖGEN – to like

| | |
|---|---|
| ich möchte | I would like (also: I should like, etc.) |
| du möchtest | you would like (familiar) |
| er möchte | he would like |
| sie möchte | she would like |
| wir möchten | we would like |
| ihr möchtet | you would like (familiar plural) |
| Sie möchten | you would like (formal or polite) |
| sie möchten | they would like |

## 12. The Compound Past tense, or Perfect tense, and general reference list of verbs

This contains the verbs used in *Mastering German*, and includes the fifty most frequently occurring verbs in spoken German.

The past participles of most of these verbs begin with ge-,
end with -en.

Some of them change the vowel sound in the du and er form of the Present tense. This is indicated.

Some of them change the vowel sound in the past participle.

Some make their Perfect tense with haben, others with sein.

### Group A

| INFINITIVE | VOWEL CHANGE in present tense | PAST PARTICIPLE | MEANING |
|---|---|---|---|
| bleiben | | geblieben (sein) | to stay; remain |
| bringen | | gebracht | to bring |
| denken | | gedacht | to think |
| essen | i | gegessen | to eat |
| fahren | ä | gefahren (sein) | to go; drive |
| finden | | gefunden | to find |
| geben | i | gegeben | to give |
| *gefallen | ä | gefallen | to like; to please |
| gehen | | gegangen (sein) | to go |
| halten | ie | gehalten | to hold |
| heißen | | geheißen | to be called |
| †helfen | i | geholfen | to help |
| kennen | | gekannt | to know someone |

## Group A cont.

| INFINITIVE | VOWEL CHANGE in present tense | PAST PARTICIPLE | MEANING |
|---|---|---|---|
| kommen | | gekommen (sein) | to come |
| laufen | ä | gelaufen (sein) | to run |
| lesen | ie | gelesen | to read |
| liegen | | gelegen | to lie; recline |
| nehmen | i | genommen | to take |
| nennen | | gennant | to name |
| reisen | | gereist (sein) | to travel |
| reiten | | geritten | to ride |
| schlafen | ä | geschlafen | to sleep |
| schwimmen | | geschwommen (sein/haben) | to swim |
| sehen | ie | gesehen | to see |
| singen | | gesungen | to sing |
| sitzen | | gesessen | to sit |
| sprechen | i | gesprochen | to speak |
| stehen | | gestanden | to stand |
| tragen | ä | getragen | to wear; carry |
| treffen | i | getroffen | to meet |
| trinken | | getrunken | to drink |
| tun | | getan | to do |
| verlieren | | verloren | to lose |
| waschen | ä | gewaschen | to wash |
| werden | i | geworden (sein) | to become |
| wiegen | | gewogen | to weigh |
| wissen | weiß | gewußt | to know something |

*The verb gefallen (to like) operates in a special way. In order to render 'I like it', one must say es gefällt mir, literally 'it pleases me'. Note that 'me' is rendered by mir (dative case).

† The verb helfen (to help) has an object in the dative case. 'He helps me' is rendered by er hilft mir.

## Group B

All these verbs make their past participle by dropping the -en at the end of the infinitive, and adding -t (or -et). They are all conjugated with haben.

| INFINITIVE | PAST PARTICIPLE | MEANING |
|---|---|---|
| arbeiten | gearbeitet | to work |
| basteln | gebastelt | to make things as a hobby |
| bauen | gebaut | to build |
| borgen | geborgt | to borrow |
| brauchen | gebraucht | to need |
| fragen | gefragt | to ask |

## Group B cont.

| INFINITIVE | PAST PARTICIPLE | MEANING |
|---|---|---|
| gehören | gehört | to belong |
| glauben | geglaubt | to believe |
| hören | gehört | to hear |
| kaufen | gekauft | to buy |
| kochen | gekocht | to cook |
| kriegen | gekriegt | to get |
| lernen | gelernt | to learn |
| malen | gemalt | to paint |
| machen | gemacht | to make, do |
| parken | geparkt | to park |
| rauchen | geraucht | to smoke |
| regnen (es) | geregnet | to rain |
| reinigen | gereinigt | to clean |
| sagen | gesagt | to say; tell |
| sammeln | gesammelt | to collect |
| schauen | geschaut | to look; see |
| spielen | gespielt | to play |
| starten | gestartet | to start |
| stecken | gesteckt | to put |
| stellen | gestellt | to put; lay |
| suchen | gesucht | to look for |
| tanzen | getanzt | to dance |
| träumen | geträumt | to dream |
| trennen | getrennt | to separate |
| wandern | gewandert | to go walking |
| wählen | gewählt | to choose |
| wechseln | gewechselt | to change (money) |
| wohnen | gewohnt | to live |
| zahlen | gezahlt | to pay |
| zittern | gezittert | to shiver |

## Group C

These verbs have separable affixes, and form their past participle by placing the -ge between affix and stem.

| INFINITIVE | VOWEL CHANGE in present tense | PAST PARTICIPLE | MEANING |
|---|---|---|---|
| abfahren | ä | abgefahren (sein) | to leave; depart |
| abholen | | abgeholt | to fetch |
| abschließen | | abgeschlossen | to lock up |
| abtrocknen | | abgetrocknet | to dry up |
| abwaschen | ä | abgewaschen | to wash up |
| anfangen | ä | angefangen | to begin |
| ankommen | | angekommen (sein) | to arrive |
| anrufen | | angerufen | to telephone |
| anziehen | | angezogen | to put on (clothes) |

## Group C cont.

| INFINITIVE | VOWEL CHANGE in present tense | PAST PARTICIPLE | MEANING |
|---|---|---|---|
| aufgeben | | aufgegeben | to give up |
| aufräumen | | aufgeräumt | to tidy up |
| aufstehen | | aufgestanden | to get up |
| ausgehen | | ausgegangen (sein) | to go out |
| einkaufen | | eingekauft | to do the shopping |
| einschlafen | ä | einschlafen | to go to sleep |
| sich hinlegen | | sich hingelegt | to lie down |
| umsteigen | | umgestiegen (sein) | to change (trains) |
| wegfahren | ä | weggefahren (sein) | to go away |
| vorstellen | | vorgestellt | to introduce |

## Group D

These verbs have no ge- in the past participle. They are all conjugated with haben.

| INFINITIVE | PAST PARTICIPLE | MEANING |
|---|---|---|
| anprobieren | anprobiert | to try on |
| beginnen | begonnen | to begin |
| bekommen | bekommen | to get |
| besuchen | besucht | to visit |
| erwarten | erwartet | to expect |
| erzählen | erzählt | to tell (a story) |
| sich interessieren (für) | interessiert | to be interested in |
| reparieren | repariert | to repair |
| reservieren | reserviert | to reserve |
| telefonieren | telefoniert | to telephone |
| verdienen | verdient | to earn |
| verschreiben | verschrieben | to prescribe |
| verstehen | verstanden | to understand |
| wiederholen | wiederholt | to repeat |

The four groups of verbs given above indicate how to form the Compound Past tense. This is the tense which you should learn to use when you want to speak or write German. There is, however, another past tense: the Simple Past tense. Some Germans use this instead of the Compound Past. At this stage of learning German it is only necessary to know how to use the Simple Past tense of the verbs haben, sein, sagen, fragen and the 'modal' verbs. It will, however, be useful for you to recognise the Simple Past tense of other verbs, if and when they are used by native speakers of German.

Simple Past of MALEN – to paint
ich mal – TE
du mal – TEST
er mal – TE
sie mal – TE
wir mal – TEN
ihr mal – TET
Sie mal – TEN
sie mal – TEN

The Simple Past tense is made by adding t to the stem of the verb, e.g. fragen – fragte (to ask).

Verbs which make their Simple Past tense in an irregular way are given as follows:

| INFINITIVE | SIMPLE PAST TENSE |
|---|---|
| bleiben | blieb |
| bringen | brachte |
| denken | dachte |
| essen | aß |
| fahren | fuhr |
| finden | fand |
| geben | gab |
| gehen | ging |
| halten | hielt |
| heißen | hieß |
| kennen | kannte |
| kommen | kam |
| laufen | lief |
| lesen | las |
| liegen | lag |
| nehmen | nahm |
| nennen | nannte |
| reisen | reiste |
| reiten | ritt |
| schlafen | schlief |
| schwimmen | schwamm |
| sehen | sah |
| singen | sang |
| sitzen | saß |
| sprechen | sprach |
| stehen | stand |
| tragen | trug |
| treffen | traf |
| trinken | trank |
| tun | tat |
| verlieren | verlor |
| waschen | wusch |
| werden | wurde |
| wiegen | wog |
| wissen | wußte |

Simple Past of HABEN – to have

| ich hatte | I had |
| du hattest | you had (familiar) |
| er hatte | he had |
| sie hatte | she had |
| es hatte | it had |
| wir hatten | we had |
| ihr hattet | you had (familiar plural) |
| Sie hatten | you had (formal or polite) |
| sie hatten | they had |

Simple Past of SEIN – to be

| ich war | I was |
| du warst | you were (familiar) |
| er war | he was |
| sie war | she was |
| es war | it was |
| wir waren | we were |
| ihr ward | you were (familiar plural) |
| Sie waren | you were (formal or polite) |
| sie waren | they were |

Simple Past of SAGEN – to say

| ich sagte | I said |
| du sagtest | you said (familiar) |
| er sagte | he said |
| sie sagte | she said |
| es sagte | it said |
| wir sagten | we said |
| ihr sagtet | you said (familiar plural) |
| Sie sagten | you said (formal or polite) |
| sie sagten | they said |

Simple Past of FRAGEN – to ask

| ich fragte | I asked |
| du fragtest | you asked (familiar) |
| er fragte | he asked |
| sie fragte | she asked |
| es fragte | it asked |
| wir fragten | we asked |
| ihr fragtet | you asked (familiar plural) |
| Sie fragten | you asked (formal or polite) |
| sie fragten | they asked |

Simple Past of KÖNNEN – to be able to

| ich konnte | I could |
| du konntest | you could (familiar) |
| er konnte | he could |
| sie konnte | she could |
| es konnte | it could |
| wir konnten | we could |
| ihr konntet | you could (familiar plural) |
| Sie konnten | you could (formal or polite) |
| sie konnten | they could |

Simple Past of WOLLEN – to want to

| | |
|---|---|
| ich wollte | I wanted to |
| du wolltest | you wanted to (familiar) |
| er wollte | he wanted to |
| sie wollte | she wanted to |
| es wollte | it wanted to |
| wir wollten | we wanted to |
| ihr wolltet | you wanted to (familiar plural) |
| Sie wollten | you wanted to (formal or polite) |
| sie wollten | they wanted to |

Simple Past of MÜSSEN – to have to

| | |
|---|---|
| ich mußte | I had to |
| du mußtest | you had to (familiar) |
| er mußte | he had to |
| sie mußte | she had to |
| es mußte | it had to |
| wir mußten | we had to |
| ihr mußtet | you had to (familiar plural) |
| Sie mußten | you had to (formal or polite) |
| sie mußten | they had to |

Simple Past of DÜRFEN – to be allowed to

| | |
|---|---|
| ich durfte | I was allowed to |
| du durftest | you were allowed to (familiar) |
| er durfte | he was allowed to |
| sie durfte | she was allowed to |
| es durfte | it was allowed to |
| wir durften | we were allowed to |
| ihr durftet | you were allowed to (familiar plural) |
| Sie durften | you were allowed to (formal or polite) |
| sie durften | they were allowed to |

## SECTION C – WORD ORDER

Many sentences in this course are short phrases consisting of one or two words only. In this respect German resembles English.

When a sentence contains a verb, however, there are certain differences. Below, you will find a list of the principal sentence types used in *Mastering German*.

### 14. Statements

| Das | ist | Fritz |
|---|---|---|
| Ich | bleibe | zwei Nächte |
| Ich | habe | Kopfschmerzen |
| Ich | weiß | es nicht genau |
| Sie | hat | schon einen Pullover |
| Ich | nehme | ihn |
| Diese blauen Schuhe | sind | sehr elegant |

subject      verb

## 15. Questions

A:

| verb | subject | | |
|------|---------|---|---|
| Ist | Herr Kirchhof | da? |
| Ist | das | mit Frühstück? |
| Haben | Sie | ein Zimmer frei? |
| Geht | es | heute nachmittag? |
| Hat | das Zimmer | einen Ausblick? |
| Haben | Sie | Gepäck? |
| Fährt | die Nummer 18 | zum Rathaus? |
| Sprechen | Sie | Italienisch? |
| Möchten | Sie | eine Vorspeise? |
| War | alles | in Ordnung? |
| Nehmen | Sie | Zucker? |

↑ verb  ↑ subject

B:

| question word or expression | verb | subject | | |
|------|------|---------|---|---|
| Wie | geht | es | Ihnen? |
| Wie | komme | ich | zur Amalienstraße? |
| Was | kostet | das Zimmer? | |
| Wann | fährt | der Zug | nach Augsburg? |
| Um wieviel Uhr | fährt | der Zug | nach Innsbruck? |
| Seit wann | haben | Sie | Kopfschmerzen? |
| Wo | tut | es | weh? |

↑ question word or expression  ↑ verb  ↑ subject

C:

| subject | verb | | |
|---------|------|---|---|
| Sie | sind | Hauptschullehrer | nicht wahr? |
| Der Glühwein | ist | schön warm | |
| Die Kirche hier | ist | schön | |

↑ subject  ↑ verb

## 16. Orders or commands

| verb | subject | |
|------|---------|---|
| Kommen | Sie | herein |
| Nehmen | Sie | Platz |
| Nehmen | Sie | die erste Straße links |
| Gehen | Sie | die Marktstraße hoch |
| Fahren | Sie | Richtung Innsbruck |
| Tragen | Sie | sich ein |
| Entschuldigen | Sie | die Störung |

↑ verb  ↑ subject

## 17. Emphasis

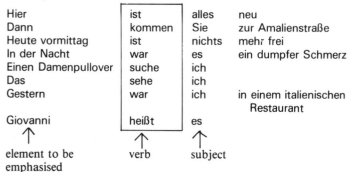

| | | | |
|---|---|---|---|
| Hier | **ist** | alles | neu |
| Dann | **kommen** | Sie | zur Amalienstraße |
| Heute vormittag | **ist** | nichts | mehr frei |
| In der Nacht | **war** | es | ein dumpfer Schmerz |
| Einen Damenpullover | **suche** | ich | |
| Das | **sehe** | ich | |
| Gestern | **war** | ich | in einem italienischen Restaurant |
| Giovanni | **heißt** | es | |

element to be emphasised     verb     subject

## 18. Modal verbs

A: **Statements**

| | | | |
|---|---|---|---|
| Ich | **möchte** | ein Zimmer | **reservieren** |
| Sie | **dürfen** | die Pumpe | **borgen** |
| Wir | **könnten** | aufs Land | **fahren** |
| Ich | **wollte** | dir nur etwas | **sagen** |
| Ich | **will** | mein neues Kleid | **anziehen** |
| Ich | **möchte** | den Arzt | **sehen** |

modal verb             infinitive

B: **Questions**

(i)

| | | | |
|---|---|---|---|
| **Darf** | ich | meine Frau | **vorstellen?** |
| **Muß** | ich | – | **umsteigen?** |
| **Kann** | ich | Ihnen | **helfen?** |
| **Kann** | ich | sie | **anprobieren?** |
| **Möchten** | Sie | etwas | **trinken?** |
| **Wollen** | wir | die Karten | **nehmen?** |

modal verb             infinitive

(ii)

| | | | |
|---|---|---|---|
| Was | **darf** | es | **sein?** |
| Wo | **kann** | ich denn hier | **parken?** |
| Warum | **möchtest** | du mit einer Straßenbahn | **fahren?** |

question word      modal verb          infinitive

C: **Emphasis**

| Hier | dürfen | Sie nicht | parken |
| Dort | können | wir | Ski-fahren |

element
to be
emphasised

modal
verb

infinitive

## 19. Verbs with separable affixes

| Der Zug | fährt | | ab |
| Der Zug | kommt | | an |
| Sie | steigen | in Koblenz | um |
| Ich | schaue | mich | um |
| Er | wäscht | die Teller | ab |
| Sie | geht | am Samstag | aus |

verb

affix

## 20. Compound Past (Perfect) tense

A: **Statements**

| Ich | habe | meine Armbanduhr | verloren |
| Ich | habe | zuerst Äpfel | gekauft |
| Wir | sind | in die Stadt | gefahren |
| Ich | bin | mit ihr zur Post | gegangen |

subject

auxiliary verb

past participle

B: **Questions**

(i)

| Sind | Sie | direkt von der Post hierher | gekommen? |
| Haben | Sie | Kaffee | getrunken? |

auxiliary
verb

subject

past participle

(ii)

| Wie lange | sind | Sie bei Schötz | geblieben? |
| Wie oft | haben | Sie Bier | getrunken? |

question word
or expression

auxiliary
verb

subject

past participle

## 21. Subordinate clauses

In theory, one could communicate perfectly well by using a whole series of very short sentences, each containing a simple idea. This would be like a very irritating train journey on a branch line, with the train stopping at every tiny wayside halt. In order to make the language flow, two or more sentences can be combined. Here is an example from Chapter 8, Dialogue 2, line 15 (p. 83):

> Was sind Sie von Beruf? Darf ich fragen? (Simple sentences)
> Was sind Sie von Beruf, wenn ich fragen darf? (Combination)

Here is another example from Chapter 11, Dialogue 2, line 7 (p. 116):

> Ich glaube. Ich möchte auch eine Suppe. (Simple sentences)
> Ich glaube, daß ich auch eine Suppe möchte. (Combination)

In each of the above examples, one sentence is neatly combined with another. In the first case, the word wenn, and in the second, the word daß signal that this is taking place. Frequently-used words which give this signal are:

wenn  — if, whenever
daß  — that
weil  — because
ob  — whether

If you wish to make your speech more sophisticated by using this technique, there are two vital rules to remember:

1. (Writing and Speaking) The main, or simple verb (or the modal verb, if there is one) goes to the end of the subordinate clause.

    . . . . . . , wenn ich fragen darf
    . . . . . . , daß ich auch eine Suppe möchte

2. (Writing only) The two parts of the sentence are separated by a comma.

The matter of subordinate clauses will be dealt with more thoroughly in *Mastering German 2.*

## SUMMARY
(a) The 'normal' place for the main verb is in the second position of the sentence.
(b) When the main verb comes to the beginning of a sentence, it signals a command, or a question (though a question can be introduced by a 'question word').
(c) Infinitives, affixes and past participles come at the end of the sentence.

## SECTION D – COMPARISONS

### 22. Comparison of adjectives

Adjectives usually make their comparative form by adding -er. The superlative form of the adjective is usually made by adding -st.

(a) Some adjectives, which end in the letters -el, -en, -er, usually drop the -e in the comparative form.

edel    edler    der, die, das edelste    noble

(b) Adjectives which end in -d, -t, or a sibilant (i.e. -s) add -est in the superlative form.

heiß    heißer    der, die, das heißeste    hot

(c) Many adjectives add an Umlaut to their principal vowel in the comparative and the superlative form. This, of course, changes the pronunciation: e.g. groß – größer, alt – älter. Here is a list of them:

| | | | | | |
|------|--------|---------|--------|--------|---------|
| arg | bad | dumm | stupid | klug | clever |
| grob | coarse | jung | young | kurz | short |
| groß | big | hart | hard | krank | ill |
| alt | old | kalt | cold | arm | poor |
| lang | long | schwach | weak | gesund | healthy |
| warm | warm | schwarz | black | | |
| stark | strong | scharf | sharp | | |

(d) Some adjectives make their comparative and superlative form in an irregular way. Unfortunately, they are very popular adjectives. Here is a list of them:

| | | | |
|--------|---------|----------------------------|--------|
| groß | größer | der, die, das größte | big |
| gut | besser | der, die, das beste | good |
| hoch | höher | der, die, das höchste | high |
| nah(e) | näher | der, die, das nächste | near |
| viel | mehr | der, die, das meiste | much |
| wenig | weniger | der, die, das wenigste | little |

(e) When adjectives in their comparative or superlative form come in front of a noun, they have to agree with the noun like ordinary adjectives. Examples:

| | |
|-------------------------|------------------------|
| eine klarere Aussicht | a clearer view |
| eine intelligentere Frau | a more intelligent woman |
| ein intelligenterer Mann | a more intelligent man |

(f) Sometimes the superlative form of the adjective is made by using -am. Here are some examples:

| | |
|-----------------------------------|------------------------------|
| Im Januar ist das Wetter am kältesten | The weather is coldest in January |
| Im Juni ist das Wetter am wärmsten | The weather is warmest in June |
| Im Juni sind die Tage am längsten | In June the days are longest |

(g) This is how you can translate the word 'most':

| die meisten Bücher | most (of the) books |

(h) Notice the way that you repeat adjectives in German:

| Die Tage werden immer länger | The days are getting longer and longer |
| Die Nächte werden immer kühler | The nights are getting cooler and cooler |

(i) Here are some important expressions for making comparisons:

| Peter ist (eben) so groß wie Klaus | Peter is just as big as Klaus |
| Klaus ist nicht so groß wie Peter | Klaus is not as big as Peter |

## 23. Adverbs

Most adjectives in German can be used as *adverbs*. Here is a normal regular comparison of adverbs.

| scharf | schärfer | am schärfsten | sharply |
| deutlich | deutlicher | am deutlichsten | clearly |
| klar | klarer | am klarsten | clearly |

| Er spricht deutlicher als sie | He speaks more clearly than she does |
| Ich spreche am deutlichsten | I speak most clearly (of all) |

Here are some irregular comparisons of adverbs:

| bald | früher | am frühesten | soon |
| gut | besser | am besten | well |

## SECTION E – THE CASES

## 24. The nominative case – the case of the *subject* of a sentence

|  | Masc. | | Fem. | Neut. | Plur. |
|---|---|---|---|---|---|
| (a) **The indefinite article** | ein | – a | eine | ein | – |
| (b) **The negative article** | kein | – not a | keine | kein | keine |
| (c) **The possessive adjectives** | mein | – my | meine | mein | meine |
|  | dein | – your | deine | dein | deine |
|  | sein | – his | seine | sein | seine |
|  | ihr | – her | ihre | ihr | ihre |
|  | sein | – its | seine | sein | seine |
|  | unser | – our | unsere | unser | unsere |
|  | euer | – your | euere | euer | euere |
|  | Ihr | – your | Ihre | Ihr | Ihre |
|  | ihr | – their | ihre | ihr | ihre |

(d) **The definite**    der   – the     die        das        die
     **article**

(e) **Adjective endings**

(i) After ein/mein, etc.:
ein—er + NOUN       eine—e + NOUN       ein—es + NOUN
                     meine—en + NOUN

(ii) After der/dieser, etc.:
der—e + NOUN       die—e + NOUN       das—e + NOUN
                     die—en + NOUN

(f) **The personal pronouns**

| Sing. | | | Plur. | | |
|---|---|---|---|---|---|
| ich | – | I | wir | – | we |
| du | – | you | ihr | – | you |
| Sie | – | you | Sie | – | you |
| er | – | he | | | |
| sie | – | she | sie | – | they |
| es | – | it | | | |

25. **The accusative case** – the case of the *direct object* of a sentence

| | Masc. | | Fem. | Neut. | Plur. |
|---|---|---|---|---|---|
| (a) **The indefinite article** | einen | – a | eine | ein | – |
| (b) **The negative article** | keinen | – not a | keine | kein | keine |
| (c) **The possessive adjectives** | meinen | – my | meine | mein | meine |
| | deinen | – your | deine | dein | deine |
| | seinen | – his | seine | sein | seine |
| | ihren | – her | ihre | ihr | ihre |
| | seinen | – its | seine | sein | seine |
| | unseren | – our | unsere | unser | unsere |
| | eueren | – your | euere | euer | euere |
| | Ihren | – your | Ihre | Ihr | Ihre |
| | ihren | – their | ihre | ihr | ihre |
| (d) **The definite article** | den | – the | die | das | die |

(e) **Adjective endings**

(i) After ein/mein, etc.:
einen—en + NOUN      eine—e + NOUN      ein—es + NOUN
                     meine—en + NOUN

(ii) After der/dieser, etc.:
den—en + NOUN       die—e + NOUN       das—e + NOUN
                     die—en + NOUN

(f) **The personal pronouns**

| Sing. | | | Plur. | | |
|---|---|---|---|---|---|
| mich | – | me | uns | – | us |
| dich | – | you | euch | – | you |
| Sie | – | you | Sie | – | you |
| ihn | – | him | | | |
| sie | – | her | sie | – | them |
| es | – | it | | | |

26. **The genitive case** – the case with which *certain relationships* of one
noun to another are conveyed

| | | Masc. | | Feb. | Neut. | Plur. |
|---|---|---|---|---|---|---|
| (a) | **The indefinite article** | eines | – of a | einer | eines | – |
| (b) | **The negative article** | keines | – of no | keiner | keines | keiner |
| (c) | **The possessive adjectives** | meines | – of my | meiner | meines | meiner |
| | | deines | – of your | deiner | deines | deiner |
| | | seines | – of his | seiner | seines | seiner |
| | | ihres | – of her | ihrer | ihres | ihrer |
| | | seines | – of its | seiner | seines | seiner |
| | | unseres | – of our | unsurer | unseres | unserer |
| | | eures | – of your | euerer | eueres | euerer |
| | | Ihres | – of your | Ihrer | Ihres | Ihrer |
| | | ihres | – of their | ihrer | ihres | ihrer |
| (d) | **The definite article** | des | – of the | der | des | der |

(e) **Adjective endings**

(i) After ein/mein, etc.:

eines–en + NOUN(e)s    einer–en + NOUN    eines–en + NOUN(s)s
                                meiner–en + NOUN

(ii) After der/dieser, etc.:

des–en + NOUN(e)s    der–en + NOUN    des–en + NOUN(e)s
                          der–en + NOUN

N.B. When the genitive case is used in the masculine and neuter singular
the noun itself is marked.

(a) If the noun ends in −s, −ß, −x, −tz, then the marker is /es/
e.g. des Hauses, des Flußes, des Platzes.

(b) When nouns end in −ld, −lg, −nd, −sch, −st, then most German-speakers prefer the marker /es/ in order to avoid having too full a mouthful of consonants
e.g. des Windes, des Landes, des Bildes.

(c) Single-syllable nouns are treated in the same way, with /es/
e.g. des Tages, des Buches, des Kopfes.

(d) However, if the noun ends in −el, −em, −en, −er, then the marker is on /s/
e.g. des Onkels, des Koffers, des Reifens.

(e) The same goes for nouns ending in −chen, −lein
e.g. des Mädchens, des Fräuleins.

(f) Also for nouns ending in −ig, −ing, −ling
e.g. des Herings, des Fruhlings.

(g) German-speakers also prefer the short /s/ marker when nouns end with a vowel
e.g. des Tees, des Schnees, des Sakkos,

or when a noun ends with a vowel + /h/
e.g. des Schuhs

or when a noun ends with a dipthong
e.g. des Baus, des Heus.

Meanings of the genitive case.

The genitive can show *possession* or *belonging*,
e.g. Ottos Buch - Otto's book; die Frau meines Bruders - my brother's wife (Do you notice the similarity with English? Easy, isn't it?)

The genitive can show that one thing is *part of* another,
e.g. ein Drittel des Weges - a third of the way; zwei seiner Bucher - two of his books.

The genitive can show possession of a *quality, property or characteristic*,
e.g. (Eine Fahrkarte) zweiter Klasse - (of the) second class; die Intelligenz der Frau - the woman's intelligence; die Schönheit des Mannes - the man's beauty.

**27. The dative case** — the case of the *indirect object* of a sentence

|  | Masc. |  | Fem. | Neut. | Plur. |
|---|---|---|---|---|---|
| (a) **The indefinite article** | einem | – a | einer | einem | – |
| (b) **The negative article** | keinem | – not a | keiner | keinem | keinen |
| (c) **The possessive adjectives** | meinem | – my | meiner | meinem | meinen |
|  | deinem | – your | deiner | deinem | deinen |
|  | seinem | – his | seiner | seinem | seinen |
|  | ihrem | – her | ihrer | ihrem | ihren |
|  | seinem | – its | seiner | seinem | seinen |
|  | unserem | – our | unserer | unserem | unseren |
|  | euerem | – your | euerer | euerem | eueren |
|  | Ihrem | – your | Ihrer | Ihrem | Ihren |
|  | ihrem | – their | ihrer | ihrem | ihren |
| (d) **The definite article** | dem | – the | der | dem | den |

(e) **Adjective endings**

(i) After ein/mein, etc.:
einem—en + NOUN    einer—en + NOUN    einem—en + NOUN
meinen—en + NOUN

(ii) After der/dieser, etc.:
dem—en + NOUN    der—en + NOUN    dem—en + NOUN
den—en + NOUN

(f) **The personal pronouns**

|  | Sing. |  |  |  | Plur. |  |
|---|---|---|---|---|---|---|
|  | mir | – | me |  | uns | – | us |
|  | dir | – | you |  | euch | – | you |
|  | Ihnen | – | you |  | Ihnen | – | you |
|  | ihm | – | him |  |  |  |
|  | ihr | – | her |  | ihnen | – | them |
|  | ihm | – | it |  |  |  |

**28. Possessive adjectives**

*Mein* Mann
*Meine* Frau

The following are the possessive adjectives with the corresponding personal pronouns:

| ich | I |  | mein | my |
|---|---|---|---|---|
| du | you (familiar) |  | dein | your (familiar) |

| er | he | sein | his |
|----|----|------|-----|
| sie | she | ihr | her |
| es | it | sein | its |
| wir | we | unser | our |
| ihr | you (familiar) | euer | your (familiar) |
| Sie | you (polite) | ihr | your (polite) |
| sie | they | ihr | their |

This is how *possessive adjectives* agree with *nouns*.

**Masc.**

| mein Mann | – | my husband |
|-----------|---|-----------|
| dein Mann | – | your husband |
| sein Garten | – | his garden |
| ihr Mann | – | her husband |
| sein Garten | – | its garden |
| unser Garten | – | our garden |
| euer Garten | – | your garden |
| Ihr Mann | – | your husband |
| ihr Garten | – | their garden |

**Fem.**

| meine Frau | – | my wife |
|------------|---|---------|
| deine Frau | – | your wife |
| seine Frau | – | his wife |
| ihre Zeitung | – | her newspaper |
| seine Küche | – | its kitchen |
| unsere Küche | – | our kitchen |
| euere Küche | – | your kitchen |
| Ihre Zeitung | – | your newspaper |
| ihre Straße | – | their street |

**Neut.**

| mein Auto | – | my car |
|-----------|---|--------|
| dein Auto | – | your car |
| sein Auto | – | his car |
| ihr Auto | – | her car |
| sein Fenster | – | its window |
| unser Haus | – | our house |
| euer Haus | – | your house |
| Ihr Haus | – | your house |
| ihr Haus | – | their house |

**Plur.**

| meine Schuhe | – | my shoes |
|--------------|---|----------|
| deine Schuhe | – | your shoes |
| seine Schuhe | – | his shoes |
| ihre Schuhe | – | her shoes |
| seine Zimmer | – | its rooms |
| unsere Autos | – | our cars |
| euere Freunde | – | your friends |
| Ihre Freunde | – | your friends |
| ihre Freunde | – | their friends |

## 29. The indefinite article

| | Masc. | Fem. | Neut. |
|-------------|-------|------|-------|
| NOMINATIVE | ein | eine | ein |
| ACCUSATIVE | einen | eine | ein |
| GENITIVE | eines | einer | eines |
| DATIVE | einem | einer | einem |

All these words mean 'a' or 'an'. The 'nominative case' is used for the subject of the sentence, and the 'accusative case' is used for the direct object of the sentence.

Examples of direct objects:

| Haben Sie ein Zimmer? (das Zimmer) | Have you got a room? |
|---|---|
| Ich möchte einen Kaffee (der Kaffee) | I'd like a coffee |

You do not use the indefinite article when you want to indicate somebody's profession:

| | |
|---|---|
| Er ist Professor | He is a professor |
| Sie ist Sekretärin | She is a secretary |

There is no direct object after the verb sein: 'to be'.

## 30. Negative ('not a . . . ')
The negative form of ein, meaning 'not a' is kein.

| | |
|---|---|
| Er ist kein Freund | He is not a friend |
| Nein, sie ist keine Sekretärin | No, she is not a secretary |

*Schmidt*: Eine Tasse Kaffee?
*Müller*: Ja, bitte.
*Schmidt*: Ugh! Das ist kein Kaffee. Das ist Tee!

## 31. The definite article

| | Masc. | Fem. | Neut. | Plur. |
|---|---|---|---|---|
| NOMINATIVE | der | die | das | die |
| ACCUSATIVE | den | die | das | die |
| GENITIVE | des | der | des | der |
| DATIVE | dem | der | dem | den |

The nominative case is used for the subject of the sentence and the accusative case is used for the direct object of the sentence.
The dative case is used for the indirect object of a sentence.

### (a) Contractions of the definite article
The definite article is often contracted with certain prepositions. E.g. an das – ans, auf das – aufs, in das – ins, um das – ums.

### (b) Definite article with countries, geographical features and streets

| | |
|---|---|
| Die Schweiz | Switzerland |
| Der Rhein | the Rhine |
| Die Donau | the Danube |
| Die Weser | the Weser |
| Die Elbe | the Elbe |
| Die Mozartstraße | Mozart Street |

### (c) The definite article is not used when two nouns are closely connected in one idea

| | |
|---|---|
| Stadt und Land | town and country |
| Hand in Hand | hand in hand |
| Wind und Wetter | wind and weather |

## 32. Adjective endings (1)
Agreement of the adjective after the words der, die or das (also after dieser, diese, dieses – *nominative case*. The adjective is part of the subject of the sentence:

Der blaue Pullover ist sehr schön
Die blauen Schuhe sind sehr elegant

Agreement of the adjective after the words der, die or das (also after dieser, diese, dieses – *accusative case*:

Haben Sie die blauen Schuhe?
Ich habe die gleichen Schuhe

Agreement of the adjective in a phrase introduced by a preposition governing the *dative case*:

Er kommt aus der schönen Stadt Bonn
Wir fahren mit dem alten Taxi

|  | **Sing.** | |  |
|--|--|--|--|
|  | **Masc.** | **Fem.** | **Neut.** |
| NOMINATIVE | der rote Rock | die schöne Bluse | das weiße Hemd |
| ACCUSATIVE | den roten Rock | die schöne Bluse | das weiße Hemd |
|  | des roten Rocks | der Schonen Bluse | des weißen Hemdes |
| DATIVE | dem roten Rock | der schönen Bluse | dem weißen Hemd |
|  | **Plur.** | |  |
| NOMINATIVE | die roten Röcke | die schönen Blusen | die weißen Hemde |
| ACCUSATIVE | die roten Röcke | die schönen Blusen | die weißen Hemde |
| GENITIVE | der roten Rocke | der schonen Blusen | der weißen Hemden |
| DATIVE | den roten Röcken | der schönen Blusen | den weißen Hemden |

Nouns in the dative plural end in -n or -en, except those which end in -s.

## 33. Adjective endings (2)

Agreement of the adjective after the words ein, kein, mein, unser, etc. – *nominative case*. The adjective is part of the subject of the sentence:

Ein *guter* Wein kostet viel Geld
Mein *altes* Fahrrad ist kaputt

The adjective is part of the direct object of a sentence, or agrees with a preposition governing the *accusative case*:

Ich habe einen *neuen* Mantel gekauft
Wir gehen eine *alte* Straße entlang

The adjective is part of the indirect object of a sentence, or agrees with a preposition governing the *dative case*:

Er gibt seiner *schönen* Sekretärin eine Kette
Er kommt mit seinem *alten* Koffer

|  | **Sing.** | |  |
|--|--|--|--|
|  | **Masc.** | **Fem.** | **Neut.** |
| NOMINATIVE | ein guter Wein | eine schöne Kette | ein altes Auto |
| ACCUSATIVE | einen guten Wein | eine schöne Kette | ein altes Auto |
| GENITIVE | eines guten Weines | einer schonen Kette | eines alten Autos |
| DATIVE | einem guten Wein | einer schönen Kette | einem alten Auto |

|  | | **Plur.** | |
|---|---|---|---|
| NOMINATIVE | meine alten Schuhe | meine schönen Blusen | unsere alten Autos |
| ACCUSATIVE | meine alten Schuhe | meine schönen Blusen | unsere alten Autos |
| GENITIVE | meiner alten Schuhe | meiner schonen Blusen | unserer alten Autos |
| DATIVE | meinen alten Schuhen | meinen schönen Blusen | unseren alten Autos |

Most nouns in the dative plural end in -n or -en.

## 34. Adjective endings (3)

Sometimes adjectives occur by themselves. That is to say, they are not preceded by the words der or dieser, or by the words ein, mein, kein, etc. In these cases the adjective is declined somewhat differently. The endings are set out for you below:

| | **Sing.** | | |
|---|---|---|---|
| | **Masc.** | **Fem.** | **Neut.** |
| | good wine | good milk | good beer |
| NOMINATIVE | gut*er* Wein | gut*e* Milch | gut*es* Bier |
| ACCUSATIVE | gut*en* Wein | gut*e* Milch | gut*es* Bier |
| GENITIVE | gut*en* Weines | gut*er* Milch | gut*en* Bieres |
| DATIVE | gut*em* Wein | gut*er* Milch | gut*em* Bier |

| | **Plur.** | | |
|---|---|---|---|
| NOMINATIVE | gut*e* Weine | schön*e* Blusen | rot*e* Hemde |
| ACCUSATIVE | gut*e* Weine | schön*e* Blusen | rot*e* Hemde |
| GENITIVE | gut*er* Weine | schoner Blusen | rot*er* Hemden |
| DATIVE | gut*en* Wein*en* | schön*en* Blus*en* | rot*en* Hemd*en* |

## 35. Prepositions governing the accusative case

The following prepositions make the definite or indefinite article occur in the accusative case:

| bis | as far as |
|---|---|
| durch | through |
| entlang | along |
| für | for |
| ohne | without |
| um | round |

*Bis*

| Er kommt bis an die Tür | He comes as far as (i.e. up to) the door |
|---|---|
| Wir bleiben bis Sonntag | We are staying till Sunday |

*Durch*

| Der Fußball geht durch das Fenster | The football goes through the window |
|---|---|
| Sie geht durch den Zug | She goes through the train |

*Entlang*

| | |
|---|---|
| Wir gehen die Straße entlang | We go along the street |
| Er kommt den Korridor entlang | He comes along the corridor |

Note that the word entlang comes after the noun.

*Für*

| | |
|---|---|
| Hier ist ein Brief für den Chef | Here is a letter for the boss |
| Ich kaufe einen Pullover für das Kind | I buy a pullover for the child |

*Ohne*

| | |
|---|---|
| Ich komme ohne meinen Mantel | I'm coming without my coat |
| Sie schwimmt ohne eine Bademütze | She is swimming without a bathing cap |

*Um*

| | |
|---|---|
| Wir sitzen um den Tisch | We're sitting round the table |
| Er geht um das Rathaus | He goes round the town hall |

## 36. Prepositions governing the dative case

The following *prepositions* govern the dative case

| | |
|---|---|
| aus | out of/from |
| außer | beside/except |
| bei | near/with/among |
| mit | with |
| nach | to/after/according to |
| seit | since |
| von | about |
| zu | to/at |
| gegenüber | opposite |

*Aus*

generally means 'out of', 'from':

(a) to express movement from a place

| | |
|---|---|
| Er kommt aus dem Zimmer | He comes out of the room |

(b) to express origin referring to time, place or material

| | |
|---|---|
| Glas aus der Römerzeit | Glass from Roman times |
| Er kommt aus Hamburg | He comes from Hamburg |
| Das Haus ist aus Stein | The house is made of stone |

(c) to express a cause – special phrases

| | |
|---|---|
| Aus diesem Grund | For that reason |
| Aus Versehen | By mistake |

*Außer*

generally means 'outside', 'out of', 'beyond':

| | |
|---|---|
| Außer Gefahr | Out of danger |
| Außer Frage | Out of the question |
| Außer sich | Beside oneself (e.g. for joy) |
| Außer Zweifel | Beyond doubt |
| Außer Kontrolle | Beyond control |

*Bei*
generally means 'by', 'near', beside:
| | |
|---|---|
| (a) Mölln bei Hamburg | Mölln near Hamburg |

(b) it means 'at the house of' or 'living with'
| | |
|---|---|
| Er wohnt bei seinen Eltern | He lives with his parents |

(c) it means 'with' or 'on', referring to persons
| | |
|---|---|
| Ich habe kein Geld bei mir | I have no money with me, or on me |

(d) other phrases
| | |
|---|---|
| Beim Frühstück | At breakfast |
| Beim Mittagessen | At lunch |
| Bei Tisch | At table |
| Bei diesem Wetter | In this weather |
| Bei dieser Gelegenheit | On this occasion |
| Bei der Arbeit | At work |

*Mit*
generally means 'with', 'by'
| | |
|---|---|
| (a) Kommen Sie mit? | Are you coming (with me or without)? |

(b) it means 'by', referring to means of transport
| | |
|---|---|
| Mit dem Zug | By train |
| Mit dem Auto | By car |
| Mit dem Rad | By bicycle |

*Nach*
(a) it means 'to' with the names of places
| | |
|---|---|
| Nach Berlin | To Berlin |
| Nach Deutschland | To Germany |

(b) it means 'after'
| | |
|---|---|
| Nach 10 Minuten | After 10 minutes |
| Nach einer halben Stunde | After half an hour |

(c) it means 'according to'
| | |
|---|---|
| Nach seinem Brief ist er krank | According to his letter he is ill |
| Nach meiner Meinung (or meiner Meinung nach) | In my opinion |
| Nach Belieben | As desired |

(d) other phrases
| | |
|---|---|
| Nach Hause gehen (fahren) | To go home |
| Nach oben | To go upwards or upstairs |
| Nach außen | To go outwards or outside |

*Seit*
generally means 'since'
| | |
|---|---|
| (a) Seit Weihnachten | Since Christmas |
| Seit Ostern | Since Easter |

(b) it also means 'for'
| | |
|---|---|
| Seit 10 Jahren | For 10 years |
| Ich wohne seit 10 Jahren in Hamburg | I have been living in Hamburg for 10 years |

Note that the Present tense is used. And note that the expression of time comes *before* that of place.

## Von

(a) it means 'of', or 'about', or 'concerning'

| | |
|---|---|
| Ich spreche von ihm | I'm speaking about him |
| Ich spreche von ihr | I'm speaking about her |

(b) it means 'by', e.g. written by

| | |
|---|---|
| Hamlet von Shakespeare | Hamlet by Shakespeare |

(c) it means 'from'

| | |
|---|---|
| von Jahr zu Jahr | From year to year |
| von Zeit zu Zeit | From time to time |

Note that the English word 'of' is sometimes omitted in German:

| | |
|---|---|
| Zwei Glas Milch | Two glasses of milk |
| Eine Menge Leute | A crowd of people |
| Eine Tasse Tee | A cup of tea |
| Die Stadt London | The town of London |
| Die Firma Schmidt | The firm of Smith |
| Der Monat Januar | The month of January |

## Zu

(a) it means 'to', when used with the names of places, or buildings in a town

| | |
|---|---|
| Ich gehe zum Rathaus | I'm going to the town hall |
| Er geht zur Haltestelle | He's going to the bus stop |

(b) it means 'at' with the names of seasons

| | |
|---|---|
| Zu Weihnachten | At Christmas |
| Zu Ostern | At Easter |

(c) it means 'at' referring to prices

| | |
|---|---|
| Fleisch zu 11 Mark das Pfund | Meat at 11 marks a pound |

(d) it means 'for' referring to purpose

| | |
|---|---|
| Zu diesem Zweck | For this purpose |
| Zum Beispiel | For example |

(e) other phrases

| | |
|---|---|
| Zu Fuß | On foot |
| Zum zweiten Mal | For the second time |
| Zum dritten Mal | For the third time |
| Zu Ende | At an end |
| Zu Hause | At home |

## Gegenüber

| | |
|---|---|
| Das Rathaus ist gegenüber dem Theater | The town hall is opposite the theatre |
| Wir sind gegenüber der Post | We're opposite the post office |

## 37. Prepositions governing either the accusative or the dative case

| | |
|---|---|
| an | by/on/at/to |
| auf | on |
| hinter | behind |
| in | in |
| neben | beside/near |

| über | over/above |
| unter | under |
| vor | in front of/before |
| zwischen | between |

When they occur with a verb which indicates *position*, they govern the dative.

When they occur with a verb which indicates *movement towards* something, they govern the accusative.

*An* with the dative
generally means 'at', 'near', by the side of

| Er sitzt an dem Tisch | He is sitting at the table |
| Das Bild hängt an der Wand | The picture is hanging on the wall |
| Er steht an dem Fenster | He is standing at the window |

*An* with the accusative
generally means 'at', 'to'

| Er setzt sich an den Tisch | He sits down at the table |
| Er hängt das Bild an die Wand | He hangs the picture on the wall |
| Er geht an das Fenster | He goes to the window |

*Auf* with the dative
generally means 'on', 'on top of'

| Das Buch liegt auf dem Tisch | The book is on the desk |

In a number of idioms, auf means 'in' or 'at'

| Auf der Straße | In the street |
| Auf dem Markt | At the market |
| Auf dem Land | In the country |

*Auf* with the accusative
generally means 'on', 'on top of'

| Er stellt die Tasse auf den Tisch | He puts the cup on the table |
| Er stellt das Radio auf den Stuhl | He puts the radio on the chair |

*Auf* also means 'for' when it refers to future time

| Er fährt auf drei Tage nach Hamburg | He is going to Hamburg for three days |

*Hinter* means 'behind'

| Er steht hinter der Tür | He is standing behind the door |
| Er geht hinter die Tür | He goes behind the door |

*In* with the dative
generally means 'in', referring to time or place.

| Das Geld ist in meiner Tasche | The money is in my pocket |
| Das Radio ist im Wohnzimmer | The radio is in the living room |

*In* also has a number of other meanings

| In der Schule | At school |
| In der Kirche | At church |
| Im Alter von ... | At the age of ... |
| Im ersten Stock | On the first floor |

| | |
|---|---|
| Im großen und ganzen | On the whole |
| Im Gegenteil | On the contrary |
| Heute in acht Tagen | Today week |

*In* with the accusative
generally means 'into'

| | |
|---|---|
| Er steckt das Geld in seine Tasche | He puts the money into his pocket |
| Er fährt das Auto in die Garage | He drives the car into the garage |

Other meanings of in

| | |
|---|---|
| Er geht in die Kirche | He goes to church |
| Sie fährt in die Stadt | She drives to town |
| Wir gehen ins Theater | We go to the theatre |

*Neben* generally means 'besides', 'by', 'at the side of'

| | |
|---|---|
| Er steht neben der Tür | He is standing by the door |
| Er stellt den Stuhl neben die Tür | He puts the chair beside the door |

*Über* with the dative
generally means 'over', 'above'

| | |
|---|---|
| Über dem Berg sind Wolken | There are clouds over the mountain |

*Über* with the accusative
generally means 'over', 'across'

| | |
|---|---|
| Er geht über die Straße | He goes across the street |
| Sie schwimmt über den Fluß | She swims across the river |

Other meanings of *über*

| | |
|---|---|
| Das Päckchen wiegt über 500 Gramm | The packet weighs more than 500 grams |
| Der Zug fährt über München | The train goes via Munich |

*Unter* with the dative
generally means 'under', 'among', 'amid'

| | |
|---|---|
| Öl ist unter dem Auto | There is oil under the car |
| Du bist unter Freunden | You are among friends |

Other meanings of *unter*

| | |
|---|---|
| Das Päckchen wiegt unter 500 Gramm | The packet weighs less than 500 grams |
| Unter dieser Bedingung | On this condition |
| Unter diesen Umständen | Under these circumstances |

*Unter* with the accusative
generally means 'under', 'among'

| | |
|---|---|
| Der Ball rollt unter das Auto | The ball rolls underneath the car |
| Die Katze läuft unter den Tisch | The cat runs under the table |

*Vor* with the dative
generally means 'before' (referring to time or place), 'in front of'

| | |
|---|---|
| Vor dem Krieg | Before the war |
| Er steht vor dem Haus | He stands in front of the house |

Other meanings of *Vor*

| | |
|---|---|
| Vor zwei Tagen | Two days ago |
| Vor langer Zeit | A long time ago |
| Sie zittert vor Kälte | She is shivering with cold |

*Vor* with the accusative
generally means 'before', 'in front of'

| | |
|---|---|
| Sie kommt vor die Klasse | She comes in front of the class |
| Er springt vor das Auto | He jumps in front of the car |

*Zwischen* means 'between'

| | |
|---|---|
| Das Fahrrad ist zwischen dem Bus und dem Auto | The bicycle is between the bus and the car |
| Er fährt das Auto zwischen die Polizisten | He drives the car between the policemen |

## 38. Prepositions governing the genitive case

Außerhalb means 'outside'

Außerhalb des Hauses — Outside the house

Diessiets means 'on this side'

Diesseits des Flußes — On this side of the river

Jenseits means 'on that side'

Jenseits des Flußes — On that side of the river

Innerhalb means 'inside'

Innerhalb des Hauses — Inside the house

Während means 'while' or 'during'

| | |
|---|---|
| Während des Winters | During the winter |
| Während des Spiels | During the game |

Wegen means 'on account of', or 'because of'

| | |
|---|---|
| Wegen des Wetters | On account of the weather<br>Because of the weather |
| Wegen des Unfalls | On account of the accident<br>Because of the accident |

Trotz means 'in spite of'

Trotz des Wetters — In spite of the weather

(N.B. trotz also governs the dative case: **trotz dem Wetter**)

# MONEY, WEIGHTS AND MEASURES

## WEST GERMAN, AUSTRIAN, SWISS AND EAST GERMAN MONEY

**West German currency**
Marks = DM; Pfennigs = Pf; DM1 = 100Pf.
DM 2,72 = zwei Mark zweiundsiebzig Pfennig.

| COINS (Münzen) | | NOTES (Banknotes) | |
|---|---|---|---|
| DM – ,1 | ein Pfennig | DM 5, – | fünf Mark |
| DM – ,5 | fünf Pfennig | DM 10, – | zehn Mark |
| DM – ,10 | zehn Pfennig | DM 20, – | zwanzig Mark |
| DM – ,50 | fünfzig Pfennig | DM 50, – | fünfzig Mark |
| DM 1, – | eine Mark | DM 100, – | hundert Mark |
| DM 2, – | zwei Mark | DM 500, – | fünfhundert Mark |
| DM 5, – | fünf Mark | | |

Currency in East Germany consists of the same coins and banknotes as in West Germany. The value and purchasing power are, however, different.

**Austrian currency**
100 Groschen = 1 Schilling.

| COINS | NOTES |
|---|---|
| 2 Groschen | 20 Schillinge |
| 5 Groschen | 50 Schillinge |
| 10 Groschen | 100 Schillinge |
| 50 Groschen | 500 Schillinge |
| 1 Schilling | 1000 Schillinge |
| 5 Schillinge | |
| 10 Schillinge | |

**Swiss currency**
100 Centimes = 1 Franc.
In German you say Rappen for centimes and Franken for francs.

| COINS | NOTES |
|---|---|
| 5 Rappen | 10 Franken |
| 10 Rappen | 20 Franken |
| 20 Rappen | 50 Franken |

| ½ | Franke | 100 | Franken |
|---|--------|-----|---------|
| 1 | Franke | 1000 | Franken |
| 2 | Franken | | |
| 5 | Franken | | |

## DISTANCES
1 mile = 1.6 kilometres                    1.6 Kilometer = 1 Meile

| Miles | 10 | 20 | 30 | 40 | 50 | 60 | 70 | 80 | 90 | 100 | Meilen |
|-------|----|----|----|----|----|----|----|----|----|-----|--------|
| Kilometres | 16 | 32 | 48 | 64 | 80 | 97 | 113 | 128 | 145 | 160 | Kilometer |

## LENGTHS AND SIZES

### General clothes sizes (including chest/hip measurements)

| GB | USA | Germany | Europe | ins | cms |
|----|-----|---------|--------|-----|-----|
| 8 | 6 | 34 | 36 | 30/32 | 76/81 |
| 10 | 8 | 36 | 38 | 32/34 | 81/86 |
| 12 | 10 | 38 | 40 | 34/36 | 86/91 |
| 14 | 12 | 40 | 42 | 36/38 | 91/97 |
| 16 | 14 | 42 | 44 | 38/40 | 97/102 |
| 18 | 16 | 44 | 46 | 40/42 | 102/107 |
| 20 | 18 | 46 | 48 | 42/44 | 107/112 |
| 22 | 20 | 48 | 50 | 44/46 | 112/117 |
| 24 | 22 | 50 | 52 | 46/48 | 117/122 |
| 26 | 24 | 52 | 54 | 48/50 | 122/127 |

### Waist measurements
(ins)   GB/USA
| 22 | 24 | 26 | 28 | 30 | 32 | 34 | 36 | 38 | 40 | 42 | 44 | 46 | 48 | 50 |
|----|----|----|----|----|----|----|----|----|----|----|----|----|----|----|

(cms)   Europe
| 56 | 61 | 66 | 71 | 76 | 81 | 86 | 91 | 97 | 102 | 107 | 112 | 117 | 122 | 127 |
|----|----|----|----|----|----|----|----|----|-----|-----|-----|-----|-----|-----|

### Shoes
GB
| 3 | 3½ | 4 | 4½ | 5 | 5½ | 6 | 6½ | 7 | 7½ | 8 | 8½ | 9 | 10 | 11 | 12 |
|---|----|----|----|----|----|----|----|----|----|----|----|----|----|----|----|

USA
| 4½ | 5 | 5½ | 6 | 6½ | 7 | 7½ | 8 | 8½ | 9 | 9½ | 10 | 10½ | 11½ | 12½ | 13½ |
|----|----|----|----|----|----|----|----|----|----|----|----|-----|-----|-----|-----|
| 36 | | 37 | | 38 | | 39 | | 40 | | 41 | | 42 | 43 | 44 | 45 |

## WEIGHTS

Some approximate equivalents – Gramm (g) (grams) and Kilogramm (Kg) (kilograms):

| | | |
|---|---|---|
| 1000 Gramm (1000g) | = | 1 Kilogramm (1 Kilo/kg) |
| 1 oz | = | 25 Gramm (g) |
| 4 oz | = | 100/125 Gramm |
| 8 oz | = | 225 Gramm |
| 1 pound (16 oz) | = | 450 Gramm |
| 1 pound 2 oz | = | 500 Gramm (½ Kilogramm) |
| 2 pounds 4 oz | = | 1 Kilogram (1 Kilo/kg) |
| 1 stone | = | 6 Kilogram |

**Body weight**
Body weight in Europe is measured in kilograms (Kilogramm). Some approximate equivalents:

| POUNDS | STONES | KILOGRAMS |
|---|---|---|
| 28 | 2 | 12½ |
| 42 | 3 | 19 |
| 56 | 4 | 25 |
| 70 | 5 | 32 |
| 84 | 6 | 38 |
| 98 | 7 | 45 |
| 112 | 8 | 51 |
| 126 | 9 | 57½ |
| 140 | 10 | 63 |
| 154 | 11 | 70 |
| 168 | 12 | 76 |
| 182 | 13 | 83 |
| 196 | 14 | 90 |

## LIQUID MEASURES

Petrol and oil are measured in litres (Liter), so are most other liquids, including milk. Wine is sometimes sold in litre bottles, but more frequently in bottles containing ¾ litre.

Some approximate equivalents:

1 pint = 0.57 Liter (litres)          1 gallon = 4.55 litres

| GB measures | Liter (litres) | GB measures | Liter (litres) |
|---|---|---|---|
| 1 pint | = 0.57 | | |
| | | 4.4 gallons | = 20 |
| | | 5.5 gallons | = 25 |
| 1.7 pints | = 1 | 6.6 gallons | = 30 |
| 1.1 gallons | = 5 | 7.7 gallons | = 35 |
| 2.2 gallons | = 10 | 8.8 gallons | = 40 |
| 3.3 gallons | = 15 | 9.9 gallons | = 45 |

## TEMPERATURE

|  | FAHRENHEIT (F) | GRAD CELSIUS (C) CENTIGRADE |
|---|---|---|
| Boiling point | 212° | 100° |
|  | 104° | 40° |
| Body temperature | 98.4° | 36.9° |
|  | 86° | 30° |
|  | 68° | 20° |
|  | 59° | 15° |
|  | 50° | 10° |
| Freezing point | 32° | 0° |
|  | 23° | −5° |
|  | 0° | −18° |

(Convert Fahrenheit to Celsius by subtracting 32 and multiplying by 5/9. Convert Celsius to Fahrenheit by multiplying by 9/5 and adding 32.)

# SOME USEFUL HINTS
# AND TIPS

Visiting a German speaking country means going into a different culture with different ways of doing things. This can sometimes be a problem, even if you know German quite well. You might like to know, therefore, of two publications which are specially prepared for prospective visitors to Germany. One is called Treffpunkt Deutschland, and the other is called Glückliche Ferientage in Deutschland. This second publication appears in English under the title *Happy Days in Germany*. Both can be obtained by sending a postcard to the German Tourist Office in Frankfurt, Beethoven Straße 69, or from its nearest branch. Many large towns also prepare brochures with useful tips and town plans, specially designed for young people who wish to visit Germany. Frankfurt produces a brochure called 16 bis 36 and Munich produces a brochure called *Young People's Guide to Munich*. These and similar brochures can be obtained by writing to the local tourist office. You should write to the Verkehrsamt der Stadt (plus name of town).

## TELEPHONING

In a public telephone box you need to put in two 10-Pfennig coins for a local call, and larger coins for trunk calls. You can make international telephone calls from many public call boxes. You should watch out for the notice on the door Auslandsgespräche.

## STAMPS

Generally speaking you can buy stamps only in post offices. They are not usually available in souvenir shops.

## SHOPPING HOURS

Shops, chemists and also travel agencies are usually open from Monday to Friday from 9 a.m. until 6 or 6.30 p.m. On Saturdays they are usually open only until midday or 2 o'clock.

## BANKING HOURS

Banks are open from 9 to 12 a.m. and from 2 until 4 p.m. They are closed on Saturdays. You can sometimes find currency-exchange kiosks in stations and airports. After 6.30 in the evening, you can buy certain things in petrol stations and newspaper kiosks.

## PUBLIC TRANSPORT

Most towns have a comprehensive system of trams, buses, underground railways and suburban railways. It is worthwhile making enquiries about tickets. Frequently you can travel right through a whole city with one ticket. Note that taxis are fairly expensive.

## REDUCTIONS

If you have an international pupils' or students' card, there are often special reductions for the theatre, museums, mountain railways and city sightseeing tours.

## HOW TO EAT CHEAPLY

Look out for snack bars. They will be called Imbiß or Imbißstube. It's worth noting that many butchers' shops often have a small table and chair where you can go to eat freshly cooked sausage. You can eat fairly cheaply in the cafeterias of large department stores, and you can go into university restaurants to eat. You simply have to buy a meal ticket as German students do. If you are in country areas, it's worth while looking out for small guest-houses. Don't forget to ask for German specialities.

## TRAVELLING

You can hitchhike in Germany, but not on the motorway. If you wish to travel long distances, you must take care to find a car before it reaches the motorway. It is allowed, however, to thumb a lift at the entries and exits to motorways. Girls are advised not to go hitchhiking alone. It is interesting to note that the first letter or letters of German registration numbers indicate the town where that car is registered.

There is a system in Germany of arranging to travel with somebody who is proposing to make a motorway journey. You give your name to a central office, and say where you want to travel to, and the office puts you in touch with someone who is going to make a journey. You often have to wait one or two days until your name comes to the top of the list, but it is cheap and safe. You should look up Mitfahrer-Zentrale in the telephone directory.

## RAIL TRAVEL

Inter Rail available up to the age of 26 years. The ticket is valid for one month in twenty-one different countries of Europe, and costs 360 Marks.

Tramper-Monats-Ticket available up to the age of 26 years, and valid for one month in the Federal Republic of Germany. Costs 198 Marks, and allows you to travel throughout Germany.

Junior-Paß available up to the age of 26 years, and is valid for one year in the Federal Republic. The ticket costs 98 Marks and allows you to buy rail tickets at half price.

## CAR RENTAL

You have to be over 21 to hire a car, and it will cost from 300 Marks a week. It is also possible to rent bicycles at more than 200 railway stations. You can leave your bicycle at the station of your destination. The cost is about 7 Marks a day, including insurance.

## LIVING IN GERMANY

There are about 600 Youth Hostels (JH) in Germany. You need a valid international Youth Hostel Membership Card, which you can obtain either in your own country or by writing to the Deutscher Jugendherbergsverband (DJH) in Detmold. The price for young people up to the age of 27 years is between 3 and 4 Marks a night. For the high season it's advisable to make a booking as early as possible. In the most popular tourist areas it's even necessary to book up a year in advance. Information about German Youth Hostels can be obtained from DJH, Bülowstraße 26, 4930 Detmold.

You can also stay at the YMCA (CVJM-Jugendheim); guest-houses for young people (Jugendgästehäuser, Jugendhotels); small overnight huts in the alps (Hütten der Alpenvereine). There are camping sites (Camping Plätze), and many private rooms and small guest-houses (Pensionen). Information about all these places can best be obtained by writing to the Verkehrsamt of the town you wish to visit.

## EMERGENCIES

If you are ill and cannot find a hospital, go to the nearest telephone kiosk or telephone directory and look for Ärztlicher Notdienst. This service is manned around the clock. In an emergency you could also try the Red Cross (Rotes Kreuz), or the Social Assistance Centre at railway stations (Bahnhofsmission). However, the best thing to do is to insure yourself against illness before travelling abroad.

If you lose your money or passport, you should report the matter to the nearest police station (Polizeirevier) or to the British Embassy or Consulate. Directory enquiries in the German telephone system is found by dialling 118 or 0118. In large cities, the police can be contacted by dialling 110. If you break down on the motorway, there are yellow emergency telephones at the roadside.

## A FEW THINGS TO SEE

Here are one or two ideas to whet your appetite. They are the sort of things which many tourists would not think of doing:

Berlin –     a stroll through the artists' quarter in Kreuzberg.

Munich –    visit the fruit and vegetable market (Viktualienmarkt) in the early morning; or go for a journey on a raft on the river Isar.

Hamburg – visit the fish market at 4 o'clock in the morning.

See some of the beautiful old towns, which have retained their ancient appearance, or been beautifully restored. For example: Freiburg with its cathedral, Bamberg with its cathedral, Passau with its three rivers, the Danube, the Inn and the Ilz, Nürnberg with its medieval castle.

Parts of Germany are already well-known for their beautiful landscapes, such as Bavaria, the Black Forest, the Rhine and the Bodensee (Lake Constance). There are, however, many other beautiful parts of Germany which are less well-known, such as the Bavarian Forest (der Bayerische Wald) with its virgin forest, or the Valley of the river Tauber in Franconia or the Hohenloher Land in Würtemberg with its many castles. Then there are the beautiful areas of the Odenwald, the Spessart, the Rhön, the Eiffel, the Lüneburg Heath and the North Sea islands (Halligen). Instead of doing a boat trip on the Rhine, why not try the river Weser? Instead of visiting Heidelberg and Rothenberg ob der Tauber, why not go to see Schwäbisch Hall, Bad Windsen on the river Nekkar, or the tiny forgotten town of Wolframs Eschenbach in Franconia, with its old town wall still intact? Celle on the Lüneburge Heide and Regensburg on the Danube are well worth a visit, both for their beauty and for their historic interest.

These are, of course, only one or two of the many attractive places you could visit in Germany. The experienced and adventurous traveller, equipped with his copy of *Mastering German* cannot fail to have a delightful holiday by taking the byroads and discovering the beautiful sights which Germany has to offer. Always try to speak a few words of German, and you will instantly make friends.

# SIGNS ON PUBLIC DISPLAY

| | |
|---|---|
| ABFAHRT | Departures |
| ABTEILUNG | Department |
| ACHTUNG | Take care |
| ADAC | German equivalent of AA RAC |
| AN | On (switches, etc.) |
| ANKUNFT | Admissions Arrivals |
| ANLIEGER FREI | Access only (i.e. only if your destination is in this street) |
| AN SONN- UND FEIERTAGEN FREI | No charge Sundays and Bank Holidays |
| APOTHEKE | Dispensing chemist |
| ARZT | Doctor |
| AUFZUG | Lift |
| AUS | Off (switches, etc.) |
| AUSFAHRT | Exit |
| AUSGANG | Exit |
| AUSKUNFT | Enquiries |
| AUßER BETRIEB | Not in use |
| AUSVERKAUF | Sale |
| AUTOBAHN | Motorway |
| AUTOBAHNKREUZ | Motorways merge |
| BAHNSTEIG | Platform |
| BAUSTELLE | Building site; road works ahead |
| BEI VERSAGEN KNOPF DRÜCKEN | Press button to get money back |
| BESETZT | Engaged; no vacancies; occupied |
| BETRETEN VERBOTEN | Keep out; no trepassing |
| BITTE MOTOR ABSCHALTEN | Please switch engine off |
| DAMEN | Ladies; Ladies' Room |
| DURCHGEHEND | Continuously |
| EIN | In |
| EINBAHNSTRAßE | One-way street |
| EINFAHRT | Way in |
| EINFAHRT FREIHALTEN | Do not obstruct entrance |
| EINGANG | Entrance |
| EINORDNEN | Get in lane |
| EINTRITT | Admission |

| | |
|---|---|
| EMPFANG | Reception |
| ERDGESCHOß | Ground floor |
| ERSATZTEILE | Spare parts |
| FAHRPLAN | Timetable |
| FAHRSPUR GESPERRT | Lane closed |
| FAHRSTUHL | Lift |
| FAMILIENNAME | Last name |
| FESTHALTEN | Hold tight |
| FLUG | Flight |
| FRAUEN | Women |
| FREI | Vacant |
| FREMDENZIMMER | Room to let (Bed and breakfast) |
| FUNDBURO | Lost property office |
| GASTHAUS | Inn; pub |
| GASTHOF | Inn; pub |
| GEFAHR | Danger |
| GEPÄCKABGABE | Left Luggage |
| GESCHLOSSEN | Closed |
| GRENZÜBERGANG | Frontier |
| HABEN SIE IHREN SCHLÜSSEL ABGEGEBEN? | Have you handed in your key? |
| HAUPTBAHNHOF | Main station (in a city) |
| HEIßE GETRÄNKE | Hot drinks |
| HERREN | Gentlemen; Gents |
| KASSE | Cash desk; till |
| KEIN AUSGANG | No way out |
| KEINE DURCHFAHRT | No thoroughfare |
| KEINE EINFAHRT | No access |
| KEIN EINGANG | Exit only; No entry |
| KEIN TRINKWASSER | Not drinking water |
| KOSTENPFLICHTIG | At owner's expense |
| LANGSAM | Slow |
| LEBENSGEFAHR | Danger |
| LKW | Lorries |
| MÄNNER | Men |
| MOTOR ABSTELLEN | Switch off engine |
| MÜNZEINWURF | Insert coin |
| MÜNZEN | Coins |
| MÜNZRÜCKGABE | Reject coins |
| MÜNZWECHSLER | Coin change |
| NICHT ANGREIFEN | Do not touch |
| NICHT BERÜHREN | Do not touch |
| NICHT RAUCHEN | Do not smoke |
| NICHTRAUCHER | Non-smoker |
| NICHT RESERVIERT | Unreserved |
| NICHT ÜBERHOLEN | No overtaking |
| NOTAUSGANG | Emergency exit; fire exit |
| NUR FÜR RASIERAPPARATE | Shavers only |
| NUR MIT SONDERGENEHMIGUNG | Permit holders only |
| OBEN/UNTEN | (This side) up; down |
| OFFEN (TÄGLICH) (BIS) | Open (daily) (till) |
| ÖFFNUNGSZEITEN | Opening hours |

| | |
|---|---|
| PARKPLATZ | Parking |
| PARKZEIT 30 MINUTEN | Waiting limited to 30 minutes |
| PKW | Cars |
| PLATZ | Seat |
| PLATZRESERVIERUNG | Seat reservations |
| POLIZEI | Police |
| POSTAMT | Post Office |
| PRAKT. ARZT | Doctor |
| PRIVATPARKPLATZ | Private parking only |
| RASTPLATZ | Lay-by |
| RASTSTÄTTE | Services (on the motorway) |
| REINIGUNG | Cleaners |
| REISEBÜRO | Travel office |
| REISEFÜHRER | Guide |
| REPARATUREN | Repairs |
| RESERVIERT | Reserved |
| RESERVIERUNGEN | Reservations |
| ROLLSPLITT | Loose chippings |
| RÜCKGABEKNOPF | Press to reject |
| RUHETAG | Rest day |
| RUNDFAHRT | Tour |
| SB-TANKSTELLE | Self-service petrol station |
| SCHLÜSSELFÄCHER | Left luggage lockers |
| SCHNELLDIENST | While you wait |
| SCHWIMMBAD | Swimming pool |
| SCHWIMMEN UND BADEN VERBOTEN | No bathing; swimming |
| SELBSTBEDIENUNG | Self-service |
| SELBST TANKEN | Self-service (petrol) |
| SONDERANGEBOTE | Bargains; special offers |
| SPARKASSE | Bank |
| SPEISEKARTE | Menu |
| SPRECHSTUNDEN | Surgery hours |
| SPRECHZEITEN | Surgery hours |
| STADTMITTE | Town centre |
| TAGESAUSFLÜGE | Day excursions |
| TANKSTELLE | Petrol station; service area |
| TREPPE | Stairs |
| TRINKWASSER | Drinking water |
| TÜRE SCHLIEßEN | Close doors (firmly) |
| ÜBERNACHTUNG UND FRÜHSTÜCK | Bed and breakfast |
| UMKLEIDERAUM | Changing room |
| UMLEITUNG | Diversion |
| UNFALL | Accident |
| UNTERFÜHRUNG | Subway |
| UNTERKUNFT | Accommodation |
| VERBOTEN | Prohibited |
| VERKAUFS- UND KUNDENDIENST | Sales and service |
| VERKEHRSAMT | Tourist office |
| VORFAHRT BEACHTEN | Give way: major road ahead |
| VORSICHT | Caution |
| WARME KÜCHE (DURCHGEHEND) | Hot meals served all day |
| WARNUNG | Warning |

| | |
|---|---|
| WARTERAUM | Waiting area |
| WARTEZIMMER | Waiting room |
| WECHSEL | Exchange |
| ZAHNARZT | Dentist |
| ZEITUNGEN | Newspapers |
| ZENTRUM | Town centre |
| ZIMMER FREI | Room to let |
| ZIMMERNACHWEIS | Accommodation bureau |
| ZIMMER ZU VERMIETEN | Rooms to let |
| ZUBEHÖR | Accessories |
| ZUFAHRT | Access |
| ZUSCHLAG | Additional charge |

# BIBLIOGRAPHY

**Books recommended for improving your spoken German**
1. *Get by in German*, BBC Publications, 35 Marylebone High Street, London W1M 4AA.
2. *BBC German Kit* (based on BBC television and radio course Kontakte), BBC Publications, 35 Marylebone High Street, London W1M 4AA.

**A small book with lots of useful vocabulary**
3. *Survive in German*, Longman.

**Grammars**
4. A. E. Hammer, *German Grammar and Usage* (Edward Arnold, 1971). A thorough and valuable book for the advanced student.
5. *Harrap's New German Grammar*, C. B. Johnson, Harrap, 1971. Thorough and clear.
6. *A Grammar of Contemporary German* (Deutsch 2000), Hueber, 1976. Adapted from the original German.

**Hints and tips about Germany**
7. *Treffpunkt Deutschland*, German Tourist Office, Frankfurt, Beethoven Straße 69.
8. *Glückliche Ferientage in Deutschland* (*Happy Days in Germany*), German Tourist Office, Frankfurt, Beethoven Straße 69.

**Dictionaries**
9. Collins *German Dictionary* (German – English, English – German, in one volume).
10. Harrap's *Standard German and English Dictionary*.
11. Langenscheidt's *New Muret-Sanders Encyclopaedic Dictionary* (four volumes).

Further information about learning German may be obtained from the Centre for Information on Language Teaching and Research, Regent's College, Inner Circle, Regent's Park, London NW1 4NS.